STUDENT AFFAIRS IN URBAN-SERVING INSTITUTIONS

Student Affairs in Urban-Serving Institutions: Voices from Senior Leaders addresses a critical gap in literature concerning the unique structure, students, and missions of urban-serving institutions (USIs). Examining the challenges and contributions of student affairs professionals in serving and meeting the needs of urban students, this volume discusses how services and interventions must reflect the reality of students, understand the sociopolitical forces that affect students' lives, and bring together a network that includes family and community. Each chapter in this volume captures the voices of student affairs leaders who not only share a range of important professional experiences, insights, and lessons learned but also unpack research and literature on competencies, knowledge bases, and experiences needed to work in urban universities and community colleges. This important book will help graduate students as well as new and continuing professionals, faculty, and scholars impact practice and policy and become agents of change in their communities.

Anna M. Ortiz is founding Director of the NASPA Faculty Division and Professor of Student Development in Higher Education and Educational Leadership at Long Beach State University, USA.

STUDENT AFFAIRS IN URBAN-SERVING INSTITUTIONS

Voices from Senior Leaders

Edited by Anna M. Ortiz

First published 2019
by Routledge
52 Vanderbilt Avenue, New York, NY 10017

and by Routledge
2 Park Square, Milton Park, Abingdon, Oxon OX14 4RN

Routledge is an imprint of the Taylor & Francis Group, an informa business

© 2019 Taylor & Francis

The right of Anna M. Ortiz to be identified as the author of the editorial material, and of the authors for their individual chapters, has been asserted in accordance with sections 77 and 78 of the Copyright, Designs and Patents Act 1988.

All rights reserved. No part of this book may be reprinted or reproduced or utilised in any form or by any electronic, mechanical, or other means, now known or hereafter invented, including photocopying and recording, or in any information storage or retrieval system, without permission in writing from the publishers.

Trademark notice: Product or corporate names may be trademarks or registered trademarks, and are used only for identification and explanation without intent to infringe.

Library of Congress Cataloging-in-Publication Data
A catalog record for this title has been requested

ISBN: 978-1-138-48738-3 (hbk)
ISBN: 978-1-138-48739-0 (pbk)
ISBN: 978-1-351-04336-6 (ebk)

Typeset in Bembo
by Taylor & Francis Books

CONTENTS

Preface *viii*

1   Introduction   1
    Jenny Jacobs and Anna M. Ortiz

2   Understanding the Urban-Serving Institution   19
    Tiffany J. Davis and Richard Walker

3   The Urban College Student   38
    Anthony Cruz and Franklyn Taylor

4   Promoting Student Success   58
    Corlisse Thomas and André McKenzie

5   Promoting Engagement and Belonging   84
    Michael A. Freeman and Anna M. Ortiz

6   Leading in an Urban Institution   105
    Larry W. Lunsford and Edward G. Whipple

7   Preparing Student Affairs Professionals to Serve in Urban
    Institutions   128
    Darrell C. Ray and Scott Radimer

8   The Vice President Experience   151
    Gail DiSabatino and Mariette Bien-Aime Ayala

vi Contents

9 Student Affairs in Urban-Serving Institutions: Reflections and
Looking Forward   176
Anna M. Ortiz

Contributor Bios   *189*
Index   *194*

PREFACE

Student Affairs in Urban-Serving Institutions is the result of a 2-year collaboration with 14 vice presidents, vice chancellors, or presidents who served as expert participants, authors, and consultants for this project. Knowing that there is a critical gap in literature about student affairs in urban-serving institutions (USIs), we sought to collect the perspectives of executive student affairs officers who could articulate the unique challenges faced by student affairs units in USIs as well as the, perhaps more importantly, contributions made by student affairs units that serve USIs. Our hope was to provide information and guidance to graduate students as well as new and continuing professionals, faculty, and scholars about the competencies, knowledge bases, and experiences needed to work in urban public universities and community colleges. We also hope this volume will be of interest to higher education academic administrators at urban institutions who may be able to use the book as a way to better understand student affairs work and partnerships.

I come to this topic in a way, I suspect, many might share. I grew up in traditional institutions of higher education (IHEs) and attended college as a traditional college student. I lived in residence halls, participated in student activities, and held student leadership positions on campus. Upon graduation, I entered a traditional student affairs master's program, where I continued that trajectory. My subsequent moves were all to traditional universities, many public and large, steeped in history and tradition. Fifteen years ago, I came to Long Beach State University as an associate professor. Here was a different kind of institution—with students who have come to exemplify the future of higher education—first-generation students, who likely live with family members, may be parenting, commute to campus, and many of whom are children of immigrants or immigrant themselves. Something else happened here: My students in the Student Development in Higher Education

viii   Preface

master's program were also different. They were excited to enter the profession of student affairs, but they were planning to do it in ways that almost never included work in residence halls, and seldom in student life, unless it was at a community college. They were interested in counseling in community college or working in outreach and TRIO programs. They wanted to help students like themselves—the urban college student. I discovered that what I taught and how I taught needed to change. I became critical of how we train student affairs professionals, finally realizing that as a field we aren't preparing them to work in urban settings or in community colleges. That sparked my interest in studying this topic in a way that would be useful to graduate students and to any professional looking to move into these institution types.

Having just admitted my relative ignorance about USIs, I sought to include folks who do the actual work in these settings. Senior student affairs officers who work in USIs have made a commitment to these unique institutions and hold much wisdom and knowledge about how they work, whom they serve, and their interplay between campus and community. But I also knew that these folks have little time to embark on traditional scholarship. Thus, I designed a project in which we could gather the voices of many and support the writers as much as I could. As will be described in more detail in Chapter 1, the project relies on conversations with these leaders who were then analyzed, along with an analyzed review of the literature for each of their chapters. We gave them everything they needed to just sit down and write, without some of the more tedious and time-consuming tasks of scholarship. The result is a volume in which the experiences of all are presented throughout, with each author bringing forward their own experiences.

What I have valued most about this project is interacting with all of these wonderful people. In my conversations with them, I learned that their drive and commitment to serve urban students was truly a life calling. Nearly all had been at more traditional universities, and all have found their passion in leading at an urban serving institution. They know they do this work in places that may not be appreciated by the state or others in higher education, but they know they are instrumental to the students and communities they serve. I am grateful to each of them for their time and energy in our conversations and am blessed to have worked with a wonderful group of them as chapter authors. The colleagues they invited to join them as authors have contributed their unique perspectives, as well. I am struck at how enthusiastically they participated in this project, many also being grateful for an opportunity to share their stories. When I met many of them at NASPA last year in our presentation there, their warmth, generous spirit, and appreciation humbled me. I thank them all for making one of my scholarship dreams come true.

I also want to thank Jenny Jacobs for all of her work on this project. At an urban-serving institution, a professor in a professional graduate program isn't often blessed to have a real graduate assistant, since most of our doctoral students work full time. I am so fortunate that I have had Jenny's talents for the past 3 years to work on this project and others. She analyzed all of the literature, was a partner in the data analysis, and kept the project on track, moving it forward. Her own experiences in urban-serving institutions and her experience on the East Coast was important to our selection of institutions and to broadening my understanding. I want to acknowledge the many cohorts of Student Development in Higher Education students at Long Beach who were my experts and teachers as I stumbled to reframe what I believed about higher education and to become a better steward for students whose diversity I had overlooked. Finally, I'd like to thank my family, friends, and colleagues who have supported me in the many hours it has taken to execute this project. A special thank you to my partner, Dan, who has had the unique experience of beginning our journey simultaneously with the chaos that comes with finishing a book.

1

INTRODUCTION

Jenny Jacobs and Anna M. Ortiz

Overview

Studying student affairs in urban-serving institutions (USIs) is especially important because their unique institutional structure, constituencies, students, and missions have been severely underrepresented in the student affairs and higher education literature, professional development, and the professional preparation of master's and doctoral students. Data tell us that the collegiate ideal of parents unpacking their first-year students from SUV to residence hall is not a reality for most of today's college students. The 2009–2011 *American Community Survey* conducted by the U.S. Census Bureau (2011) reported that 63.3 percent of all college students live with their parents or other relatives. Thus, the context for collegiate involvement for most students in urban institutions, the vast majority of whom commute to campus, does not begin in residence halls; rather, it follows nontraditional trajectories that do not usually include the typical collegiate activities such as student group membership, participating in student government, or association with Greek-letter organizations. The lives of USI students are highly differentiated and complex, often with jobs, families, and community expectations and obligations that can exert multiple and sometimes competing demands on students' time. The needs of USI students are unique and so, too, must be the approach to student affairs work in the USI. The institutions themselves are also worthy of study and attention. Often, in the shadows of their states' flagship universities, these institutions play special, fundamental roles in the communities they serve, becoming beacons of hope for first-generation college students, avenues for social mobility and career re-training, and drivers of economic development in their cities.

In this chapter we begin with an explanation of the conceptual foundation that undergirds this project and the collective knowledge of the vice presidents, vice chancellors, and presidents who have participated in our work. We also explain the project itself in more detail by outlining how we defined *urban-serving institutions*; collected data; and collaborated with participants, contributors, and authors. Throughout the volume, we use quotes and exemplars from participants and authors, most of which have been edited for clarity. There are a variety of titles and names associated with student affairs and student services units and professionals within academia and in the institutions in this project; for this text we have selected *student affairs* as a representative name for all units and their leaders. We also use the title of *senior leader* or *vice president* interchangeably, knowing that there are also several terms for the senior student affairs officer.

Conceptual Foundation

Our aim in this project is to consider urban-serving institutions differently than they have been studied or written about in the past. We embrace a two-fold conceptual framework to analyze an approach to student affairs work: one that mirrors culturally relevant pedagogy (Ladson-Billings, 1995), a leading perspective that informs K–12 practices, and the other that brings the early work of Alexander Astin on counterproductive views of excellence (Astin, 1985) to a contemporary understanding of urban-serving institutions.

Culturally Relevant/Responsive Student Services

Inspired by Ladson-Billings' (1995) seminal work reconsidering teaching pedagogy by applying the tenants of culturally relevant pedagogy (CRP), our aim with this project was to first acknowledge that student affairs must operate differently in USIs in order to truly serve the students who make up this unique population. Ladson-Billings' original work called on educators to focus on the academic efficacy and potential of their students, developing cultural competence with deep knowledge about the culture of their students, becoming a part of the communities that they serve, and to consider the sociopolitical consciousness of using knowledge to analyze societal forces that affect the lives of students and their families. CRP challenges educators to refrain from considering students who are different from the White, middle-class norm through deficit terms, such as *deprived, disadvantaged, at risk*, or *chronically underachieving* (Ladson-Billings, 2014), and instead to understand that the perceived success of this "normal" conceptualization of student is largely attributable to their social and cultural advantages.

When we consider higher education, and our work in student affairs in particular, through the lens of CRP, we can see the ways in which our education and training has relied primarily on theories and practices that reflect the experiences of traditional college students: those who attend elite private colleges or universities or large public

Introduction **3**

research universities by moving to campus, completing college within 4–5 years, and engaging in a range of high-impact practices (Kuh, 2008).

Research, texts, and training that fail to recognize the wide variation among students and institutions where student services are practiced mimics the deficit perspective that necessitated a transformation in teaching pedagogy, calling us to offer what we propose as *culturally relevant or responsive student services*. We use both terms, *relevant* and *responsive*, in this volume as appropriate in particular contexts. At times, a service needs to be culturally responsive and at other times, usually in the context of programming or staff training, being culturally relevant seems more accurate. Through culturally relevant/responsive student services (CRSS), underprepared students are not viewed as less capable of learning but, instead, more in need of support to overcome past educational inequities such as underfunded urban elementary and secondary schools, credentialed teacher shortages, and broken college preparation pipelines. Additionally, CRSS requires that student affairs professionals are able to (a) permeate cultural boundaries in ways that are informed and respectful; (b) work to gain knowledge about how practices have disserved students; and (c) develop a willingness to examine their own values, dispositions, and competencies in order to better serve urban students. Ultimately, student affairs professionals change their practices by recognizing students' cultures as valuable contributions to the higher education setting, and then offering congruent support and opportunities that enable students to thrive.

Engaging With a Counterproductive Hierarchy

Building on this conceptual framework, we consider the urban institution itself using an antideficit lens. To do so, we draw on Alexander Astin's concept of counterproductive views of excellence (Astin, 1985), which remains profoundly significant nearly 35 years later. Astin described a hierarchy rooted in a "shared belief system" (p. 4) in which the reputation and resources of an institution are the measure of excellence and quality rather than the impact of an institution upon its students. The shared belief system became a kind of shared mythology about what constitutes excellence in U.S. higher education and which of our 4,000+ institutions of higher education (IHEs) are *the best*. In *Achieving Educational Excellence* (Astin, 1985), Astin described a parlor game in which guests are asked to list the top five or ten IHEs in the country and expressed no surprise that the lists were almost uniform: Harvard, Yale, Princeton and publics like Berkeley and Michigan as top universities. These institutions still enjoy a cycle of privilege, where they attract "the best" faculty and students, large endowments, excellent track records of securing government and philanthropic grant monies, and grandiose, state-of-the art facilities. Outcomes such as graduation rates, graduate entry exam scores, and prominent job placement are also excellent, largely attributable to the pre-college characteristics of their students rather than what the institution actually contributes to student outcomes. Indeed, all these factors, which can be found in

Astin's conceptualization of the counterproductive hierarchy, are a part of the formula the *U.S. News and World Report* uses in its annual ranking of universities. The notoriety that top-ranked institutions receive from these "Best Colleges" lists then becomes the basis for attracting more resources, more applicants, and even more of "the best."

Furthermore, this hierarchy promotes the notion that underprepared students are a liability to institutions, faculty, and staff, who will have to spend excess resources to raise those students up to the mythological notions of quality and excellence. Astin warned that this counterproductive hierarchy of shared beliefs promotes institutional conformity (Astin, 1985, p. 12) and leaves many IHEs at lower rungs of the hierarchy striving to match the metrics of their more prestigious peers (e.g., raising admission standards, spending institutional resources to attract faculty from more highly ranked institutions, offering merit scholarships to attract highly qualified and highly advantaged students). This belief system and the practices it engenders often leaves the institutions most willing to admit the underprepared student at the bottom of the hierarchy "treated with something not far from contempt" (p. 13) or focused on seeking the resources generously afforded to those institutions at the top instead of their own students.

This counterproductive hierarchy becomes the basis for reputation, ranking, and resource distribution rather than assessment of the unique needs of different institutions and their unique student populations, goals, and needs. When institutions do not meet the normalized standards of higher education they are seen as inefficient, struggling, or *less than* and thus underserving of resources. These under-resourced institutions are then perceived as lacking or insufficient when their student outcomes look different from other well-resourced institutions. Astin (1985) said that,

> we are inclined to believe that the goal of equality has been attained when opportunities are made available to all who desire them and when no person is denied access to higher education because of race, gender, income, or social status. [However,] given the great diversity in the faculties, facilities, and other resources of American colleges and universities, it seems necessary to expand the concept of quality of opportunity to take into account the relative quality or excellence of the opportunities provided.
>
> *(p. 18)*

In 1985, the concept of equity had yet to take strong hold in higher education, but Astin described it well here. Simply making higher education accessible to all potential students does not mean that all the opportunities are equitable. Some opportunities unfairly benefit some, while systemically denying them to others, not because the institution, such as a USI, is insufficient, but because the system that distributes resources is inequitable.

Astin (1985) believed that if most people stopped to really think about the meaning of excellence or quality in higher education that they would see the intellectual and personal development of students as paramount to the educational goals and mission of any institution. He called this the *talent development approach* for considering institutional excellence. We are used to thinking about institutional excellence through a lens of resources and reputation, but if institutional excellence were to be considered through a lens of equity, the talent development approach would likely reign supreme (Astin, 1985, p. 62). Considering USIs through the lenses of CRP and CRSS allows us to see past the hierarchical conceptualization of higher education in our nation to understand what higher education is really about: the development and education of students. If institutional excellence was determined by what institutions do for their students, with whatever resources they receive, the reputation hierarchy of higher education institutions in this nation might dramatically shift. USIs might be recognized and rewarded because they have an additive effect for students who are in greater need whereas higher ranked and more prestigious institutions maintain a status quo of privilege and exclusion by simply confirming social status for the already privileged.

Because higher education opportunities are not equitable, the work of the USI as an equitable opportunity provider becomes more important, and thus the work of student affairs in these institutions becomes critical. The services and interventions enacted by student affairs staff have to reflect the reality of student needs and circumstances, and use skill sets to bring together a network that includes family, community, and cultural groups from the urban centers in which these institutions are located. The programs, processes, and practices for supporting student development rely on analysis of sociopolitical forces such as racism, poverty, blight and gentrification, local and national legislation, and institutional resourcing models that affect the lives of, and opportunities available to students attending USIs. Employing CRSS in USIs could shift the ways students are perceived and the ways their development is supported; such a shift would mirror the impact of CRP on classroom-based student learning outcomes. Furthermore, reconsidering the reputations of USIs through CRSS and CRP, empowers these institutions to become agents of change in their communities by providing continuing education programs and social services for local residents and resources for the highly varied constituencies that traditional universities struggle to adequately serve.

The Case for Reconsidering the Urban-Serving Institution

Higher education institutions have experienced increases in enrollment, despite fears of a decrease in the number of high school graduates, in the last 10 years for which data is available. Integrated Postsecondary Education Data System (IPEDS) data show that U.S. institutions have seen a 14.5 percent increase in enrollment since 2006 and that, despite being a smaller group, urban institutions saw more enrollment growth than their nonurban peers (NCES, 2019). This demonstrates the continued relevance of USIs in higher education. All institutions have experienced increased enrollment among low-income students, as measured by

Pell Grant status. Over the last 10 years, urban institutions have outpaced the increases in Pell Grant awardees of their nonurban peers and enroll 58 percent of the nation's college-going Pell Grant recipients (NCES, 2019). By 2016, urban institutions had also seen steady increases in the enrollment of students who identify as women, as well as minoritized racial/ethnic identities such as Asian, Hawaiian, Pacific Islander, Black or African American, Hispanic, or two or more races; with Native American enrollment remaining relatively the same. In 2016, urban institutions enrolled 58 percent of college-going women and 62 percent of college-going students who identified with a minoritized race or ethnicity (NCES, 2019).

Pressure to Perform

In addition to meeting the unique internal demands and needs of a nontraditional student population and institutional structure, the vast majority of USIs are public institutions and must navigate government regulations in our current "era of accountability." Many new state initiatives across the nation are calling for an increase in graduation rates and a reduction in time to degree, with some states tying future funding to an institution's ability to meet specific goals. This pressure to perform is complex for the public USI. In both 2- and 4-year institutions, the needs of the urban college student reflect the context in which they live and work and the public systems in which they have been educated, a context that is beyond the control and even influence of an institution that is often tasked to "make-up the difference" and compel USI students to match their more traditional peers. Student affairs units are tasked to create environments in which students thrive—those that engender a sense of belonging and engagement—and to offer innovative programs that support student success. In the USI environment, student affairs units become partners within the academic enterprise that can reach beyond classroom and on-campus services in order to provide support that is vital not only for students to succeed but also for these institutions to meet the demands and expectations of regional, state, and even national legislative and accreditation bodies.

A Dearth of Literature for Student Affairs in Urban Institutions

Peggy Gordon Elliott noted in her 1994 book *The Urban Campus* that at the brink of a new century the changing times heralded the emergence of a *new majority* of students who no longer fit the traditional college student model. While emphasizing the importance of understanding the growing new majority student population, as well as the diverse needs and unique characteristics of the urban campus, Elliott (1994) also cautioned that "we cannot, with any degree of success, educate students while operating under the same assumptions and with the same models that were successful in the much different past" (p. xiii). What was abundantly clear to Elliott 25 years ago is now clearer to more researchers in the last 3 decades who have sought to understand not only the characteristics and needs of the students and institutions themselves but the vital contributions these intuitions make to the lives and families of students, the local communities, the regional workforce, and higher education (Anderson-Butcher, Iachini, Ball, Barke, & Martin, 2016; Buendia, 2010; Newbold, 2015; Perry & Wiewel, 2005; Rodin, 2007). However, despite the growing number of USIs across the country, and the continued evolution of the needs and characteristics of the USI student population, there are virtually no texts currently used in any student affairs preparation program that focus on urban institutions (Ortiz, Filimon, & Cole-Jackson, 2015).

Mind the Gap: A Review of Existing Literature about USIs

While we may be deepening our understanding of the important differences between urban-serving institutions and their traditional counterparts, there is very little literature about what to do to mitigate the differences that may negatively impact students, and even less literature specifically about the role of student affairs units and student affairs leaders at urban institutions. After Elliott's 1994 description of the imminent shift in higher education, Perry and Wiewel (2005) and Rodin (2007) explored the surroundings and the effect of urban institutions on their neighborhoods and local communities in two, of very few, books that address the characteristics, challenges, lessons learned, and potential future of USIs. Both texts explore the world of USIs through other disciplines such as urban planning, leadership, and real estate, further emphasizing the need for texts that explore urban institutions from a student affairs perspective.

Perhaps most interesting about the 2005 and 2007 texts is the multidisciplinary approach used by the authors. In *The University as Urban Developer*, Perry and Wiewel (2005) examined the role of the USI as an integral player in real estate development and a potential antidote for urban blight if leveraged thoughtfully in the process of urban planning and development. In *The University and Urban Revival*, Rodin (2007) echoed some of the ideas of the role that higher education institutions can play in urban neighborhood and community development, especially those areas challenged by poverty, crime, and deteriorating neighborhood relationships. However, the singular focus on the leadership and management of a major development campaign at one Ivy League institution makes for a fascinating case study about the role of an institution that is uniquely positioned to serve its urban community through a vast array of resources that most institutions, especially USIs as defined in this project, are without.

What becomes most clear when reviewing the literature that does look at USIs is that the most recent text that explores the full identity of the USI is 25 years old, and, since that time, the other texts that are often referenced and cited have written extensively about USIs from a limited external perspective that leaves the internal world of USIs to remain mysterious, unacknowledged, and misunderstood. While all of these authors acknowledged the multifaceted and complex nature of USIs, none of these texts thoroughly, if at all, acknowledged the role of student affairs as a vehicle for contributing to the institutional mission and outcomes for USIs.

A great deal of research connected to USIs focuses on the differences that exist between the experiences of commuter students compared with residential students. However, most of these rest on the notion that the residential student experience is the norm, while the commuter student experience is an "alternative" or "other" experience (Gefen & Fish, 2013; Lonn, Teasley, & Krummc, 2010; López Turley & Wodtke, 2010; Palmer, 2012; Sparks & Nuñez, 2014). Research about the commuter versus residential student experience can be generalized into two types of studies: student profile studies that compare the characteristics and traits of commuter and residential students (Alfano & Eduljee, 2013; Gianoutsos & Rosser, 2014; Lonn et al., 2010; López Turley & Wodtke, 2010) and student outcomes studies that compare the academic and developmental outcomes of students living off and on campus (Martin & Kilgo, 2015; Nelson, Misra, Sype, & Mackie, 2016; Palmer, 2012; Sparks & Nuñez, 2014). While studies like Alfano and Eduljee (2013) and Krause (2007) found that commuter students are often less engaged with their institutions, studies by Martin and Kilgo (2015) and Nelson, Misra, Sype, and Mackie, (2016) found that commuting to campus does not necessarily negatively affect those students' psychological well-being or academic proficiency.

Student affairs professionals are taught that belonging and engagement are crucial to student success; in fact, the importance of belonging and engagement could be considered the keystone of the very existence of student affairs units (Tovar, Simon, & Lee, 2009; Melendez, 2016). However, it is important to remember that the act of driving to campus is not as significant as facts such as where these commuting students are coming from, who they are, what their competing interests are, and how their social identities, employment status, goals, and needs impact the way they interact with their institutions. A better understanding of the role of student affairs in the success of students at USIs in which the student population is predominantly commuter is certainly needed, but it is important to remember that most USI students are dealing with far more than just a drive to campus in their pursuit of education.

Seemingly, the majority of research that relates to the urban institution consists of that which evaluates and recommends best practices for commuter campuses and minoritized student populations. Several works related to activities and services available to students at USIs, most of which focus on engagement and support, are highlighted throughout the chapters in this volume (Barbatis, 2010; Clark, 2006; Donaldson, McKinney, Lee, & Pino, 2016; , Perrakis, & Maxwell, 2007; Kretovics, 2015; Newbold, 2015; Nicpon et al., 2006). All of these texts are referenced in Chapter 3 and Chapter 4 as the authors explore the unique identities, experiences, and challenges of the urban college student.

The topic of belonging is perhaps one of the most frequent themes that appears throughout research about urban college and commuter students. Kretovics (2015) and Newbold (2015) focused particularly on the challenges of and new efforts being made toward developing a sense of belonging for commuter students, while Nicpon et al. (2006) examined the relationship between belonging and academic success specifically for first-year students. Clark (2006) and Hagedorn, Perrakis, and Maxwell (2007) explored best practices specifically for urban campuses to engage their majority commuter student population and promote student success. Two other qualitative studies that are frequently cited throughout this volume (Barbatis, 2010; Holland, 2016) explore notions of belonging and student success through student perspectives that provide great insight for student affairs professionals and leaders to consider. While in-depth and informative for the topic of USIs, the majority of these studies explores topics in isolation without making deeper connections across institutional types, student experiences, student and academic affairs programs and initiatives, and institutional goals and mission; and without acknowledging that student affairs leadership lives at the heart of these connections. Our work here aims to combine these different bodies of literature and develop a clearer picture of the ways in which USIs can achieve greater institutional success for the benefit of their students.

The qualitative research about student affairs in USIs offers clear examples of what works for students attending these institutions as well as the unique challenges these students face throughout their collegiate experiences. Several qualitative studies found that nontraditional support is meaningful to nontraditional students attending nontraditional institutions (Pratt, 2015; Villarreal & Garcia, 2016) because the unique experiences of USI students become validated when the services available fit and acknowledge their lived experiences. Most quantitative research that investigates the experiences of students in USIs can speak to one of two topics: the challenges and barriers that most commuter and/or minority student populations face (Fischer, 2007; Ross et al., 2012; Whalen, Saunders, & Shelley, 2009) or the tactics that students attending USIs and students services units can and do employ to manage those challenges and barriers (Darling, 2015; Dugan, Garland, Jacoby, & Gasiorski, 2008; Grutzik & Ramos, 2016; Hensley, Shaulskiy, Zircher, & Sanders, 2015; Torres, 2006). Findings from these quantitative studies support the notion that the USI student's persistence, retention, or the decision to leave college is affected by circumstances beyond their control, such as racial and ethnic identity (Fischer, 2007; Torres, 2006), personal finances (Hensley et al., 2015; Whalen, Saunders, & Shelley, 2009), and institutional support programs (Darling, 2015; Grutzik & Ramos, 2016).

These studies play an important role in gaining a better understanding of students and institutions that reach beyond the traditional collegiate model. However, understanding the uniqueness of a student population, or an institution, or a practice, is only a first step. There remains a significant lack of practices, methods, or even suggestions for how to increase the size and scope of programs and services to serve the broader institution populations of USIs and the local communities that they serve. Chapters 2 and 3 set the stage by diving more deeply into understanding the USI and USI student. Subsequent chapters deeply explore vital issues related to student success, engagement, and belonging in USIs, as well as the training, leadership, and partnerships needed for student affairs units within USIs.

Student Affairs in Urban-Serving Institutions

Currently, the extant research focused on USIs explores which students succeed and which students do not or what interventions do and do not work for students. We are attempting to fill gaps with expertise from leaders who have spent most of their careers in USIs and can share from their own experiences how student affairs units can play an important role in urban institutions and how student affairs leadership can dramatically impact the success of the urban institution. We know from the participants in this project that student affairs training programs rarely prepare student affairs practitioners for work outside a traditional-collegiate environment; we also know that the experiences of students attending urban institutions vary greatly from those attending traditional universities, especially when those students commute to campus and/or come from minoritized identity groups.

By highlighting the voices of student affairs leaders in USIs, we are able to better contextualize what the sparse literature related to USI demographics and programs is telling us. The successful practices and lessons learned within urban student affairs units need to be heard in order to bring to life what is missing in the current literature: connection. To better serve USI students and institutional goals, we need to start connecting our understanding of the multifaceted experiences of USI students with the variety of institutional types that exist within the USI sector. We also need to connect best practices, recommendations, and lessons learned from the literature and student affairs leaders to institutional missions, national standards, and the broader goals of higher education.

Description of the Project

Tasked with the goal of deepening the understanding of (a) USIs, (b) the impact student affairs can have in attaining student development goals at these institutions, and (c) the positive impact of these institutions on the local community, we began to research the limited literature on urban-serving institutions. The literature review helped to refine our definition of *urban-serving institution* as the following:

1. Located in a major urban area
2. Primarily a commuter campus, with a very small percentage of residential students, if any.
3. A campus that has a significant proportion of students from underserved populations in regard to race, ethnicity, and/or socioeconomic status
4. A place where there is an ethos of serving the urban area through leadership, research, and service to address a wide range of localized issues and improve the quality of life for communities and their members
5. Offers a variety of undergraduate, graduate, and/or extended education programs that are relevant to the members of urban centers

The first three elements of this definition were assessed through institutional demographic information about location, city size/population, and student population demographics. The fourth element related to an "ethos of serving" was assessed through qualitative evaluation of each institution's mission statement, as well as vision, values, and strategic goals statements (where available). Each institution's mission statement and supporting information was uploaded to NVivo, where the documents were evaluated for information related to service for the community and population beyond the limits of the campus footprint. Finally, the fifth element of the definition was assessed by searching for and tracking the number and type of education programs provided by the institution—looking specifically for those that extended beyond traditional educational models such as those programs seen at Virginia Commonwealth University (VCU, 2019), which ultimately led us to include this institution in our sample.

An initial search for institutions that met these criteria began with a review of the member list for the Coalition of Urban Serving Universities (USU) and Coalition of Urban and Metropolitan Universities (CUMU). The names of 109 institutions were combined and organized according to the U.S. Census Bureau's National Regions and Divisions in order to ensure regional and geographical representation. The list of urban-serving institutions organized by region was cross-referenced with a list of minority-serving institutions created by the Penn Graduate School of Education Center and a list of institutions catalogued in the Carnegie Community Engagement Classification. Cross-referencing yielded a list of 27 institutions that met the project's criteria for urban-serving institution (see Table 1.1). From this final list, the contact information for the senior leaders of the Student Affairs divisions at each institution were found and these officers were invited to participate in the project.

In the summer of 2017, conversations with participants, using a standard protocol, were recorded primarily via phone, although two were conducted in person. Interviews were recorded and transcribed verbatim. Preliminary data analysis resulted in the chapter structure for the book and helped to guide subsequent analysis. some participants in the interview phase of the project elected to serve as chapter authors—and are introduced subsequently—or as consultants for the development of this volume.

Those who elected to serve as authors were given the opportunity to identify which chapters they would like to author. All participants identified colleagues with whom they elected to write the chapters. Coded data from the interviews and the literature review were distributed to each chapter team for the development and writing of each assigned chapter. All participants had opportunities to contribute through a review and consultation process, and many authors have served as resources for each other as the chapters developed, thus creating a text that represents the experiences of many, rather than the perspectives of individual chapter authors. We believe the utility of this work is enhanced by a participatory research process that has, in many ways, modeled a circle of inquiry that is representative of action research, a style of research that is often best suited to address the realities of an institution's work and settings.

TABLE 1.1 Disaggregated Project Sample Data for All 27 Institutions

Institution name	% commuter student population	Underserved populations		
		% students from minoritized race/ethnicity	Institutional designation	% of students awarded Pell Grants
California State University, Fullerton	98%	74%	AANAPISI, HSI	47%
California State University, Long Beach	92%	77%	AANAPISI, HSI	51%
California State University, Los Angeles	96%	89%	AANAPISI, HSI	67%
City Colleges of Chicago, Harold Washington College	100%	87%	AANAPISI, HSI	44%
City Colleges of Chicago, Malcolm X College	100%	91%	HSI, PBI	43%
CUNY, City College	98%	83%	AANAPISI, HSI	53%
Community College of Philadelphia	100%	72%	PBI	61%
Coppin State University	79%	98%	HBCU, MSI	57%
Florida International University	92%	88%	HSI	49%
Georgia State University	82%	69%		49%
Long Beach City College	100%	87%	AANAPISI, HSI	34%
Metropolitan State University	100%	45%	★	42%
Morgan State University	75%	94%	HBCU, MSI	52%
Northeastern Illinois University	100%	61%	HSI	48%
Rutgers University, Newark	Yes	66%		50%
Saint Louis Community College	100%	89%	PBI	35%
San Francisco State University	89%	75%	AANAPISI	43%
San Jose State University	87%	76%	AANAPISI	41%

Institution name	% commuter student population	Underserved populations		
		% students from minoritized race/ethnicity	Institutional designation	% of students awarded Pell Grants
Seattle Central College	100%	56%	^	20%
Southern University at New Orleans	~75%	86%	HBCU	60%
University of Central Florida	83%	48%		38%
University of Houston, Downtown	81%	82%	AANAPISI, HSI	46%
University of Massachusetts, Boston	100%	53%	AANAPISI	40%
University of Memphis	86%	50%	PBI	46%
University of Nevada, Las Vegas	93%	61%	AANAPISI	36%
University of the District of Columbia	96%	85%	HBCU, MSI	47%
Virginia Commonwealth University	79%	46%	★	28%

Source: Commuter student population statistics from https://nces.ed.gov/collegenavigator/. Institutional Designation from www.gse.upenn.edu/pdf/cmsi/MSIs_Location_Map.pdf. Percentage of students from minoritized race/ethnicity and percentage of students awarded PELL Grants came from https://nces.ed.gov/ipeds/datacenter/Institutionbyname.aspx

★ *Indicates a student population where minoritized racial/ethnic identity is significantly higher than state population demographics.*
^ Indicates a large population of students designated as "Non-Resident Alien" status

Data Analysis and Chapter Structure

After interviews were transcribed, initial data analysis saw the emergence of major themes that would later become chapters. Chapter 2 provides context for the urban serving institution by discussing the unique characteristics and qualities of these institutions that distinguish USIs from the more "traditional" institutional model. Chapter 3 emerged from the discussion of the particular characteristics of the urban college student and the acknowledgement, by many of the leaders who contributed, that while most college students face some of the same basic challenges, attending a USI adds a level of complexity that students at traditional institutions do not face.

Chapters 4 and 5 emerged from discussion that focused on the role and purpose of student affairs units in USIs. Leaders who were interviewed shared examples of best practices, successful programs, and lessons learned in their units that were seen as contributing to student success. Leaders were also able to articulate the specific ways in which their units worked to promote student engagement and belonging through independently and in partnership with other units on campus and within the local community.

A set of themes emerged around the duties associated with leading student affairs units in USIs, duties such as establishing strategic goals, fostering change, staffing, fundraising, data driven decision-making, and division promotion and management. These themes originally emerged as ideas that could be complemented by another theme related to partnerships within, across, and beyond the institution. However, as the chapter writing progressed, it became clear that the duties associated with leading a student affairs unit were not separate from the importance of creating partnerships across the institution, nor was this work separate from strengthening the pipeline from local school districts into the institution. Eventually, what would have been two different chapters became Chapter 6, an exploration of the multifaceted nature of the role of senior student affairs officer (SSAO).

Chapter 7 emerged from recurring themes among contributors, that the experience of the SSAO is deeply influenced by familial, educational, and professional background and experiences. Most contributors traced their professional evolution as a varied journey from which they acquired new knowledge through steep learning curves, included a great deal of professional isolation, and was fueled by a personal mission to serve. Chapter 8 was devised from themes that emerged during discussion of preparation for this work. Leaders who were interviewed shared the educational experiences and professional development opportunities that were most important in their preparation and work, as well as any theory and curricula that they found particularly useful. Many leaders also shared insight about programs and trainings that they perceived as beneficial for their staff, colleagues, and peers. Chapter 9 serves as a summary of the major themes in the volume with careful attention to themes and issues that occur across the chapters. Select recommendations from the individual chapters are reinforced. The future of urban-serving institutions is considered with an eye toward implications for the profession of student affairs.

Conclusion

Our hope is that this volume will prove a helpful resource for student affairs professionals who work in or seek to work in urban institutions and perhaps as a resource for student affairs faculty facilitating the graduate preparation of future student affairs professionals. In addition, the volume will likely be of interest to higher education graduate students, scholars, and faculty members who have an interest in urban education. Academic administrators at urban institutions may also be interested in using this work as a way to better understand student affairs work and partnerships. Scholars and graduate students who study urban education at the PreK–12 level may also find value in this volume as they support their students on the path toward higher education.

Each chapter in this volume addresses a particular topic relevant to urban-serving institutions, student affairs, and leadership. But, perhaps additionally unique to this volume, it is the individual voices of the leaders who participated in the research and writing of this volume that we hope will be received as equally important to this work. In addition to the research, scholarship, and literature presented in each chapter is a personal introduction written by each chapter author/participant so readers may get to know the leader authoring the chapter.

Each chapter includes suggestions and questions intended to stimulate discussion or further consideration of the ideas presented in the chapter. Broadly speaking, our aim in writing this volume was to explore questions such as: How do we prepare our graduate students to work with underprepared students? How are we helping student affairs professionals new to USIs learn to connect and support students who find it hard to get involved in traditional activities because they live at home or have significant work commitments? How are we helping student affairs staff learn to collaborate with faculty and academic departments to support students when their primary point of connection is the classroom and not a residence hall, student union, or a student organization? And how do we prepare to help close the opportunity gap that results in disparity in graduation rates for specific racial and ethnic groups? Such questions became the cornerstones of our project for this volume.

This project illuminated the importance of capturing the voices of student affairs leaders who can not only share a range of important professional experiences, insights, and lessons learned, but who are also wrestling with important questions about leading, managing, and working in USIs. We also hope that the circular-inquiry approach to researching and representing the experiences of the student affairs leaders who participated in the crafting of this volume will inspire readers to embrace various forms of action research projects in their own work to foster change and growth in their unique education environments. Most importantly, we hope this volume will inspire readers to continue to wrestle with important questions, especially those questions that reach into the uniqueness of urban educations pursuit of a more equitable future for all of our students.

References

Alfano, H. J., & Eduljee, N. B. (2013). Differences in work, levels of involvement, and academic performance between residential and commuter students. *College Student Journal*, 47(2), 334–342.

Anderson-Butcher, D., Iachini, A. L., Ball, A., Barke, S., & Martin, L. D. (2016). A university-school partnership to examine the adoption and implementation of the Ohio community collaboration model in one urban school district: A mixed-method case study. *Journal of Education for Students Placed at Risk*, 21(3), 190–204.

Astin, A. E. (1985). *Achieving academic excellence: A critical assessment of priorities and practices in higher education.* San Francisco, CA: Jossey-Bass.

Barbatis, P. (2010). Underprepared, ethnically diverse community college students: Factors contributing to persistence. *Journal of Developmental Education*, 33(3), 16–26.

Buendia, E. (2010). Reconsidering the urban in urban education: Interdisciplinary conversations. *Urban Review*, 43(1), 1–21. doi:10.1007/s11256–11010–0152-z

Clark, M. R. (2006). Succeeding in the city: Challenges and best practices on urban commuter campuses. *About Campus*, 11(3), 2–8.

Darling, R. A. (2015). Creating an institutional academic advising culture that supports commuter student success. *New Directions for Student Services*, 150, 87–96. doi:10.1002/ss.20130

Donaldson, P., McKinney, L., Lee, M., & Pino, D. (2016). First-year community college students' perceptions of and attitudes toward intrusive academic advising. *NACADA Journal*, 36(1), 30–42. doi:10.12930/NACADA-15–012

Dugan, J. P., Garland, J. L., Jacoby, B., & Gasiorski, A. (2008). Understanding commuter student self-efficacy for leadership: A within-group analysis. NASPA Journal, 45(2), 282–310.

Elliott, P. G. (1994). *The urban campus: Educating the new majority for the new century*. Phoenix, AZ: The Oryx Press.

Fischer, M. J. (2007). Settling into campus life: Differences by race/ethnicity in college involvement and outcomes. *The Journal of Higher Education*, 28(2), 125–156. doi:10.1353/jhe.2007.0009

Gefen, D. R., & Fish, M. C. (2013). Adjustment to college in nonresidential first-year students: The roles of stress, family, and coping. *Journal of the First Year Experience & Students in Transition*, 25(2), 95–115.

Gianoutsos, D., & Rosser, V. (2014). Is there still a considerable difference? Comparing residential and commuter student profile characteristics at a public, research, commuter university. *College Student Journal*, 48(4), 613–628.

Grutzik, C., & Ramos, S. (2016). The role of the student support specialist: The possibilities and challenges of a long-term, proactive, and scaffolded relationship. *Community College Journal of Research and Practice*, 40(2), 113–132. doi:10.1080/10668926.2014.997842

Hagedorn, L. S., Perrakis, A. I., & Maxwell, W. (2007). The negative commandments: Ten ways urban community colleges hinder student success. *Florida Journal of Educational Administration & Policy*, 1(1), 25–35.

Hensley, L., Shaulskiy, S., Zircher, A., & Sanders, M. (2015). Overcoming barriers to engaging in college academics. *Journal of Student Affairs Research and Practice*, 52(2), 176–189. doi:10.1080/19496591.2015.1020246

Holland, N. E. (2016). Partnering with a higher power: Academic engagement, religiosity, and spirituality of African American urban youth. *Education and Urban Society*, 48(5), 299–323.

Krause, K. D. (2007). Social involvement and commuter students: The first-year student voice. *Journal of the First-Year Experience & Students in Transition*, 19(1), 27–45.

Kretovics, M. (2015). Commuter students, online services, and online communities. *New Directions for Students Services*, 150, 69–78.

Kuh, G. D. (2008). *High-impact educational practices: What they are, who has access to them, and why they matter*. Washington, DC: Association of American Colleges and Universities.

Ladson-Billings, G. (1995). Toward a theory of culturally relevant pedagogy. *American Educational Research Journal*, 32(3), 465–491. Retrieved from www.jstor.org/stable/1163320

Ladson-Billings, G. (2014). Culturally relevant pedagogy 2.0: A.K.A. the remix. *Harvard Educational Review*, 84(1), 74–84.

Lonn, S., Teasley, S. D., & Krummc, A. E. (2010). Who needs to do what where? Using learning management systems on residential vs. commuter campuses. *Computers & Education*, 56(3), 642–649. doi:10.1016/j.compedu.2010.10.006

López Turley, R. N., & Wodtke, G. (2010). College residence and academic performance: Who benefits from living on campus? *Urban Education*, 45(4), 506–532. doi:10.1177/0042085910372351

Martin, G. L., & Kilgo, C. A. (2015). Exploring the impact of commuting to campus on psychological well-being. *New Directions for Student Services*, 150, 35–43.

Melendez, M. C. (2016). Adjustment to college in an urban commuter setting: The impact of gender, race/ethnicity, and athletic participation. *Journal of College Student Retention: Research, Theory & Practice*, 18(1), 31–48. doi:10.1177/1521025115579671

National Center for Education Statistics (NCES). (2019). Compare institutions by degrees of urbanization [Data file and code book]. *U.S. Department of Education, Institute of Education Sciences*. Retrieved from https://nces.ed.gov/ipeds/datacenter/mastervariablelist.aspx?stepId=2

Nelson, D., Misra, K., Sype, G. E., & Mackie, W. (2016). An analysis of the relationship between distance from campus and GPA of commuter students. *Journal of International Education Research*, 12(1), 37–46.

Newbold, J. J. (2015). Lifestyle challenges for commuter students. *New Directions for Student Services*, 150, 79–86. doi:10.1002/ss.20129

Nicpon, M. F., Huser, L., Blanks, E. H., Sollenberger, S., Befort, C., & Kurpius, S. E. R. (2006). The relationship of loneliness and social support with college freshmen's academic performance and persistence. *College Student Retention*, 8(3), 345–358.

Ortiz, A. M., Filimon, I., & Cole-Jackson, M. (2015). Preparing student affairs educators. In J. H. Schuh & E. Whitt (Eds.), *Reflections on the past 20 years in student services. New Directions for Student Services* (pp. 79–88). San Francisco, CA: Jossey-Bass.

Palmer, S. (2012). Understanding the context of distance students: Differences in on- and off-campus engagement with an online learning environment. *Journal of Open, Flexible and Distance Learning*, 16(1), 70–82.

Perry, D. C., & Wiewel, W. (2005). *The university as urban developer: Case studies and analysis*. New York: Routledge.

Pratt, K. (2015). Supporting distance learners: Making practice more effective. *Journal of Open, Flexible and Distance Learning*, 19(1), 12–26.

Rodin, J. (2007). *The university & urban revival: Out of the ivory tower and into the streets*. Philadelphia: University of Pennsylvania Press.

Ross, T., Kena, G., Rathbun, A., KewalRamani, A., Zhang, J., Kristapovich, P., & Manning, E. (2012). *Higher education: Gaps in access and persistence study (NCES 2012–2046)*. Washington, DC: NCES, IES, & U.S. Department of Education.

Sparks, P. J., & Nuñez, A. M. (2014). The role of postsecondary institutional urbanicity in college persistence. *Journal of Research in Rural Education*, 29(6), 1–19.

Torres, V. (2006). A mixed method study testing data-model fit of a retention model for latino/a students at urban universities. *Journal of College Student Development*, 47(3), 299–318. doi:10.1353/csd.2006.0037

Tovar, E., Simon, M. A., & Lee, H. B. (2009). Development and validation of the college mattering inventory with diverse urban college students. *Measurement and Evaluation in Counseling and Development*, 42(3), 154–178. doi:101177/0748175609344091

U.S. Census Bureau. (2011). 2009–2011 American community survey 3-year data. Retrieved from www.census.gov/content/dam/Census/library/working-papers/2013/acs/2013_Bishaw_01.pdf

Villarreal, M. de Lourdes, & Garcia, H. A. (2016). Self-determination and goal aspirations: African American and Latino males' perceptions of their persistence in community college basic and transfer-level writing courses. *Community College Journal of Research and Practice, 40*(10), 838–853. doi:10.1080/10668926.2015.1125314

Virginia Commonwealth University (VCU). (2019). Virginia Commonwealth University mission statement [webpage]. Retrieved from http://bulletin.vcu.edu/about/mission-vision-core-values/

Whalen, D., Saunders, K., & Shelley, M. (2009). Leveraging what we know to enhance short-term and long-term retention of university students. *Journal of College Student Retention, 11*(3), 407–430.

2

UNDERSTANDING THE URBAN-SERVING INSTITUTION

Tiffany J. Davis and Richard Walker

As coauthors, our paths to this topic were different, yet our commitment to this work and our institution is the same. We have the privilege of working at the nation's second most diverse public university. The University of Houston (UH) holds the designations of a Hispanic-serving institution (HSI) and an Asian American and Native American Pacific Islander–Serving institution (AANAPISI). On our campus, no single racial or ethnic group is a majority, and, as a result, diversity and inclusion is a cornerstone of our identity. Tiffany is a faculty member in our Higher Education, Leadership, and Policy Studies graduate program and Richard is the Vice President for Student Affairs and Enrollment Services.

I (Tiffany) have worked in both administrative and faculty positions within student affairs for over a decade and UH is my first urban-serving institution context. I was drawn to the University of Houston because of its deep commitment to access, diversity, and community. From my engagement on campus and within the greater Houston community, I am even more committed to helping train and socialize future scholar-practitioners to develop the knowledge, competencies, and mindsets that are necessary to develop and sustain transformative, inclusive, and equity-oriented programs, practices, and policies while thriving in the USI work environment.

Over the course of my (Richard) 36-year career working in student affairs, I have had the opportunity to work at two regional institutions, a Tier-1 private research university, and for the past 8 years at UH, a large, public, Research-1 urban-serving institution. Working with a large population of first-generation, undocumented, foster care, and historically underrepresented racial/ethnic student populations has been a true motivation and passion for me. It pushes me to make certain that we are enacting our mission to ensure these students' access and success. I, along with the other vice presidents in this project, have a shared commitment to the historical USI mission, yet can acknowledge that USIs are changing and evolving as a type of institution within the higher education landscape.

> *Our hope is that this contextual chapter helps frame for readers the historical and current positioning and significance of the urban-serving institution.*
>
> *—Tiffany J. Davis, Ph.D., Clinical Assistant Professor of Higher Education and Program Director of Higher Education Master's Programs, University of Houston and*
> *Richard Walker, Ed.D., Vice President for Student Affairs and Enrollment Services and Vice Chancellor for Student Affairs and Enrollment Services, University of Houston System*

Institutional diversity remains a distinguishing characteristic of the American higher education system. Exemplified by over 4,300 degree-granting postsecondary institutions (NCES, 2018, Table 317.10), the large number and wide range of community college, public, private, and for-profit institutions offer both access and choice for today's college-going population (Eckel & King, 2004). Urban-serving institutions (USIs), formed to meet the increasing demands of diverse and growing enrollments in the mid-twentieth century, represent 68 percent of colleges and universities in the United States and serve approximately 20 million students (APLU, 2018a). Our goal is to provide context around the urban-serving institution that helps to better situate and understand the findings and implications from the leader interviews that are discussed throughout this book. In this chapter, we discuss the institutional characteristics of USIs, including student profile and institutional type, and how the urban context influences structures and activities of these institutions. We also address leadership and governance issues, such as institutional sustainability and health, tensions affecting mission, and the influence of presidential leadership.

What Is the Urban-Serving Institution?

Urban-serving institutions (USIs) represent the third wave of the American higher education movement, following the colonial colleges and public land-grant colleges and alongside the development of a community college model. They were established and grew "in response to urbanization, mass migration to urban areas, increased enrollments primarily fueled by returning GIs during the post–World War II era, and unprecedented access extended to women and people of color" (Zerquera, 2016, p. 140). Also called *metropolitan universities*, some might narrowly classify these institutions on the basis of their location in a major urban area; however, defining characteristics of an urban-serving institution extend beyond the setting and include an access-oriented mission, a diverse and largely commuter student profile, and a symbiotic connection to the community.

Urban-serving institutions are considered "anchor institutions" with significant impact on the city in which they reside (Friedman, Perry, & Menendez, 2014, p. 22), influencing economic progress and social potential by generating jobs, attracting industry, providing cultural opportunities, and working to improve the condition of a community (Harris & Holley, 2016). The concept of anchor institutions incorporates the potential benefits of universities for city-regions and outlines the need for leaders of urban universities to integrate this "anchoring" role into the fabric of their institution through the mission and in their leadership structure, curriculum, policies, budget, and commitment to evaluation (Craft, Garmise, Modarres, Perry, & Villamizar-Duarte, 2016). According to Harris and Holley (2016), the anchor institution concept idealizes the belief in the power of place-based institutions to support social and economic growth because "when universities serve as community anchors, they make specific decisions to leverage various forms of capital, including economic, human, and intellectual, to advance the well-being of their local communities" (p. 402).

The label of "urban-serving institution" is not homogeneous, as there are different institutional types that compose this group, and as such, the unique ways they enact their access-oriented mission are also diverse. For example, this project includes leaders from public community colleges, research universities, and minority-serving institutions, including historically Black colleges and universities (HBCUs), Hispanic-serving institutions (HSIs), and Asian American and Native American Pacific Islander–Serving institutions (AANAPSIs) that represented varying Carnegie institutional designations related to enrollment profile and institutional size. Some of these institutions, such as community colleges, continue to be open access, while others had varying levels of selectivity. Moreover, whereas HBCUs espouse a specific mission for providing educational access and educating Black students, community colleges senior leaders discussed the focused ways their campuses attracted working adults and provided access to life-long learners through continuing education in addition to traditional academic and vocational education.

Broad-Based Access and Equity Mission

There is widespread belief in the power of education for reducing economic inequality and increasing social mobility in America; thus, making college accessible to everyone is one of the most pressing challenges facing U.S. higher education (Eckel & King, 2004). For USIs, this is foundational, as Zerquera emphasized: "A key and significant part of the urban-serving research university mission is to provide access to urban and historically marginalized students in their regions, populations typically underserved by higher education" (2016, p. 137). These populations include students from historically underrepresented racial/ethnic backgrounds, first-generation students, low-income students, and adult learners. According to the APLU (2018a), urban-serving institutions strive to narrow the achievement gap between students in regard to race, ethnicity, and socioeconomic status by addressing the challenges facing these students, ultimately hoping to eliminate educational disparities and inequities.

For example, one institution in this study instituted an automated process in their admissions cycle for the university system. If a student applies to the main campus and is not admissible, they do not receive a denial letter, which could hinder student matriculation. Instead, the institution informs such students of the schools within the system where they are admissible and offers to forward their applications to the different campuses for admissions consideration free of charge. The senior leader went on to share the rationale behind this decision:

> [The chancellor] wanted to make sure that what we say to folks is, there is a place for you if you want a higher education degree in the university system. It might not be on the main campus where you really want to be, but we have a place for you. We are really cognizant in looking at not omitting people.

This type of process supports greater access and choice for students and increases the likelihood of students enrolling in or transferring into a 4-year institution.

The culture of urban-serving institutions is evolving and deepening. Rather than a series of functions, a mode of social responsibility and community responsiveness drives the actions and choices of these institutions. Administrative leadership must understand this evolution and clearly articulate a vision for success, as they have an obligation by the nature of their mission to advance equity and opportunity within the city of residence. The idea that educational opportunity and access should be upheld is a given. However, one of the challenges is that some view the context of higher education as shifting from being considered a public good that serves society as a whole to a private good that primarily benefits individuals (Zerquera, 2016). USIs need to maintain a focus on equity and opportunity for the communities they serve. One example of an institution supporting economic and cultural advancement is Florida International University (FIU), an institution in this project. In 2006, FIU established its region's first public medical school to increase access to medical education for the South Florida community and improve medical practice for the diverse populations it serves (Zerquera, 2016). Another example is the University of Houston's Third Ward Initiative, which is a collaborative partnership with the Third Ward, a historically African American community, and the community in which the University of Houston is located. This initiative is focused on a sustainable partnership that demonstrably improves the quality of life in the shared neighborhood by improving educational outcomes; securing jobs; developing and strengthening businesses; and celebrating the arts, culture, and history of the region.

Diverse Student Profile

In USIs, *diversity* refers to a wide range of student characteristics, explored in more depth in Chapter 3, but emphasized here by one of our senior leaders: "When you're working in a big city, you're going to get the gamut. You're going to get people who come from very different backgrounds, very different experiences. And you have to be comfortable with that." The American student population continues to grow in diversity and size (Wood, 2017) and urban institutions continue to reflect this diversity, given their access-oriented mission and their location in densely populated urban centers. Furthermore, the desirability of urban life—racial/ethnic and socioeconomic diversity, cultural attractions, restaurants, museums, nightlife—also attracts students to these institutions. As one leader remarked, "There's an energy here. I think there are opportunities in the community that are appealing to [students]." The diverse student profile of urban institutions includes students of color, first-generation, low-income/Pell-Grant-eligible, commuter, and adult learner students. In addition to racial, ethnic, and socioeconomic diversity, institutional leaders in this study also observed the rise of undocumented and DACA students, foster care students, and students with mental health needs on their campuses. For example, one leader wondered about the connection between the urban context and student population: "The number of students here who have mental health needs is much greater. And I don't know if that is because cities tend to have more services that it attracts more students with need."

The diversity of the student population, in terms of demographics and academic interests, influences the ways these institutions serve and retain these students. A senior leader made the following observation:

> The reality is that we need to be creative in how we think about serving students, with different and alternative program delivery methods, because we are more likely to see students who are working more hours, if not full time, commuting from home, and more likely to be attached to families or other commitments.

The succeeding chapter explores in depth the unique needs of the urban college student and subsequent chapters address current approaches to serving this population.

The Influence of the Urban Context

Images of tall buildings situated in close proximity within a city center with minimal green space often come to mind when thinking about the design of urban campuses. To some extent, this image is accurate, as one senior leader shared the following:

> Well, of all the public universities in the state, we have the smallest land mass. When all universities opened, they were given a thousand acres, but we were only given about 400, so we're land locked. For expansions, we have to go up.

He explained that in response to this land-locked challenge, his campus has "gradually been building throughout the city, almost becoming the city." One reason for the building phase of many institutions is the desire to add residential spaces to the campus plan. As urban campuses begin to see more traditional-aged students, campus leaders are wanting to become more residential to increase engagement among what was historically a primarily commuter population.

Urban environments are complex, diverse, fast paced, and dense; social issues and problems related to poverty, crowding, crime, housing, public education, traffic, health issues, and transportation often plague these urban areas. The urban college campus is not insulated and faces many of these social issues that affect their ability to serve students and create safe and inclusive campus environments. In particular, institutional leaders in this study articulated concerns related to gang activity, crime, drug culture and drug use, homelessness, and the use of public spaces. While the increased risk of criminal activity may be real for most USIs, many of the institutional leaders did not characterize their campuses as being or feeling "unsafe." In fact, one leader shared a story about employing a supportive chief of campus police with prior city policing experience:

> He's very innovative and has been a real advocate for sexual abuse and violence victims. And so, when people get on our campus and they hear from our police, they don't really have the concerns they initially had. He does a perception of campus safety survey every year, and 97 or 98 percent of faculty, staff, and students report feeling safe on campus. I think what happens outside our core campus is sometimes what's more concerning to folks.

This story demonstrates the importance of urban-serving institutions enacting community-oriented policing, a strategy wherein police focus on building relationships and getting to know members of the community.

The open nature of public, urban institutions presents additional challenges because of problems related to crime, drug use, and homelessness in the areas surrounding these campuses. For example, one leader indicated,

> Folks in our area come here to use the restroom or to get warm or to use the library. We've found people hiding in the ceilings . . . people come into the lab, and someone's in there sleeping. A lot of drug activity in the restroom. And it's not hidden. We're trying to grapple with how we mitigate risk with open access.

For some campuses, mitigating risk may involve increased policing of public spaces or a total campus lockdown, while others attempt to limit access from unaffiliated persons through key-card scans and sign-in procedures. The issue of public space highlights the shadow side of how the urban campus, particularly those located in the heart of the city, must always consider how the urban context can sometimes disrupt "business as usual."

The blurred boundaries between the city and the USI is more than a physical phenomenon. "We've become a point of contact for support and so students [even if they are no longer enrolled] come back to us, because they don't know where else to go." This senior leader's reality resonated with many of our interviewees—in particular, those who worked at urban community colleges. They said that serving community college students is akin to a life-time commitment; students see the community college as a resource even if they are not enrolled in that semester, even if they took classes 2 years ago. Alumni and students came to trust these urban community college staffs as sources for assistance and resource hubs.

The urban campus may serve the city, but also looks to the city to provide assistance, as is discussed in chapters throughout this volume. The aforementioned urban social problems not only impact safety and security on the college campus but also student learning, which may result in the need to activate community resources to benefit students. For example, since the cost of living tends to be greater in urban settings, students might face issues with finding affordable housing or navigating food insecurity. While initiatives such as food pantries and free-meal programs are growing and becoming institutionalized on campuses, it is often not enough to fully support students trying to stay focused on their academic goals. Therefore, colleges rely on their network of government and nonprofit agencies to assist in providing resources to students. For example, some community colleges, in particular, have partnered with organizations such as Single Stop USA (2014); these colleges utilize a case management approach to connect students to local resources in the community for housing, transportation, childcare, health insurance, legal aid, nutrition services, and financial literacy.

A Resource for the City

"Sometimes it's hard to know where the campus ends and city begins and vice versa." This senior leader's observation reflects not only the physical space of an urban campus but also the presence these institutions have in their regions. Urban-serving institutions contribute to their local cities using leadership, research, and service to address a wide range of localized issues to improve the quality of life, as well as by focusing on workforce development to assist in economic development of the area. For example, the University of Houston System Board of Regents recently approved the establishment of a College of Medicine at the University of Houston (UH), an urban-serving and Hispanic-serving institution (HSI). The new medical school will focus on preparing primary care doctors to practice in communities with significant health and health-care disparities (i.e., underserved urban and rural communities) in Houston and across Texas, as the state ranks 47th out of 50 states in primary care physician-to-population ratio. Furthermore, "as one of the most ethnically diverse universities in the nation, a primary goal is to graduate more physicians from underrepresented minorities in medicine, so the workforce better mirrors the population" (Rosen, 2017, para. 10). The distinctive focus of the newly created UH medical school to address community needs to improve health outcomes, demonstrates the ways in which USIs are responsive to the needs of their local cities and exist for the public good. In fact, according to the Coalition of Urban Serving Universities (USU), "the majority of USUs are involved in public health partnerships, investing an average of $2.6 million annually on efforts that range from providing services and clinical trials to advocating for minority representation in the health-care industry" (2019, para. 12).

In developing partnerships, campus-based community service offices and service-learning opportunities at urban-serving institutions are central to enacting their "anchor" role by serving as a resource to the city. While most institutions traditionally have these types of offices, USIs are demonstrating the ways in which these initiatives can be intentional rather than broad based. For example, one senior leader shared, "We do a lot with the community; we have over 500 student organizations. We have a really well-developed service-learning program; a lot of that is based in schools or with philanthropic ventures with community partners." Like others in the project, this leader highlighted the two-fold impact of a service-learning program that provides health services via pre-health student volunteers: communities benefit from these services and students learn and grow through the experiences. Another senior leader in this project shared information about their Center for Leadership and Service:

> Any time community agencies want assistance with anything, they can go to this office and we'll provide whatever assistance they need: from student volunteers, to mentors, to reading assistants, as well as [matching students with agencies for the] many classes that require service learning. Our office will take care of that, the instructor has to do nothing.

As these examples demonstrate, being responsive to the city's needs remains a core commitment of the USI, and this duty begins at the top levels of leadership. Thus, USI administrators are engaged in the community at the highest level and an administrative infrastructure is present to coordinate, improve, and make visible the depth of these universities' community engagement work (Craft et al., 2016, p. iii). One senior leader discussed how the president was working in the community and making the university an essential part of the fabric of the city. Another shared how executive leaders from their campus attended neighborhood meetings throughout the year and hosted an annual meeting where the president would attend and provide updates on the university's building plans and other university initiatives. Another leader shared how their campus mobilized an inclusive excellence commission composed of 25 community leaders, industry leaders, government officials, and community-based organizers from across the state to guide the institution in becoming a regional leader. These examples provide some evidence for Friedman et al.'s (2014) work that found leaders of urban-serving institutions are dedicated to their communities and are involved in multiple partnerships with other public, private, and not-for-profit entities. In fact, according the USU (2019), institutions who are members of the Coalition of Urban Serving Universities collaborate with community partners nationwide, each providing an average of $733,000 in support to nonprofits. Additionally, community support initiatives coordinated by urban institutions centered on bettering the quality of life in the community exist and, in many cases, involve working to address key health, economic, social, and educational disparities as demonstrated by the earlier example of the development of the new University of Houston Medical College.

An essential focus within the realm of community engagement is economic development and human capital; urban colleges and universities are often among the largest employers in their cities. According to the USU (2019), in 2010–2011, urban-degree granting institutions employed 2.6 million people, and paid over $190 billion in salaries, wages, and benefits to over 1.9 million full-time equivalent staff. Our home institution, the University of Houston (UH), again illuminates the relationship an urban-serving institution has within its host city. UH is considered Houston's institution (e.g., one of our institutional hashtags is #ForTheCity) and has a strong effect on the local workforce and the economy. According to an economic value study conducted using 2012–2013 data, UH employed 4,687 full-time and part-time employees with 98 percent of the employees living in the region and UH spent $484.1 million on payroll (EMSI, 2015). Additionally, the accumulated contribution of former students of UH employed in the regional workforce amounted to $4.3 billion in added regional income for the UH service region economy, which is equivalent to 55,994 jobs (EMSI, 2015).

In addition to the human capital impact, Friedman et al. (2014) suggested that "much attention centers on the role universities play in innovation and technology development and transfer" (p. 13). In 2010–2011, the average urban-serving institution submitted 59 inventions, filed 50 patents, had 17 active licensing agreements, netted $2.5 million in income from royalties, and spent $1 million on technology transfer activities (Friedman et al., 2014). Simply put, urban-serving institutions are serving as dynamic sources of knowledge ensuring that our research is translated to marketable products and services to benefit communities and society through inventions, industrial technology, and scientific discovery.

University and K–12 partnerships also reflect the access mission of urban-serving institutions as they are uniquely positioned to provide faculty and students who can offer direct support and resources to local schools and educators (Borrero, 2010). In many urban environments, quality public education and educational opportunity is lacking for students, especially for historically underserved populations; this results in a leaky pipeline for students to postsecondary education. According to the National Center for Education Statistics (NCES, 1996), "urban educators report the growing challenges of educating urban youth who are increasingly presenting problems such as poverty, limited English proficiency, family instability, and poor health" (p. v). Not much has changed, as today's educators report these same challenges, possess fewer resources and less control of teaching curricula, and work amid low student-performance rates and deteriorating physical spaces as urban schools continue to receive unequal fund allocations (Duncan & Murnane, 2014; Gorski, 2008).

Friedman et al. (2014) found that many urban college leaders developed a variety of initiatives that respond to the continuing education gap that exists among their cities' public secondary schools. Urban colleges such as University of Central Florida (UCF), Johns Hopkins University, and University of California, Los Angeles (UCLA; Korn, 2017) have embarked on new initiatives that not only aim to improve the local school system and surrounding community but also to strengthen the student pipeline to their institutions. These institutions have helped to create new schools (as in the case of Johns Hopkins) or overhaul troubled schools (in the case of UCLA and UCF) by providing curriculum guidance, contributing volunteer hours, and raising donor funds. As the president of Johns Hopkins University remarked, "Our fate is inextricably linked to the fate of Baltimore. . . . As goes Baltimore, so goes Hopkins" (Korn, 2017, para. 25), because as the pipeline for historically underserved students from the local public education system becomes strengthened, urban institutions will continue to serve even more of the diverse student population that is characteristic of the urban-serving institution in part because of the access mission of these colleges.

It is clear that urban-serving institutions contribute to the public good by helping to shape their local and regional communities through a deep commitment to making college accessible for everyone, support for an increasingly diverse student population, the cultivation of community partnerships, and workforce development.

Institutional Leadership and Governance

Urban institution leaders, especially the president, must set the vision and pay attention to student-focused functions, academic and research support services, and community engagement—both strategy and infrastructure (Craft et al., 2016). Given the distinctive profile of underserved students who disproportionately attend urban-serving institutions (i.e., first-generation, low-socioeconomic status, nontraditional students, students of color, etc.), an institutional commitment to provide the support services necessary to foster their student success is important. Colleges that attract and enroll more "traditional" students (i.e., 18–24-year-olds, residential, predominately White, middle- to high-socioeconomic status students) may not develop culturally responsive policies, programs, and practices in the same way as urban-serving institutions. One senior leader indicated that "it's really important to have the leadership of an institution on board with what it means to be an urban institution and to live it." Leadership must understand their students and must consider the needs of all students inclusive of race, ethnicity, gender, sexual orientation, and socioeconomic status, especially as these characteristics are known to influence student success. In fact, urban-serving institutions are often leading the way in promising practices focused on the needs of historically underserved populations and communities—programs that are highlighted in Chapters 4 and 5.

Presidents and senior leaders at urban-serving institutions are also accountable for keeping the costs of higher education affordable and being conscious of rising student debt. As a result, leadership must be able to increase fundraising, reduce expenditures, and stabilize—actually minimize—tuition increases. For instance, one leader shared, "The current president has been able to reduce institutional expenditures by almost $20 million, cutting out some excess waste and duplication." In an attempt to stabilize tuition, some USIs have established fixed tuition rates, which allows a student to enter under a rate and hold it steady for a defined period of time, usually for a period of 4 years. One leader shared,

Several years ago, the tuition increases were anywhere from 7–10%; for the past couple of years under [the president's] leadership, it's been 3% or less. Which is the lowest in the state. So, I think that is shifting the priority and focus to retain students and to get them graduated.

Here at the University of Houston, we have UHin4, a program created to simplify the process for students to earn both a high-quality and affordable education. This program allows students to budget accurately, incentivizes them to finish in a timely manner, saves families money and time, and allows them to enter the workforce earlier or begin graduate studies earlier.

The unique missions of USIs necessitate being visionary and thinking "out of the box" in order to be successful serving both campus constituents and the broader community. Leadership, especially presidential leadership, needs to be comfortable charting a path that is not traditional in order to accomplish the value-rich missions of the urban-serving institution. One leader stated, "The administrative functioning here is extremely participatory, and as an institution, we are comfortable with a view that is not traditional." Urban planning and community development are two areas in which USIs have embraced this role and responsibility of thinking beyond the box. For example, the University of Illinois at Chicago's South Campus/University Village project introduced new residential development to a formerly depressed part of the city (Perry, Wiewel, & Menendez, 2009). In Baltimore, Maryland, higher education institutions are part of the East Baltimore Revitalization Initiative, which is a 10- to 15-year effort to invest $1.8 billion to redevelop the 88-acre Middle East neighborhood adjacent to the Johns Hopkins Medical Institutions (Perry et al., 2009). In both of these instances, the results were because of the universities' efforts and from the ongoing relationships between universities and multiple institutions and stakeholders.

Institutional Governance

Leaders of urban-serving institutions must function under a governance structure both internally, relative to shared governance within the institution, and externally, relative to the formal governance of a board of trustees or regents. The shared governance structure within institutions usually consists of faculty, staff, and student senates or organizations. Therefore, having a shared understanding and commitment to the mission and strategic direction of the institution is essential. One leader remarked,

The shared governance model here is extremely healthy in the way that the committee structures work, it's also the way that the university works, and so there's not only the organic and the informal, there's the formal and non-organic steering of all those people.

Boards of trustees or regents can take on a variety of organizational structures—from locally governed boards to state boards—which may impact the scope and influence of the governing boards. One leader indicated that,

> the university switched to a locally governed board. So now, the institutions in the state have their own board of trustees; whereas [the previous state-wide governing board] was highly ineffective, very politicized. Decisions were not necessarily made in the best interest of some institutions.

Another leader agreed and expressed having a localized board allowed for a stronger commitment to the institutions within the system and the communities in which the institution is situated, thus better meeting the needs of the community. It appears from the leaders in our project that localized board structures might better understand the mission, context, and community in which urban serving institutions function in contrast to state governing boards that have purview over diverse institutional types and profiles.

Some institutions also function within a system or district approach. College/university systems of higher education typically comprise a number of individual institutions overseen by system leadership as well as institutional leadership. Some examples of college/university systems include: Georgia Board of Regents, University of Texas system, University of California system, and the University of Houston system. The district approach is particular to most community/technical colleges, such as the St. Louis Community College District and Miami Dade College District. The City University of New York system includes 2- and 4+-year institutions, many of which have specific foci. Each district often consists of a particular geographic area of a state and operates the public community college system in its district. One leader commented thusly: "Each college is part of the state board community/technical college system and we have a district office."

System or district approaches may present a different set of challenges for USIs and for the leadership to maneuver. Our University of Houston System serves as a unique case. The system consists of four distinct institutions: UH, the flagship institution of over 46,000 students (a USI); UH-Downtown, an institution just a few miles from the flagship institution serving approximately 14,000 students in the heart of the city (also a USI); and two regional institutions, UH-Clear Lake and UH-Victoria (which are not USIs). From a leadership perspective, the president and the vice presidents of the flagship institution also serve in a system role with the president serving as the chancellor of the system and the vice presidents serving as vice chancellors of the system. There is one Board of Regents for the University of Houston system. Having administrators serve in dual-leadership roles requires everyone to understand the unique mission of each institution, while developing policies and processes that best serve all four universities. From a governance perspective, how then do administrators ensure that the USIs within the system/district are enacting their mission, when there are other institutional missions, such as that of regional institutions, to uphold? Moreover, if the flagship institution is not the USI, administrative leaders must not allow the flagship campus to become an over-shadowing force to the USI mission.

Institutional Sustainability and Health

The urban-serving-institution mission, while having distinguishing and unifying characteristics, contains aspects that sometimes contradict one another when the purpose of these institutions and their precarious situation within the higher education context are considered (Zerquera, 2016). A key issue in this tension centers on access versus selectivity. As many states have already developed or are in the process of exploring performance-based funding, some senior leaders expressed concern about fairness for USIs relative to the metrics being developed and utilized. One leader remarked, "Our board of governors has clamped down. We have a metrics system now in our funding metrics and so they've insisted that we go to a four-year graduation rate on which we're judged, which is not fair." While the concept of performance-based funding to focus institutions on out-comes has merit, one of the issues of fairness centers on the fact that institutions within a given state have varying missions and serve distinctive populations of students. For example, it is unimaginable that a selective institution would be similar to an open access institution on graduation, retention, and persistence measures. The latter institutions serve a more diverse student population that traditionally has lower levels of college readiness, tend to be students from his-torically underserved populations, and need more intrusive and holistic support processes to ensure success. Therefore, two unintended effects of performance funding have been institutions increasing their admissions requirements (admis-sions restrictions) and changing academic policies and expectations in order to meet these new performance metrics, specifically retention and graduation rates (Dougherty et al., 2016). Moving USIs to respond to external pressures and become more selective institutions is a point of tension that has an impact not just on the access-oriented mission but also on institutional financing and function. According to Dougherty et al. (2016), performance-based funding leads to "changes in colleges' revenues from the state, in their awareness of the state's priorities and of their performance in relation to those priorities, and in their organizational capacities" (p. 149). Thus, from a financial standpoint, the sustainability of urban institutions could be significantly impacted. Until state legislatures reject a "one size fits all" approach for accountability in favor of mission-centric performance measures, USIs may have to reconcile how to serve their increasingly diverse populations with decreased state funding.

The history of urban-serving institutions, especially urban-serving research universities, has contributed lasting tensions on their missions (Zerquera, 2016). On one hand, the USI mission prioritizes community engagement and economic development of the region; on the other hand, a research institution is distinguished by a comprehensive research enterprise inclusive of cited publications, federally funded research, and renowned scholars. Therefore, the sustainability and health of urban serving institutions may rest on being susceptible to the expectations of the value systems of more prestigious institutions situated "higher" in the academic hierarchy. Yet, these are the same institutions that have historically been criticized for lack of opportunity and access, particularly for minoritized and marginalized students. For instance, San Diego State University achieved higher graduation rates and narrowed achievement gaps among students; however, it did so while raising selectivity and excluding groups of students whom it typically served in the past (Nelson, 2011). The University of Texas–San Antonio stated in its *Graduation Rate Improvement Plan* that it would improve student success, in part, through the use of greater selectivity in admissions (Zerquera, 2016). These institutions are not isolated examples; colleges and universities across the nation have articulated increasing admissions selectivity as an institutional strategy for not only positioning themselves better in performance-based funding environments but also enhancing institutional prestige.

Of paramount importance is consideration of access by policymakers and practitioners. By some estimations, many urban institutions are participating in what O'Meara (2007) termed *institutional striving*, a process of pursuing prestige within the academic hierarchy within five areas of institutional operations: student recruitment and admissions; faculty recruitment, roles, and reward systems; curriculum and programs; external relations and shaping of institutional identity; and resource allocation. According to one leader,

> as higher education institutions have been allowed to occupy multiple spaces, everyone is trying to be all things to all people. Everyone is trying to compete with each other, and it's why there is so much duplication and waste in higher education as a whole-urban institutions are not urban any more. Urban is the setting not the mission or function.

The leader who commented that the board of governors in the state has clamped down and created a metrics system said that the board expects students at the USI who have to work, "to graduate at the same pace as [the flagship where] students come from wealthy backgrounds, for the most part, and don't work; it's hurting our mission to some extent."

The idea that student recruitment and admissions is critical to the sustainability of urban-serving institutions is supported in the interviews with senior leaders for this project. One leader noted the differences in "the dynamic of coming to an environment where you have to fight for students, versus one where they're just going to come." Some leaders expressed the concern that there are so many options for students that urban institutions are vying for enrollment and must demonstrate that the institution is more welcoming and responsive, requiring many to create a culture shift. As indicated by institutional leaders, this speaks to the need to provide a better student experience across all areas of academia and connects to enrollment management and changes in institutional culture. At many urban-serving institutions, there is a desire to build new or more student housing on campus and/or off campus near the institution. A number of leaders named housing as a priority because of the desire to enhance and improve the student experience—a significant component of student success initiatives—by changing campus "into 24/7 thinking," and as one leader put it, wanting the campus "to be more than just a basic 24/7 environment, but a real thriving environment."

The institutional health and sustainability of urban-serving institutions hinges on whether they can continue to aim to be all things to all stakeholders in their regions, yet fulfill their historical—and critical—role in eliminating educational disparities for historically underserved student populations through affordable and accessible post-secondary education. Failing to preserve the mission of these institutions "jeopardizes the roles these institutions fulfill within society more generally and warrants better recognition and support" (Zerquera, 2016, p. 149).

Networking Between Urban-Serving Institutions

The instrumental role and responsibility of the urban-serving institution in urban areas and in higher education overall is well documented (APLU, 2018a; Eckel & King, 2004; Friedman et al., 2014; Zerquera, 2016). One of the senior leaders shared, "I think urban education—urban institutions—really are becoming the leaders for the future of American higher education. You're seeing cities invest more in their urban centers." Two professional organizations, the Coalition of Urban Serving Universities (USU) and the Coalition of Urban and Metropolitan Universities (CUMU), provide an excellent avenue for this work, a space for institutional leaders to network with each other and collectively advance the mission and goals of urban-serving institutions.

Coalition of Urban Serving Universities (CUSU)

The Coalition of Urban Serving Universities is one of seven commissions of the Association of Public and Land Grant Universities (APLU) that allows leaders from across institutions to connect in order to address critical issues and expand their knowledge base (APLU, 2018a). The USU is a president-led organization of more than 35 public urban research institutions across the country. Members of the coalition must be located in metropolitan areas with populations of 450,000 or greater, enroll ten or more doctoral students per year, conduct at least 10 million dollars in research activities, and demonstrate a commitment to their urban areas (APLU, 2018b). The work of the USU centers on two pillars: initiatives working to advance student success through innovation, and initiatives aiming to achieve community transformation through partnerships. The USU's four primary areas of focus include "(1) Improving the Health of a Diverse Population, (2) Fostering Student Achievement, (3) 21st Century Workforce Development, and (4) Building Smart Resilient Cities" (APLU, 2018c, para. 1). In each of these areas, USU partner institutions generally collaborate with urban community leaders to assess community needs, increase the use of data and evidence to develop interventions and solutions, and disseminate scalable best practices and information to assist other campus leaders in strengthening America's urban centers.

Coalition of Urban and Metropolitan Universities (CUMU)

The Coalition of Urban and Metropolitan Universities is an international organization of universities in large metropolitan areas that share a common understanding of their distinct mission and values, which sets them apart from many traditional models of postsecondary education. According to their website, the coalition is "the longest-running and largest organization committed to serving and connecting the world's urban and metropolitan universities and their partners. CUMU focuses on strengthening institutions that are developing new responses to the pressing educational, economic, and social issues of the day" (CUMU, 2017). The CUMU comprises more than ninety member institutions that represent the diverse range of academic institutions, from small, private liberal arts colleges and Ivy League institutions to historically Black colleges and universities and large research institutions. They present an annual conference that is focused on CUMU member institutions, their community partners, and their work addressing contemporary challenges through dialogue and presentations that allow participants to think of actionable steps to address these challenges.

Words of Advice

In this chapter, we have accomplished a number of objectives related to understanding the urban-serving institution and its role in and importance to both the city in which it is located and within the higher education landscape broadly. We have discussed the USI's broad access and equity mission; described the diverse student profile; identified the ways the urban context influences USIs; and have outlined the evolving context of institutional leadership, governance, and sustainability. Our advice to professionals who work within these institutional types and for the administrators trusted to provide visionary leadership for them, centers on continually enacting the place-based and access mission of the USI. First, it is important to reflect on the power of place and its influence on the nature of work at USIs—the relationship to and with the community is central. As more of our nation's urban areas are in the process of revitalization, the USI is playing a central role in contributing to these efforts through economic development, technology transfer, and human capital. We need to be mindful about the ways in which our work has the potential to both help and harm the communities we are committed to serving. Therefore, it is important that professionals at all levels within the institution reflect on their relationship to the community—from public outreach and civic engagement to strategic planning and decision-making. We advise professionals involved in these initiatives and practices to enact a culturally relevant approach in working with and alongside community leaders.

We know that students and their needs are constantly evolving. In enacting the access and equity mission of the USI, it is imperative for professionals to understand the distinctive population of students they are serving. Urban-serving institutions have historically offered access and served the most marginalized and/or vulnerable populations of our nation. With the projected population shifts and demographic changes, these are the same students who are needed to ensure the future of our nation's economic competitiveness and social advancement by reducing, and ultimately eliminating, disparities and inequities. Currently, there is a movement based on the concept of "institutional striving," which has the potential to alter some of the focus of USIs away from this broad-access mission. As student affairs professionals, it is important to maintain the focus on student access and success and be prepared to advocate for the needs of students, even as some governance structures want to move in a different direction that may not be beneficial to the populations of students attending USIs. Leaders within student affairs have a voice and influence their institutions as policies and programs are developing and evolving. Use your voice and influence to ensure that students succeed.

An urban-serving institution is more than just a university located in an urban area; to be urban serving means to be, and to be seen as, an "anchor institution—whose physical presence is integral to the social, cultural, and economic wellbeing of the community" (Friedman et al., 2014, p. 1) in which the institution is located. Student access and success, applied research, meaningful community partnerships, and economic development are key elements to the mission of an urban-serving university, which distinguishes the USI from other institutional types within the American higher education structure. Urban-serving institutions play a significant role in educational enterprise and will continue to hold an essential place in higher education as long as institutional leaders, state politicians, and community partners continue to understand their responsibility for contributing to the public good and embrace this responsibility by advocating for increased fiscal, human, and community resources that are critical for their continuing success. What we have learned from our work in and study of the urban-serving institution is that it reflects the ethos of an urban center: complex, diverse, and fast paced. This type of context requires professionals who are visionary and not afraid to change, yet who will continue to honor the work and importance of a USI to the local community and to higher education.

Discussion Questions

- What are the most important contributions of urban-serving institutions to higher education and society?
- Understanding the power of place, how have urban-serving institutions formed symbiotic relationships with the communities in which they are located? What are some innovative ways that they can continue to forge these partnerships?
- What new vision and changes are needed for urban-serving institutions to continue to play a significant role in higher education?

References

Association of Public and Land-Grant Universities (APLU). (2018a). Why public urban research universities? Retrieved from www.aplu.org/members/commissions/urban-serving-universities/why.html

Association of Public and Land-Grant Universities (APLU). (2018b). Coalition of Urban Serving Universities. Retrieved from www.aplu.org/members/commissions/urban-serving-universities/index.html

Association of Public and Land-Grant Universities (APLU). (2018c). USU initiatives. Retrieved from www.aplu.org/members/commissions/urban-serving-universities/usu-initiatives/index.html

Borrero, N. (2010). Urban school connections: A university-K-8 partnership. *Catholic Education: A Journal of Inquiry and Practice*, 14(1), 47–66.

Craft, A., Garmise, S., Modarres, A., Perry, D., & Villamizar-Duarte, N. (2016). *Anchoring the community: The deepening role of urban universities*. Retrieved from http://usucoalition.org/documents/Anchoring_the_Community_APLU_USU_2016_Survey_Report_fnl.pdf

Coalition of Urban and Metropolitan Universities (CUMU). (2017). [CUMU homepage.] Retrieved from www.cumuonline.org/

Coalition of Urban Serving Institutions (USU). (2019). Who we are. Retrieved from http://usucoalition.org/about/who-we-are

Dougherty, K. J., Jones, S. M., Lahr, H., Natow, R. S., Pheatt, L., & Reddy, V. (2016). Looking inside the black box of performance funding for higher education: Policy instruments, organizational obstacles, and intended and unintended impacts. *RSF: The Russell Sage Foundation Journal of the Social Sciences*, 2(1), 147–173.

Duncan, G. J., & Murnane, R. J. (2014). Growing income inequality threatens American education. *Phi Delta Kappan*, 95(6), 8–14.

Eckel, P. D., & King, J. E. (2004). An overview of higher education in the United States: Diversity, access, and role of the marketplace. Retrieved from www.acenet.edu/news-room/Documents/Overview-of-Higher-Education-in-the-United-States-Diversity-Access-and-the-Role-of-the-Marketplace-2004.pdf

Engineering, Math, Science Institute (EMSI). (2015). Demonstrating the economic value of the University of Houston. Unpublished report. Houston, TX: University of Houston.

Friedman, D., Perry, D., & Menendez, C. (2014). The foundational role of universities as anchor institutions in urban development: A report of national data and survey findings. Retrieved from http://usucoalition.org/images/APLU_USU_Foundational_FNLlo.pdf

Gorski, P. (2008). The myth of the "culture of poverty." *Educational Leadership*, 65(7), 32–36.

Harris, M., & Holley, K. (2016). Universities as anchor institutions: Economic and social potential for urban development. In M. B. Paulsen (Ed.), *Higher education: Handbook of theory and research* (pp. 393–439). New York: Springer.

Korn, M. (2017, July 30). Urban colleges move into K-12 schools to help kids and themselves. *Wall Street Journal*. Retrieved from www.wsj.com/articles/urban-colleges-move-into-k-12schools-to-help-kids-and-themselves-1501448250

National Center for Education Statistics (NCES). (1996). Urban schools: The challenge of location and poverty. Retrieved from https://nces.ed.gov/pubs/web/96184ex.asp

National Center for Education Statistics (NCES). (2018). Table 317.10. Degree-granting postsecondary institutions, by control and level of institution: Selected years, 1949–50 through 2016–17. Retrieved from https://nces.ed.gov/programs/digest/d17/tables/dt17_317.10.asp?current=yes

Nelson, L. A. (2011, May 21). Raising graduation rates, and questions. *Inside Higher Ed*. Retrieved from www.insidehighered.com/news/2011/05/27/san_diego_state_raises_graduation_rates_in_part_by_becoming_more_selective

Perry, D. C., Wiewel, W., & Menendez, C. (2009). The university's role in urban development: From enclave to anchor institution. *Land Lines*, 21(2), 2–7.

O'Meara, K. (2007). Striving for what? Exploring the pursuit of prestige. In J. C. Smart (Ed.), *Higher education: Handbook of theory and research* (Vol. 22; pp. 121–179). New York: Springer.

Rosen, M. (2017, November 16). UH creates college of medicine to address shortage of primary care physicians. *University of Houston*. Retrieved from www.uh.edu/news-events/stories/2017/november/11172017BORMedSchool

Single Stop USA. (2014). [Single Stop homepage.] *Single stop*. Retrieved from http://singlestopusa.org

Wood, M. (2017, March 24). The changing face of today's student: More diverse, older and requiring more personalized learning. *Arobatiq*. Retrieved from http://acrobatiq.com/the-changing-face-of-todays-student-more-diverse-older-and-requiring-more-personalized-learning/

Zerquera, D. (2016). Urban-serving research universities: Institutions for the public good. *Higher Learning Research Communications*, 5(2). Retrieved from https://files.eric.ed.gov/fulltext/EJ1133105.pdf

3

THE URBAN COLLEGE STUDENT

Anthony Cruz and Franklyn Taylor

We have always cared about the entire student experience, the challenges students face on their educational journey, and the difference we can make in their lives. Moreover, as we were working on this project, we realized that our urban community college experiences gave us a unique perspective that is both insightful and rewarding. In our daily work we are confronted with the issues described in this chapter, namely low-income status, commuter status, multiple identities, and first-generation status. We have come to expect these characteristics and work very hard with our teams to overcome the challenges they generate. In the end, we strive to engage our urban college students to better understand their attitudes, wants, needs, and aspirations. This helps us advocate for the things they need to create a vibrant college experience that ultimately leads to student success.

*– **Anthony Cruz**, Ed.D., Vice Chancellor for Student Affairs, St. Louis Community College District and **Franklyn Taylor,** Ed.D., Campus Vice President of Student Affairs, St. Louis Community College, Forest Park*

The urban college student is far more complex than most imagine. They attend college with many of the same dreams and aspirations as those students who attend rural and suburban institutions, but their life experiences are more varied and unique. Urban college students have multiple identities and the intersectionality of their lives make them unique individuals with interconnected life experiences. The intersectionality creates opportunities for students to be advocates for the programs and services they need, as they partner with staff to create change by using their experiences to support improvements and new directions. These students partner with staff in advocacy and activism to create change by using their experiences to support these changes. One of the vice presidents said, "There are all kinds of backgrounds, every student I've met, there's been a story that has been different. There's nothing homogeneous about our population in terms of the stories that they bring to us when they get here on campus." According to the Coalition of Urban and Metropolitan Universities (CUMU, 2018), 38 percent of urban students receive Pell Grants, 46 percent of students are from minoritized groups, and 25 percent of undergraduate students are over the age of 25. In this project, the institutions mirror these figures, as shown in Chapter 1. Their diversity includes more than these basic demographics. They also inhabit contextual spaces that are more common to the urban environment, such as home and food insecurity and first-generation status, among others. They also lead complex lives; they more than likely commute and have responsibilities that come with living with their families or having families of their own. They also are pretty settled in their community, with many reluctant to leave town after graduation for employment opportunities in other cities. One of our vice presidents said, "We can't get our students to leave the city. We can't even get Coca-Cola to come here and recruit from [a neighboring state] because our students won't move." In this chapter, we explore what characterizes the life of students in USIs and provide recommendations for working effectively with these students.

The Diversity of Our Students

Leaders in this project represent institutions with student populations that are representative of other urban institutions across the United States. The average undergraduate student population across all of our institutions is 20,196. Since nearly all our institutions are designated as minority-serving institutions, many with more than one designation, they are highly racially and ethnically diverse, as Table 3.1 shows.

In fact, as was shown in Table 1.1, minority populations for the institutions ranged from 45 percent to 98 percent, with all but two being less than 50 percent. The average gender population is 43 percent men and 57 percent women, and the

TABLE 3.1 Average Racial/Ethnic Identity Across Sample Institutions

Identity	%
American Indian/Alaskan Native	0.2%
Asian	11.7%
Black/African American	26.8%
Hispanic/Latino	25.1%
Native Hawaiian/Pacific Islander	0.2%
White	23.2%
Two or more races	3.8%
Unknown	3.4%
Non-resident alien	5.7%

Source: Aggregate data based on NCES classifications accessed via *https://nces.ed.gov/collegenavigator/*

average student age is 67 percent who are 24 and under and 33 percent who are 25 and over. The average commuter population is 90 percent. The financial aid need for the participating institutions is higher than the average urban institution, with 63 percent of the students receiving financial aid including loans, grants, and scholarships while 47 percent of the students receive Pell Grants. One of the vice presidents shared that at their institution about 60 percent of their students come from low-income families and qualify for Pell Grants and 40 percent of their entire student body had household incomes below $20,000. Even though the economy has improved since the Great Recession of 2008, and the situation has improved for many people across the country, our urban students are still challenged with many of the same financial issues that go beyond what is happening in the classroom.

As far back as the 1990s there has been a change in the student demography as suggested by Rendon (1994). She stated that the majority of college students are women, immigrants, adults, African Americans, Mexican Americans, Puerto Ricans, American Indians, Asian, first-generation students, and, increasingly, non-racial minorities, which includes students with disabilities, LGBTQ students, and Jewish students. This continuing trend in demographic changes is exemplified in the urban environment as well. The racial/ethnic makeup of our urban student populations is reflective of the communities in which our urban institutions are located because these students largely live in the community while attending college, living with their families or other relatives or on their own outside of campus housing. We have worked diligently to increase diversity on our campuses, and it remains a very significant mission to vice presidents in this project. While many urban institutions are situated in cities that have large African American populations, African Americans are underrepresented in the student body. Many of the vice presidents are concerned with African American and Latinx men and see the recruitment, retention, and success of this student population as a priority not only for student affairs divisions but for the entire college or university as well. Urban institutions are constantly creating strategies to increase outreach, recruitment, and support for these students.

As urban institutions have become increasingly more diverse over the last few decades, we cannot deny that equity issues exist for our students of color. Several vice presidents mentioned that they are concerned with the academic success of students of color. At most urban institutions, African American male students have the lowest persistence and completion rates (Shapiro et al., 2017). We are having conversations on our campuses and addressing biases that may be contributing to these lower success rates. Some institutions originally created multicultural affairs offices to support African American students when the numbers of African Americans were relatively low and, "there were more elements of racism embedded into the ethos of institutions." Unfortunately, despite the length of time these supports have existed, their efforts have not had the desired outcomes, and we need to continue to work on solutions to improve the support we provide to our African American students. Furthermore, in recent years at many of our institutions, Latinx students have surpassed the percentage of white students and have become the largest racial/ethnic group, and at times, experience similar challenges with positive outcomes and institutional racism that their African American peers have experienced. Programs and supports that have been shown to be successful for these students are reviewed in Chapter 4.

Additionally, increased diversity at our urban institutions is also reflected by more Muslim students on our campuses, as noted by several of the vice presidents. Their Muslim students, at times, feel marginalized and our vice presidents want to make sure that their campuses provide a good home and a safe space for them. Many Muslim students have some of the fears shared by our undocumented students about being singled out and being deported. One vice president shared that "they're scared to death that Trump's going to deport them, and we have 349 students from the seven countries that he identified [in the travel ban executive order] and 25 faculty members." One way to alleviate these fears is to establish a safe zone on our campuses; locations on campus where Muslim students know they can be themselves without fear of discrimination, where they can explore their personal identities together, gather for religious related events and host Islam awareness events. Similarly, the newly established Dream Centers on campuses in the project provide similar supports for undocumented students.

First-Generation Status

As the first person to attend college in their family, first-generation students must navigate the complexities of college while shouldering the responsibility to translate the essence of college to their families and justify a myriad of decisions including the decision to attend, persist, and what to study and be involved with while they are there. All vice presidents talked about serving the needs of first-generation college students, one of them discussed:

> I think that just understanding how differently you need to structure what you do. When you hold an orientation, realizing that half of the folks in here, their parents did not go to college, so they don't have the understanding of terms and terminology and what all this means? What's the FAFSA? And so, we've tried to also structure things remembering who's in your audience, who these students are or who they are not.

Pascarella, Pierson, Wolniak, and Terenzini (2004) concluded that when you compare first-generation students and their peers on their knowledge of postsecondary education, knowledge about cost of attendance, income support and their level of preparation for college, their college-experienced peers are further ahead.

When 30 to 40 percent of the student body is first-generation, as was the case for many of these urban campuses, they wrestle with the meeting challenges and resolving issues that emanate from familial inexperience with college. One vice president connected this phenomenon to some of the issues at hand:

> I think there's a lot of students that are attracted to us because we're in an urban setting. But again, because we have a high number of first-generation students with a lot of financial need, a lot of them don't have the familial experience of what it means to be in college, how you navigate college. They might not be as knowledgeable about networking. And sometimes there's educational preparation issues that they face.

The challenges of being first-generation can be exacerbated by a lack of familiarity with campus engagement. Peer to peer learning is more challenging when students are on campus solely to attend class. Sometimes engagement with faculty may be also be challenging for the same reason. This is more prevalent in the community college setting because most students are commuters and have family and work obligations.

Food and Home Insecurity

In his seminal work, Maslow (1943) introduced us to human motivation and the hierarchy of needs. This theory can be applied to urban college students. According to Maslow, our needs are placed into a hierarchy: physiological needs, safety and security, love and belonging, self-esteem and self-actualization. His theory suggests that our urban students must have these needs met to achieve success and thrive (Maslow, 1943). For more than 15,000 college students, the basic physiological needs of healthy and plentiful food are not being met. At least 20 percent of community college students have very low levels of food security (Broton & Goldrick-Rab, 2018). A recent survey of more than 4,000 undergraduate students at ten community colleges across seven states indicates that approximately half of students are food insecure (Goldrick-Rab, Broton, & Eisenberg, 2015). In a comprehensive study of more than 24,000 students across the California State University system, Crutchfield and Maguire (2017) found that nearly 42 percent of the students surveyed experienced some level of food insecurity. Further, the CSU study confirmed the far-reaching effects of a lack of basic resources documenting poor academic performance, as well as mental health concerns and physical illness because of these circumstances. The levels of food insecurity are different at institutions across the country (Goldrick-Rab, Broton, & Eisenberg, 2015). While most of these students receive financial aid, a very small percentage use public assistance to meet some of their most basic needs. Many of our institutions have created food pantries. At St. Louis Community College, more than 10 percent of our students take advantage of our food pantries called Brown Bag Cafés. Unfortunately, this 10

The Urban College Student **43**

percent is not truly indicative of the number of our students who are experiencing food insecurity. It is very challenging to capture the actual number because many students are reluctant to share their need with college faculty or staff. Food insecurity at urban institutions is often more prevalent among African American and Latinx students. A survey of CUNY undergraduate students indicates that African American and Latinx students were about 1.5 times more likely to report food insecurity than White and Asian students (Freudenberg et al., 2011). In addition, rates of food insecurity were higher among those reporting health problems. "Students who reported that their health was fair or poor were more than 1.5 times more likely to report food insecurity than those who rated their health as excellent or good" (Freudenberg et al., 2011, p. 4).

The rise in food insecurity is compounded by increases in homelessness. Several vice presidents stated that the increase in homelessness amongst our students in the urban environment is prevalent and a challenge for urban institutions. This goes back to Maslow's hierarchy of needs and human motivation. The need for shelter, food, and clothing is of primary importance and relevance to this population. One vice president exemplified what many talked about in our project:

> For the student affairs profession—the difference between working at this institution versus a traditional . . . my most pressing issue has to do with finding solutions for dealing with hunger and homelessness . . . as opposed to alcohol abuse and Greeks! Both are taxing and important to be addressed . . . but very different!

Crutchfield and Maguire (2017) found that almost 11 percent of students in their study had experienced homelessness in the previous twelve months. Data from the NCES Condition of Education report and the Digest of Education Statistics report illustrate that student homelessness is a challenge that begins when students are still in high school. In 2014–2015, the rate of homelessness among U.S. public school students was highest in city school districts at 3.7 percent or 578,000 students (NCES, 2016). Many of these students will enroll at our urban colleges and universities as commuter students while continuing to struggle to find a place to live. One of our vice presidents confirmed this by stating that "[We are] struggling with the number of homeless students [particularly] the number of young people that are homeless.]" When Jacoby (2015) applied student development theories to commuter students, she alluded to Maslow's theory when she explained that for one to self-actualize one must meet the basic needs of food, shelter and clothing. Extending her line of thought, without basic needs and the safety and security that housing security brings, a sense of belonging-so important for urban college students-is nearly impossible.

Several vice presidents also mentioned their concerns about students who were recently foster youth. An increasing number of young adults transition out of foster care every year. The number of foster youth transitioning is estimated to be between 20,000 and 25,000 per year. Former foster youth are more likely to attend community colleges because four-year institutions are costlier (Dworsky, 2017). Unfortunately, community colleges are more likely to encounter former foster students who are homeless and in need of food on a regular basis. Goldrick-Rab, Richardson, and Hernandez (2017) stated that former foster youth who attend community college are at greater risk for food shortage and homelessness. In their study, 29 percent of students who were former foster youth were homeless. Urban community colleges rarely have on-campus housing, which limits their ability to respond to this important need with institutional resources.

As mentioned elsewhere in this volume, urban university and college leaders must connect with their local communities to create partnerships that support college students who struggle with food insecurity and homelessness. Institutions need to create campus food banks or form strong partnerships with local food banks to serve students. Creating a food bank on campus reduces not only time and transportation costs but it also reduces the stigma associated with accessing these support systems. Students report an increased sense of belonging and integration when colleges advertise poverty-alleviation supports as just another student support service like advising or tutoring. Another strategy would be to coordinate with college culinary programs to provide healthy-cooking demonstrations in partnership with food banks.

Undocumented and Deferred Action for Childhood Arrival (DACA) Status

According to data collected by Educators for Fair Consideration published in 2018, an estimated 65,000 undocumented immigrants graduate from high school each year, but only 10,000 graduate from college (Educators for Fair Consideration, 2018). The election of President Trump in 2016 caused a great deal of speculation about the fate of these undocumented college students. The president's strong views on illegal immigration created uncertainty for thousands of undocumented college students. This uncertainty was further exacerbated by the decision to end the DACA program in March of 2018. Our urban institutions have been particularly impacted by this decision because we have a significant number of DACA recipients due to the location of our largest urban centers and their high proportion of recent immigrants. Some institutions in California have more than 1,000 DREAMers enrolled on their campuses. One of our vice presidents describes the situation:

> Our DREAMers feel very insecure, unsafe, they distrust our campus police, for good reason. But . . . trying to rebuild those bridges is very important. So, we've been doing a lot of work in that area. So, we know our DREAMer students feel unsafe.

To create a safer environment, urban institutions put extra thought into programmatic and staffing decisions because we know that these students need a highly individualized approach. While the Midwest has a smaller population of undocumented students, we have put into place support systems to assist our undocumented students, despite not having support from state laws. To overcome the fact that the state of Missouri does not allow state institutions to charge in-state tuition to DACA students, St. Louis Community College created a DACA scholarship fund through the College's foundation, recently changing the scholarship's focus to include all undocumented students. This has mitigated the cost of attendance for many of our DACA and undocumented students.

Lesbian, Gay, Bisexual, Transgender, Queer, Intersex, Asexual (LGBTQIA) Students

The last 10 years have seen an increased awareness of transgender students and their needs. Some of our more progressive urban institutions have been helping transgender students much longer. While working in the Midwest in 2009, I (Anthony) had my first experience trying to find the appropriate restroom accommodations for a transgender student. I faced opposition from many at the college, but I was able to convert one of restrooms to an all gender restroom. This experience broadened my horizons as to the scope of student issues. It was more about the personal aspects and the personal challenges that students face to achieve their goals. Many urban institutions have developed a welcoming environment for LGBTQIA students by creating LGBTQIA centers, safe zone ally training, and other initiatives (Taylor, 2015). One our vice presidents mentions that "LGBTQIA students report feeling attracted to us because of the kind of climate we've been able to create. We have a lot of staff that are invested in that." Although there is not extensive research literature on the likelihood that these students attend urban institutions, one small study did show that experiences with discrimination pushed LGBTQIA students away from rural areas (Winstead, 2015) and the 2018 Campus Pride Index showed that LGBTQIA-friendly campuses were more likely to be located in large cities.

Low-Income Students

One of the characteristics of urban college students is that many come from low-socioeconomic status (SES) households. This creates more complex issues when coupled with other challenging characteristics that have been discussed in this chapter. Ziskin, Fischer, Torres, Pellicciotti, and Player-Sanders (2014) stated that students from all income levels understand how a second job can assist and contribute to the financing of college and that students from all income levels may not contact a financial aid advisor or consider changing the way they are financing their education if their circumstances change. Low-income students should be encouraged and guided to reconsider their financial situation when the situation warrants or the opportunity comes up. This is consistent with the literature and as one of the vice presidents in the interviews for this project suggests:

> Our students are very loan averse; it's very interesting. But a lot of times what they do is they use their financial aid refunds to help support the family. And that might be well and good but what happens when you have to pay the deposit for housing the next semester and you don't have that. That's the kind of financial aid planning I'm talking about. How to manage the financial award you have. And because many of our students get healthy refunds, after they pay for their books and things, we want to try and get them to save.

Many lower income, first-generation students see loans as a last resort even though they may need a loan to bridge the gap left between their need-based awards and cost of attendance. This reluctance causes some students to take fewer credits per term and can result in lower completion rates. The notion that student borrowing is excessive across the board is not true. The media's constant attention on excessive student borrowing deters many students from making a rational decision to invest in their educational future (Avery & Turner, 2012).

Another issue that low-income students face is poor college outcomes even when they enter college with strong academic preparation. The college outcomes of affluent students are much more positive when compared with lower SES students. Hoxby and Turner (2015) stated that in the urban community college, the disparity may start at the admissions application stage where the low-income students take a different path from students in the higher income bracket, but continue on a path toward a less positive outcome through their entire college experience (Hoxby & Turner, 2015, p. 514). From our experience, low income students are often the last to register for classes which causes them not to get the classes they need to stay on track and graduate on time. These students are more likely to depend on financial aid and many ultimately drop their classes if their financial aid is not approved.

Moreover, many students feel that financial aid offices are barriers for receiving the necessary financial aid. This sentiment is greater amongst lower income students because of their negative experiences with financial aid offices (Ziskin et al., 2014). There are occasions when a new student submits a document to the financial aid office and are not told about the additional documents that are required to process and finalize their financial aid award. The student's lack of knowledge about the process coupled with the staff member's failure to appropriately inform the student about additional missing documents may result in the student not getting their aid on time or not receiving it at all. These types of adverse interactions lead students to mistrust the financial aid office. Students gather financial aid information from family members, friends, and their colleges and universities. Since many urban students are first-generation college students, they do not rely on parental knowledge and depend more on their friends and peers to acquire financial aid advice. This approach can result in misinformation or applying their friend's situation to theirs even though they may have very different financial circumstances.

Complexity of the Urban Commuter Student

Like most urban institutions, those in our project primarily serve commuter students, with the average commuter population at 90 percent. Urban commuter students face a myriad of challenges that add to the complexity of their lives as college students. Burlison (2015) suggested that there are many nonacademic commitments that impact the commuter student's level of involvement and engagement in the campus environment. To better assist these students Jacoby (2015) suggested that the use of theories and intentional practices are inextricably bound for students to succeed.

Multiple Identities

Urban commuter students are confronted daily by the challenges posed by their multiple social identities. Some are from minoritized groups, first-generation students, some are low income, some from single family households, or have families of their own, and many having developmental, physical or learning disabilities—most have some combination of all these characteristics. A secondary aspect is that these students are navigating the demands of two worlds as described by one vice president who stated that students need:

> To navigate two worlds because they are in college and their friends are not. And so, having to kind of code switch or operate in two identities—needing to be one way at home versus another way on campus. Without really being able to fully accept the fact, yes, you are different from your friends. [When they] maybe do some bad things at home, [we remind them] but you are here for a reason, you chose to be here.

Helping students attend to, manage, and develop these multiple identities creates opportunities for institutions to improve the life and experiences of these students. Garland used this opportunity in a 2015 study to explore some of the identity issues that exist and how to provide the necessary resources and create opportunities for students (Garland, 2015). One example is informing student affairs front line staff of resources and referrals to better assist students who need multiple and different sources of support. Likewise, student affairs units can make faculty more aware that students are not defined by just one characteristic and that they should be on the alert for students who may be experiencing many challenges at one time.

Work and Family Responsibilities

One of the complexities of the urban college student is that most work and have family responsibilities. These added responsibilities, when coupled with their multiple identities and first-generation status, create interesting dynamics and challenges as they navigate college. According to one of the vice presidents, urban college students come with a host of responsibilities and commitments that are different from the traditional on-campus residential student. Families must deal with the cost of college, which then becomes closely associated with their students working part time, full time, or even more. Alfano and Eduljee conducted a study in 2013 that addressed differences in work, levels of involvement and academic performance between residential and commuter students. Surprisingly, they found no significant relationship when comparing the hours that each group worked and their GPA. But the study did show that the residential students felt better in being part of the college community and that their level of stress was significantly less than the commuter student (Alfano & Eduljee, 2013). This may be due to extensive commutes or long days of work and study with minimal sleep. Moreover, research shows that students living on campus have a greater chance of not dropping out than students who live with families at home. One such study by Ishitani and Reid suggested that students who live with their parents are 23 percent more likely to drop out (Ishitani & Reid, 2015). Leveson, McNeil, and Joiner (2013) further focused on the external factors that affect students who work, commute, live at home and care for dependents. Their study suggests that those who commute, work, and have family caregiving responsibilities, in excess of 16 hours per week are more likely to withdraw.

Given the substantial body of research reviewed throughout this volume that demonstrates the positive outcomes of social and academic involvement, the lack of involvement due to time spent commuting, working, and managing family responsibilities is bound to complicate student success. This calls for student affairs professionals to ameliorate the effects of off-campus responsibilities when working with these students (Burlison, 2015). Considering the intersection of race, culture ethnicity, Kodama (2015) suggests that students of color as commuters in the urban environment have demonstrated special needs that may sometimes be misunderstood and sometimes overlooked. It is an unfortunate, but common occurrence that staff members may blame families for putting extra pressure on students to attend to younger siblings, participate in family activities, or for household maintenance. It is important to remember the work of Tara Yosso (2005) which shows that family, home, and culture offer important forms of capital for student success and that Rendon (1994) found external agents were important validators for students. Burlison (2015) also found that those living with supportive parents experienced less stress than those who have unsupportive parents.

The combination of multiple identities, first-generation status, working families or employment status creates a special dynamic of multiple, often competing, priorities that must be juggled by urban commuter students. Students must make choices, sometimes difficult choices that have severe unintended consequences. Competing priorities create a challenging situation that urban commuter college students must navigated by, so that when challenges collide with their academic pursuits, their academic success remains intact.

Serving Urban College Students

The diversity of our students creates the need for culturally sensitive student affairs professionals, as discussed in Chapter 1. One vice president stated that culturally responsive student affairs services need to apply to all, and that student affairs staff need to be creative about how students are served and realize that traditional models may not apply. This also applies to our faculty colleagues as they are called to strive for culturally relevant pedagogy (Ladson-Billings, 1995) and culturally responsive teaching. Shevalier and McKenzie (2012), suggested that culturally responsive teaching is neither simply about "what" or "how" nor solely an abstract or theoretical "why" it is really the nexus of "what" and "why", and is, at its core, about the ethical practice of instruction. Culturally responsive teaching responds to students in ways that will help build and sustain meaningful positive relationships; making a difference in urban schools in the areas of academic achievement, social and emotional growth, and empowerment.

Validation is an important aspect of the urban students' quest for success. When staff and faculty validate students' experiences, self-efficacy, and prior knowledge and confirm their place in the institution, sense of belonging is enhanced and students are in a better position to thrive and succeed. Rendon (1994) stated that culturally diverse students need and should be validated in and outside of the classroom, particularly when these students express doubts, because helping and assisting students to build trust and confidence enhances their success. The validation process is best enacted when faculty and student affairs staff work in concert with important people in students' lives. Rendon highlighted that family and community members are also critical validation agents for college students and that faculty and staff should be encouraged to help students access these sources of validation.

Urban students need a caring staff that are multiculturally competent. Pope, Reynolds, and Mueller (2004) suggested that multicultural competency combines awareness, knowledge, and skills that are necessary for a student affairs professional to be effective. Like cultural responsiveness, these skills are important in the services rendered to urban college students, particularly to effectively address varying student characteristics and the challenges students face. As vice presidents suggested, understanding different cultures is critical because these urban students come from unique schools, communities, and cultures. Creating an affirming and more welcoming environment is the goal, and we must make sure our staffs have the necessary skills, knowledge, and awareness to effectively assist our urban students in a multi-cultural environment (Pope et al., 2004).

Validating and culturally responsive faculty and staff are more likely to become role models for urban college students and their care for students goes a long way in meeting their needs. However, students are also seeking diversity in those role models. When urban students see someone who looks like them or someone who comes from the same neighborhood thriving and succeeding as faculty and staff in the same environment in which they are trying to succeed, they are motivated to succeed and make their role models proud.

Words of Advice for The Urban Student Affairs Professionals

It goes without saying that to combat and cater to the needs of our urban college students, professional development must be utmost in our quest to serve students. As the student population changes and the depth of the challenges deepen, particularly from the themes that emerged from the interviews conducted for this project, professional development becomes a required endeavor and a moral imperative for urban institutions. Generally, professional development is important for student affairs professionals to be trained in numerous and multiple areas such as sensitivity, cultural competencies, navigating theoretical concepts and connecting these theories on a practical level to assist these students. We have experienced this at our own colleges and practice. Supervisors and administrators need to make resources available and give staff time away from their daily duties to be involved in meaningful and intentional training. Urban institutions should also introduce student affairs professionals to the student affairs competencies to accelerate the skills, knowledge and ability to enhance the performance of the profession (ACPA & NASPA, 2015). Although all competencies are important and relevant to student success and the making of a consummate student affairs professional, we believe that Advising and Helping, Personal and Ethical Foundations, Social Justice and Inclusion, Student Learning and Development and Values, Philosophy and History are the most relevant to the development, growth and ultimate success of the urban students as it relates to the skills, knowledge and ability of our student affairs professionals.

Another critical area that should be explored and emphasized in developing staff at all levels is to be cognizant of the developmental needs of the urban college students, which are reflected in this chapter. Staff should be trained in student development theories and how to apply them to situations in the urban environment. Let staff understand their own stories, backgrounds and past experiences and at the same time help students see themselves in all these theories (Patton, Renn, Guido, & Quaye, 2016).

Chavez and Longerbeam (2016) suggested that for students to succeed, faculty should integrate different cultural strengths in their teaching and learning process. In their view this will ultimately lead to student success particularly amongst students of color who make up a vast segment of the urban student profile and population. They further state that this is important because more and more diverse students are enrolling in our institutions. Cultural teaching enhances student learning, success and retention. We agree with Chavez and Longerbeam when they call for a sense of urgency in adopting this cultural approach to teaching, and we suggest extending those tenants to the work of student affairs. The pedagogical designs that they suggest require transformation in the way we usually teach and practice to confront the challenges of teaching across cultural frameworks. Student affairs professionals can partner with academic affairs to offer workshops and training for faculty to accelerate and enhance learning across cultural strengths and also providing resources to achieve this goal. Furthermore, student affairs professionals should continue to work with students, giving them the tools and coaching them to ask meaningful questions to faculty and to self-advocate inside the classroom.

With declining college enrollments and reduced funding from local, state and federal sources, urban institutions have a tremendous task of exploring outside funding sources. This includes private grants from all other sources and non-profit organizations. This should be an institutional priority and endeavor that has departments working together to eradicate silos and create strong partnerships. We recommend that institutions set aside seed money and college initiative funds to start food pantries on campus, scholarships and stipends for daycare and micro loan programs. These programs could be scaled up to provide campus wide outreach and opportunities. Urban institutions should strive to tap into alumni to donate to increase scholarship opportunities that can be used for deserving urban college students. Urban institutions can also provide micro loans on a short term basis to assist students with short term needs such as rent and child care. Many students drop out or stop out because they need less than a thousand dollars to take care of their needs.

For urban colleges and universities to increase student success and meet the needs of their diverse communities, they must examine how their policies, processes, and practices impact their students. The impact must be examined by disaggregating their student data, so that student success disparities between student groups is transparent, with the expectation of increasing student success levels for all students. This equitable student success approach is being used by Portland Community College through their Achieving the Dream initiatives. We are firm believers that aligning urban student needs with institutional financial aid processes and practices is a key to improving student success outcomes for lower-income and first-generation college students.

Student affairs leaders need to work with stakeholders across their campuses to develop a financial education strategy that makes sense for their student populations. We should consider integrating financial literacy into campus life and on-campus activities. Campuses may want to consider financial management education sessions for both incoming students and their parents at student orientations. Many urban college students find themselves either running out of financial aid or with unexpected financial obligations as they are finishing their degrees. Unfortunately, these financial constraints prevent many students from graduating. Many institutions across the country have established emergency funds to cover these expenses when students are close to graduation (Krueger, Parnell, & Wesaw, 2016). At St. Louis Community College we have initiated an emergency fund called the Retention Grant that we offer to students who have less than a $500 balance, have a 2.75 GPA, and have earned more than 30 credits. The Retention Grant has allowed more students to return to college for their next semester and continue their studies. These Retention Grants are funded by generous donations to the College Foundation.

It is well understood in higher education that the Free Application for Federal Student Aid (FAFSA) is complex and not very easy to navigate for most students and their families. It is even more challenging for our first-generation students who may lack the knowledge and cannot rely on their parents for assistance. This issue is further exacerbated when the student must convince their parents that providing their personal and financial information will not put them in jeopardy. While there have been attempts to simplify the FAFSA, we still yearn for a major overhaul. Many of our lower income students with the biggest need simply do not fill out the FAFSA (McKinney & Novak, 2015). According to the American Council on Education, every year over a million students who would likely qualify for Pell Grants fail to receive aid because they do not complete the application. College Goal Sunday is a national effort that targets lower income students and encourages them to apply for financial aid. The issue with College Goal Sunday is that it is focused only on one weekend in the entire year.

Advocacy for The Urban College Student

Urban institutions must reexamine their policies, practices, procedures, and politics that affect the provision of services to students. These policies are normally impacted by internal and external conditions. It is our assertion that urban institutions need to use their leverage, administrative oversight and remedies to confront and change some of the anachronistic and outmoded policies that normally impact their practices. Urban college administrators must advocate for change and use their leadership capacity to enact changes that will ease the challenges that urban institutions and their students face. Urban colleges should work closely with state governments to align policies with the students' needs. In some cases, the state rules, regulations and policies are not student friendly or applicable to the college environment. This creates road blocks and unfinished policies and practices that are undertaken by urban institutions to meet the needs of its students.

The interviews and current literature suggest that the provisions of basic and essential services such as food pantries and child care needs are important services that could be provided to lessen the challenges faced by the urban college students. An article in the Chronicle of Higher Education titled "Campus Child Care, a critical student benefit, is disappearing" states that cities with immigrant populations who are below the poverty line face numerous challenges. One such challenge is child care needs and services. Without these services some students will not be able to complete college or manage their college responsibilities. In many states campus child care is hard to find for the 30 percent of community college students are parents. The article also states that "students say that if they don't have child care, then other services just don't mean that much" (Carlson, 2015). We feel that it is very important to take a close look at these services and make every effort for these services not to be provided in isolation. A comprehensive array of services will create the condition for our urban college students to succeed.

There is also an opportunity for institutions to provide virtual connections to commuter students allowing them to connect to a community or the urban campus. Kretovics suggested that institutions should devote resources that will create opportunities for all in the campus community to be connected and be engaged (Kretovics, 2015). Jacoby stated, "As commuter students continue to become more diverse and attend an increasingly wide variety of institutions, educators, administrators, and policy makers must develop a thorough understanding of their needs, relevant theoretical frameworks, and strategies to increase their persistence and engage them deeply and productively in learning" (2015, p. 10). Jacoby (2015) also suggested that institutions should provide opportunities for theoretical knowledge and frameworks that will be used in these environments to exercise success and educational goals.

Families should be integrated into the fabric of urban institutions. Regular and consistent programming should occur within this integrated approach. Institutions should have the will to create offices of family involvement and programming. This idea is gaining momentum in four-year institutions where parental involvement offices and committees are normal occurrences and staples. This will allow parents and families to be integrated into the fabric of the institution thereby providing programming that will assist in the transition and success of the urban college students. Barbatis (2010) highlighted a recommendation that family advisory councils should be created, students co-enrolling with parents and children in life skills courses. This will create habits of success that could be replicated at home (Barbatis, 2010).

We believe that urban institutions need a paradigm shift and culture change in the provision of services to urban college students. This entails academic course planning, registration hours, orientation hours and course scheduling. Urban institutions are making efforts in this regard to change course. More must be done to achieve the goal of catering to the needs of the urban college students and fostering their success. Provisions should be made for alternate night schedules and weekend colleges in which urban college students can start and complete their program by only attending on the weekend. Provisions should also be made for when classes start and finish. In 2015, Darling explored academic advising strategies that enhance student success and persistence. One such finding was that academic advisors should consider commuter students as a cohort and strive to examine data that are pertinent to commuter students. The study also found out that advisors could assist with the marginalization and mattering challenges that these commuter students face. Darling listed several recommendations that include reviewing of policies and assessment plans (Darling, 2015). Grutzik and Ramos (2016) stressed that intensive academic advising, clear articulation, and adequate information to students are important. This, when added with the other mentioned changes in processes and practice, contributes to the paradigm shift in the provision of services to students.

Campus and institutional leaders in the urban environment should engage the community to provide the needed services to ease the challenges and increase the success of our urban students. Some of these services include regular, frequent bus services and routes to the urban college, with discount tickets and passes for their students. In short, leveraging our impact on the community and requesting reciprocal returns in resources and policies and bringing the community to the college. Steinacker (2005) stated that universities can be valuable contributors to a city or local economy. Colleges and universities should leverage their contribution and showcase studies that include student commuter impact and student resident impact.

Finally, those who work in USIs need to know as much about their students as they can. We have outlined what we and the other VPs have learned and experienced in this chapter, but we also know students in your setting are unique. Depending on your location, you might have a significant number of immigrant students and their needs will vary. Or perhaps, you are near a large military based and thus veteran status becomes important to attend to. In our experience it is also important to adopt an air of authenticity in working with students, they can see through us very easily. We have found that being straightforward and transparent, while being respectful is most effective. Allowing for differing expressions in response to authority, stress, and other challenges also makes building trust an easier task. After all, trust is the basis for developing a sense of belonging which we know is foundational for the success of our students.

Discussion Questions

- Describe ways that urban serving institution can create stronger partnerships and community engagement to meet the needs of urban college students.
- Describe some of the unique challenges faced by commuter students attending urban institutions and how can we assist them in managing their complex lives.
- How might we make diverse student bodies feel safer and more welcome?

- What types of assessments and evaluative measures can be administered on an ongoing basis to gain more knowledge about your student population?
- What ways of working with students may not be successful in an urban serving institution?

References

ACPA & NASPA. (2015). *Membership of ACPA and NASPA joint task force on professional competencies and standards. Professional competency areas for student affairs practitioners.* Washington, DC: Author.

Alfano, H. J., & Eduljee, N. B. (2013). Differences in work, levels of involvement, and academic performance between residential and commuter students. *College Student Journal*, 47(2), 334–342.

Avery, C., & Turner, S. (2012). Student loans: Do college students borrow too much or not enough? *Journal of Economic Perspectives*, 26(1), 165–192.

Barbatis, P. (2010). Underprepared, ethnically diverse community college students: Factors contributing to persistence. *Journal of Developmental Education*, 33(3), 16–26.

Broton, K. M., & Goldrick-Rab, S. (2018). Going without: An exploration of food and housing insecurity among undergraduates. *Educational Researcher*, 47(2), 121–133.

Burlison, M. B. (2015). Nonacademic commitments affecting commuter student involvement and engagement. *New Directions for Student Services*, 150, 27–34.

Campus Pride Index. (2018). LGBTQ-friendly campus search. Retrieved from www.campusprideindex.org/searchresults/display/670316

Carlson, S. (2015, May 22). Campus child care, a 'critical student benefit,' is disappearing. *The Chronicle of Higher Education*. Retrieved from https://www.chronicle.com/article/Campus-Child-Care-Is/230135

Chavez, A. F., & Longerbeam, S. D. (2016). *Teaching across cultural strengths: A guide to balancing integrated and individuated cultural frameworks in college teaching.* Sterling, VA: Stylus.

Coalition of Urban and Metropolitan Universities (CUMU). (2018). Retrieved from www.cumuonline.org/cumu-members/membership-data-dashboard/

Crutchfield, R. M., & Maguire, J. (2017). Researching basic needs in higher education: Qualitative and quantitative instruments to explore a holistic understanding of food and housing security. California State University, Basic Needs Initiative. Retrieved from www2.calstate.edu/impact-of-the-csu/student-success/basic-needs-initiative/Documents/researching-basic-needs.pdf

Darling, R. A. (2015). Creating an institutional academic advising culture that supports commuter student success. *New Directions for Student Services*, 150, 87–96.

Dworsky, A. (2017, December 11). Foster care youth and postsecondary education: The long road ahead. *Higher Education Today*. Retrieved from www.higheredtoday.org/2017/12/11/foster-care-youth-postsecondary-education-long-road-ahead/

Educators for Fair Consideration. (2018). Retrieved from http://www.e4fc.org/home.html

Freudenberg, N., Manzo, L., Jones, H., Kwan, A., Tsui, E., & Gagnon, M. (2011, April 11). Food insecurity at CUNY: Results from a survey of CUNY undergraduate students. Healthy CUNY Initiative, City University of New York. Retrieved from http://web.gc.cuny.edu/che/cunyfoodinsecurity.pdf

Garland, J. L. (2015). Commuter students with disabilities. *New Directions for Student Services*, 150, 57–67.

Goldrick-Rab, S., Broton, K., & Eisenberg, D. (2015). *Hungry to learn: Addressing food and housing insecurity among undergraduates.* Madison: Wisconsin HOPE Lab.

Goldrick-Rab, S., Richardson, J., & Hernandez, A. (2017). *Hungry and homeless in College: Results from a national study of basic insecurity in higher education.* Madison: Wisconsin HOPE Lab.

Grutzik, C., & Ramos, S. (2016) The role of the student support specialist: The possibilities and challenges of a long-term, proactive, and scaffolded relationship. *Community College Journal of Research and Practice, 40*(2), 113–132. doi:10.1080/10668926.2014.997842

Hoxby, C. M., & Turner, S. (2015). What high-achieving low-income students know about college. *American Economic Review, 105*(5), 514–517.

Ishitani, T. T., & Reid, A. M. (2015). First-to-second year persistence profile of commuter students. *New Directions for Student Services, 150,* 13–26.

Jacoby, B. (2015). Enhancing commuter student success: What's theory got to do with it? *New Directions for Student Services, 150,* 3–12.

Kodama, C. M. (2015). Supporting commuter students of color. *New Directions for Student Services, 150,* 45–55.

Kretovics, M. (2015). Commuter students, online services, and online communities. *New Directions for Students Services, 150,* 69–78.

Krueger K., Parnell, A., & Wesaw, A. (2016). Landscape analysis of emergency aid programs. *National Association of Student Personnel Administrators.* Retrieved from https://www.naspa.org/rpi/reports/landscape-analysis-of-emergency-aid-programs

Ladson-Billings, G. (1995). Toward a theory of culturally relevant pedagogy. *American Educational Research Journal, 32*(3), 465–491.

Leveson, L., McNeil, N., & Joiner, T. (2013). Persist or withdraw: The importance of external factors in students' departure intentions . *Higher Education Research & Development, 32*(6), 932–945. doi:10.1080/07294360.2013.806442

Maslow, A. H. (1943). A theory of human motivation. *Psychological Review, 50*(4), 370–396. doi:10.1037/h0054346

McKinney, L., & Novak, H. (2015). FAFSA filing among first-year college students: Who files on time, who doesn't, and why does it matter? *Research in Higher Education, 56*(1), 1–28.

National Center for Education Statistics (NCES). (2016). *Digest of Education Statistics.* Washington, DC: U.S. Department of Education.

Pascarella, E. T., Pierson, C. T., Wolniak, G. C., & Terenzini, P. T. (2004). First-generation college students: Additional evidence on college experiences and outcomes. *Journal of Higher Education, 75*(3), 249–284.

Patton, L., Renn, K. A., Guido, F. M., & Quaye, S. J. (2016). *Student development in college: Theory, research, and practice.* San Francisco, CA: Jossey-Bass.

Pope, R., Reynolds, M., & Mueller, J. (2004). *Multicultural competence in student affairs.* San Francisco, CA: Jossey-Bass.

Rendon, L. (1994). Validating cultural diverse students: Towards a new model of learning and student development. *Innovative Higher Education, 19*(1), 33–51.

Shapiro, D., Dundar, A., Huie, F., Wakhungu, P., Yuan, X., Nathan, A., & Hwang, Y. A. (2017). Completing college: A national view of student attainment rates by race and ethnicity – Fall 2010 cohort (Signature report No. 12b). Herndon, VA: National Student Clearinghouse Research Center.

Shevalier, R., & Mckenzie, A. B. (2012). Culturally responsive teaching an ethics-and care-based approach to urban education. *Urban Education, 47*(6), 1086–1105. doi:10.1177/0042085912441483

Steinacker, A. (2005). The economic effect of urban colleges on their surrounding communities. *Urban Studies*, 42(7), 1161–1175.

Taylor, J. (2015). Call to action: Embracing an inclusive LGBTQ culture on community college campuses. *New Directions for Community Colleges*, 172, 57–66.

Winstead, R. (2015). *Queer spaces in Kentucky: Understanding LGBTQ migration* (Unpublished master's thesis). University of Kentucky, Lexington, KY.

Yosso, T. (2005). Whose culture has capital? A critical race theory discussion of community cultural wealth. *Race Ethnicity and Education*, 8(1), 69–91.

Zisken, M., Fischer, M., Torres, V., Pellicciotti, B., & Player-Sanders, J. (2014). Working students' perceptions of paying for college: understanding the connections between financial aid and work. *The Review of Higher Education*, 37(4), 429–467.

4

PROMOTING STUDENT SUCCESS

Corlisse Thomas and André McKenzie

As a first-generation college student from New York City, I quickly learned from my family and teachers that education was the answer to almost every question I posed. I grew curious and then fascinated by the books and spaces, teachers and classrooms, that could open whole worlds to me and transport me back to the past and into the future, connecting the two along the way, in a single day. I selected a career in student affairs because of the administrators, faculty, and programs that supported me as both an undergraduate and graduate student. The power of higher education to change the course of a life was a reality for me that I wanted other students to experience. My coauthor's personal and professional background also propelled him to his life's work promoting and supporting student success. Though he attended a large state institution in the heartland of Illinois as an undergraduate, his early foray into a career in higher education as a student affairs professional was at a 4-year institution in the city of Chicago. Being a native of the city, he was quite familiar with the student population the school served and the challenges they faced as students in urban settings. Our combined histories tell a story of a passion for having an impact on and, further, creating pathways to success for students for whom the way is not always clear. Of particular importance to us both is our belief in the need for colleges and universities to speak to students with one voice and serve them on the basis of one set of beliefs rather than our now typically fragmented messaging and motivation. This belief has urged us from our disparate roles as senior administrators in student affairs and academic affairs to explore how institutions can truly collaborate across boundaries to contribute to student success at urban-serving institutions.

*— **Corlisse Thomas**, Ed.D., Vice Chancellor for Student Affairs, Rutgers University-Newark, and*
***André McKenzie**, Ed.D., Vice Provost for Academic Support Services and Faculty Development, St. John's University*

The challenges that urban-serving institutions face in providing their students with academic and other supports to ensure their success has been well documented. Citing some of the distinctive characteristics that often typify this population, discussed in Chapter 2, coming from underrepresented and low-income households; having to balance school, family, and work responsibilities; and often being the first in their families to attend college—aptly illustrates how this student demographic differs from that of its nonurban counterparts (Flynn, 2015; Conway, 2009; Benson & McClendon, 2008; Clark, 2006). Given this, higher education leaders must creatively determine how to alter traditional models of programs and services to appropriately meet institutional needs and support student success.

Success in the academic setting is normally defined in terms of retention, program completion and graduation. If a student completes their postsecondary goal within a reasonable time frame, we typically consider them to be successful. Though this traditional definition of success holds in the urban setting, the needs and characteristics of students at urban-serving institutions require that university leaders promote student success from a perspective that looks well beyond academic ability. At its core, Student Affairs' purpose is to encourage and support student success. In urban settings, student affairs work and the methods we employ to do that work often determine whether a student will be successful in the classroom. What we know in urban settings is that the nature of our student populations dictates that we employ a multifaceted and collaborative approach to supporting student success.

This chapter provides a discussion of seven critically important programmatic and conceptual elements that are foundational to promoting student success in the urban setting. They are: (1) structural challenges in promoting student success; (2) financial aid programs, policies, and initiatives; (3) wrap-around support and advising; (4) wellness and mental health programs and services; (5) career education and life skills planning; (6) culturally relevant/responsive student services; and (7) graduation and academic support initiatives. The chapter also suggests that purposeful programs and strategies in these areas will definitively contribute to student success at urban-serving colleges and universities.

Structural Challenges in Promoting Student Success

Promoting student success at USIs requires that numerous institutional factors are aligned to address the needs of students. Among these factors are the structural and cultural characteristics that often impede our ability to effectively design programs, services, and environments that support students. Perhaps the most salient structural challenge, noted both by senior leaders in this project and the higher education literature, involves the institutional silos that are prevalent at most colleges and universities, and particularly the separation that often exists between student affairs and academic affairs. These silos are rooted in the disparate purposes these areas have historically served at universities and the cultural differences between these functions. However, leaders are learning that these silos no longer serve their institutional missions, nor fulfill university goals to be student centered and ensure student success.

Eliminating silos was important to our senior leaders, or vice presidents (VPs). One VP spoke of cross-training staff in career and academic advising so that "they can help students at multiple points." Another discussed the numerous connections that the student affairs department has in the local community and with other departments on campus so that it can help students in a variety of ways. Programmatically, one senior leader spoke of an early alert program, a common best practice at many universities, that in this particular case is "interconnected, between student services, staff, and counselors and faculty." Another described the importance of academic advising, an area that is considered sometimes "outside of the realm of traditional student affairs," as a central touchpoint for students that could be utilized to provide students with far more than academic advising. Conceptually, one spoke of the imperative that student affairs and academic affairs has to be "married at the hip, whether we like it or not, appreciate it or not," in order to best serve the wide-ranging needs of TRIO students (those enrolled in any of the eight federal programs designed to serve and assist individuals from disadvantaged backgrounds to progress through the academic pipeline from middle school to postbaccalaureate institutions) at the university. Higher education research also recognizes the need for coordination on the college campus. Clark (2006) concluded the following:

> Powerful educational experiences cannot be left to happen by chance, so educators must be intrusive and intentional in their efforts to foster students' success across semesters. Institutional approaches that dedicate, combine, and coordinate physical, social, and academic spaces for urban commuter students offer exciting possibilities for building connections and increasing student success during the first year and beyond.
>
> *(p. 8)*

Further, Newbold's (2015) look at commuter student characteristics challenged "the inclination to see students only as learners" (p. 83). If we view students holistically, we then must move beyond silos to fully address their needs.

Institutions also need the technological capacity to remain connected departmentally in a way that provides students with a cohesive college experience. While students may expect that information they have shared with one division of the university travels with them to other divisions, institutions often have systems that do not "speak" to one another, causing students to have to share the same information repeatedly, or start from the beginning of their narratives during each encounter with a new institutional department or service. This technological disconnection, a structural challenge for urban-serving institutions, leads to an experiential challenge for students, many of whom are still being acclimated to the collegiate environment. They must reliably and repeatedly present the specifics of a number of issues and concerns—almost akin to the improbable notion of hospital patients knowing and explaining every aspect of their medical chart for a variety of medical professionals. The technological disconnect we speak of now becomes a very real and human disconnect for students, perpetuated by the institution's inability to offer them a sense of continuity of experience. The documented alienation from their colleges that students at urban-serving institutions feel (Clark, 2006; Hagedorn, Perrakis, & Maxwell, 2007; Newbold, 2015) is heightened by this reality. In short, how can students feel connected to an institution that does not know them? Some institutions are tackling this by employing online-advising case management software that connects institutional service providers and enables them to utilize predictive analytics to know when students need help and what kind of help they need. These online systems allow advisors to keep a record of specific student interactions, making information available to any office that has access to the system. Still others recognize the problem but have yet to address it. Technology is also a key consideration in how we publicize and make services available to students. Given the prominence of technology in everyday life, our connection to students is enhanced when we can offer them information, programs, and services online (Yearwood & Jones, 2012).

Another consistent structural challenge in the urban-university or college setting is related to issues of scale. While there is no shortage of good ideas and variety of pilot programs that employ best practices or utilize assessment data to design interventions that are responsive to student needs, student affairs leaders consistently express concern about the scalability of such interventions. The size of the student population at many institutions prohibits making these programs available to all students. The lack of resources in many urban settings causes some schools to make-do or create patchwork programs in an attempt to give students *some* help rather than none, if help in its ideal format is not a financial possibility. This structural reality is an argument for college-wide collaboration and more resources overall to maximize limited resources. One VP characterized the high number of very successful intrusive advising programs on their campus as "boutique programs," illustrating the challenge of having successful interventions that only reach specific segments of large student populations.

Administrative bureaucracy is another structural challenge that administrators learn to manage, however it often deters student success. Hagedorn et al. (2007) specifically included this problem as one of their *negative commandments* when reviewing the issues that affect urban community college student success. Specifically, they command, "Though shalt NOT prolong unnecessary bureaucracy which takes time away from student services and administration" (p. 28). One senior leader recalled having student affairs staff state the three top things they could do in a single week to support student success, and yet found that the staff had no scheduled time to do any of those things. Another noted that we often bombard students with bureaucracy before even getting to know them, describing an initial student encounter as follows:

> You have to take a test. Here you go. Fill that out. Now you need to go to testing and you need to take math, and you need to take reading and writing so they can determine what classes you get to take. And [the students] just want to sit down and talk to someone about [their] career.

This example illustrates the need to be attentive to the quality of the student experience in addition to the content. Achieving essential tasks—like placement testing—must be couched in activities that recognize the aspirations that students bring to the college experience and that foster a relationship with the university that is not transactional in nature.

Finally, a structural challenge that several VPs mentioned was the difficulty in accessing services that many students experience. Many senior leaders questioned themselves and their campuses regarding where, physically, on campus they are located, whether they are open at appropriate hours, and whether the traditional learning formats they provide are working for the diversity of students that attend their institutions. Given that many of our students are working, living at home with their parents, or are parents themselves, or commuting, sometimes long distances, and many times are first-generation college students, senior leaders in this study have seriously grappled with whether and how their campuses have integrated the diverse needs, characteristics, and experiences of their students into the way that they are supported. Senior Leader observations clearly show that institutions, if they have not already done so, should conduct a critical analysis of their organizational and administrative structures and their capacity to meet diverse student needs. Throughout the remainder of this chapter we highlight examples of innovative practices enacted by institutions to integrate diverse student needs and manage the structural challenges that often impede student success.

Financial Aid Programs, Policies, and Initiatives

For many students at urban-serving institutions navigating the financial aid process—an essential element of college attendance—is often mysterious and complicated. It is critical for students and their families to understand how scholarships, grants, and loans work. Increasing student success has become a priority for all higher education institutions, as many face declining enrollments, and public institutions are experiencing less state support. Making sure that all students are given the appropriate level of financial aid advice is essential and vital to their success. It is even more important to urban college students because they have a greater need for financial aid. Unfortunately, the actual policies that dictate the awarding of student financial aid at our colleges and universities has made the process, and its consequences, even more onerous for urban commuter students. For decades, the primary model used in the development of financial aid policies at the federal or state level has been based on the assumptions and expectations of the "traditional" college student experience. These assumptions and expectations include the time needed for degree completion (a challenge for community college transfers), minimum course credit enrollments, and credit completion (a challenge for working students or those who experience crisis during the term)—all of which are directly tied to the type and amount of financial aid ultimately awarded. These assumptions fail to take into account the lives, experiences, and demands placed on students at urban-serving institutions. Their inability to fit neatly into the established financial aid model has resulted in punitive measures and consequences that disproportionately affect this population. Missteps, unforeseen events, and limited resources can have severe consequences on these students' academic progress. A lack of cultural capital in obtaining financial aid information, learning about the process of applying, and submitting materials on time can present significant obstacles to the goal of college completion. Additionally, family responsibilities and work obligations often exacerbate the educational and economic challenges these students face, necessitating that institutions implement financial aid strategies and practices to better support the needs of this population, particularly those from low-income households (Ziskin et al., 2014). Efforts spearheaded by organizations such as the Working Students Success Network (WSSN)—a consortium of 19 community colleges in Arkansas, California, Virginia, and Washington—address the broad financial insecurities of low-income students by providing information about and assistance in applying for public benefits, offering financial literacy training and personalized counseling, and delivering these nontraditional support services in an integrated or bundled manner (Price, Roberts, Kraemer, & Chaplot, 2018).

Assisting students in identifying financial support for basic needs outside of academic costs is critical to their academic success. Establishing partnerships with local organizations and agencies is one way that institutions have approached this issue, as one of the VPs explained:

> We knew a large number of students were eligible for public benefits, legal/financial counseling, food assistance, tax preparation support, and so we engaged with a not-for-profit, the Robin Hood Foundation, and then later Single Stop USA, to connect students across our seven community colleges to public benefits. On average, students who were eligible received about $5,200 in additional resources and benefits, essentially, we doubled the Pell Grants for the lowest income students. That had a huge impact.

This is an excellent example of one institution's success in minimizing the often-negative consequences of financial aid policies that disproportionately affect students at urban-serving institutions. Seeking resources outside more traditional forms of financial aid, as illustrated here, can provide these students with a broader range of financial support to meet their educational costs. As a result of their level of income, family size, or other qualifying factors, many students may be eligible for benefits provided by municipal or other social services agencies.

On the basis of their report of microgrant student aid programs at ten public urban research institutions, Anderson and Steele (2016) detailed the impact of this strategy on their efforts at student retention and degree attainment. Often referred to as *retention grants* or sometimes *gap grants*, these programs are specifically designed to target students who have unmet need, are on track for graduation and have a financial gap that will require them to drop out. Because many low-income students lack the necessary savings and/or family financial support to pay unexpected emergencies or shortfalls, they frequently are at a loss to identify additional financial resources. These grants are a resourceful, best-practice financial aid strategy that institutions employ to support degree completion.

Anderson and Steele (2016) noted that while these grants and other strategies are considered critical tools, they are ineffective as standalone efforts, and they urge campus leaders to engage in creating a campus culture in which there is dedication to and resources invested in increasing retention, graduation, and overall success for students. A 2016 NASPA study found that 532 of 706 participating colleges reported having some type of emergency fund for their students (Krueger, Parnell, & Wesaw, 2016). Illustrating this particular practice, one of our VPs commented:

> We know in the long run it's better for us for you to be here, and for us to find a way for you to find $500, $600, $700 than not. I think that those initiatives have been in place for a couple of years. I think they are continuing to refine them, so that they are a little bit faster, to try and intervene.

Another participating institution takes this approach even further in its Run to the Top initiative, a financial aid program that provides a "last-dollar" scholarship, meaning that the scholarship will cover the cost of in-state tuition and mandatory school fees after all federal, state, and internal/external scholarships and grants have been applied. A further example was expressed by yet another leader:

> We have a program that assists students in need—a homeless student program, as well as a foster student program. I believe that we reach every group that you find at an urban setting. Our students' [financial need] is close to probably 75%, if not higher.

These comments point out that financial aid policies and programs need to be nimbly applied to the plethora of student circumstances at USIs to create a campus culture that supports retention and graduation.

Educating students on the financial aid process and financial literacy is vital to providing students with the skills to better navigate and manage their financial obligations. Potter's (2017) study on support for low-income students at an urban public university resulted in an action plan for his institution that makes students' financial literacy one of its major goals. Likewise, one of our VPs stressed the need for financial literacy thusly:

> They're thinking about money-in-hand and what can I do with my money right now? It is helping them plan. I think, when you don't have parents who went to college themselves, they don't understand all these things; about how to be planful and making sure that you make good choices about the classes you take. So, we've put a lot of money into [financial] advising.

She went on to emphasize that students work a lot and prioritize "work rather than school, and we have to shift that thinking." At her institution they are working on time, financial, and stress management to build "financial literacy as early as possible." By connecting financial literacy to degree completion, she said, staff then try to get students to, "understand the value of saving for summer so that they can decrease time to degree."

The Coalition of Urban Serving Universities and the Association of Public Land-Grant Universities (2016), agreed that institutions need to do more to help students understand the impact their decisions can have on their academic success and financial stability. They concluded that 50 percent of the institutions that participated in their study cited unmet financial need as a "significant challenge" for their entering classes. Recommendations from the report include finding ways to provide additional grant support and funding; linking funding renewal to student progress and academic advising; offering students personal financial literacy courses that count as credit toward their degree; and making financial aid information easier to find and accessible to students. The institutions that participated in the 2016 USU study shared what strategies they have used or are currently using to promote retention and graduation. These common strategies—organized into ten categories (e.g., need-based aid, noncurricular financial literacy, increasing awareness of student financial difficulties, FAFSA completion, and assistance with student employment, among others)—underscore the need for these and other practices to be utilized when working with students at urban-serving institutions.

Wrap-Around Support and Advising

Wrap-around support and advising services address the range of needs that a student may have in order to support their academic success. These needs range from enrollment and registration services to classroom support, wellness, mental health, and career advising. Individualized programs and services that are collaborative and intensive offer "clear pathways to student success" (Kuh, Kinzie, Schuh, & Whitt, 2005, p. 109) and communicate the institution's ability to understand student needs and provide interventions that address them. These services often are administered with a case management approach and cross departmental lines, pulling in a wide range of institutional partners to contribute to student success. Many institutions employ the case management model as a primary strategy for managing student issues, providing intervention, and crisis prevention. In most instances, case managers in student affairs take the lead in addressing student concerns by triaging referrals and coordinating with other departments to gather available information and determine an appropriate response or support plan for the student. Once an intervention has been initiated and support structures are in place, the case manager provides further follow-up with the student as needed.

In many ways these programs exemplify "shared responsibility for educational quality and student success" (p. 157), one of the common elements that Kuh et al. (2005) found at successful schools. They described this signature contributor to success in many ways, including,

> The collaborative spirit and positive attitude that characterize DEEP [Documenting Effective Educational Practices] campuses are evident in the quality of working relationships enjoyed by academic and student affairs which operate on many campuses as functional silos, a situation that is all too common in higher education.
>
> *(Kuh et al., 2005, p. 172)*

Among other things, Kuh et al. (2005) found that successful wrap-around support and advising are antithetical to institutional compartmentalization.

Programmatically, many senior leaders in this project discussed established wrap-around programs that address the needs of their students while acknowledging some of the structural challenges that students face. These programs combine a variety of purposes, with an aim to maximize the time that students spend at school. Some, for instance, described orientation programs that combined transcript evaluation, registration, advising, financial aid, and other essential business in a single- or half-day program. They recognize that, most times, their students have limited time to complete essential college business. Although many campuses are reluctant to make programs mandatory, this is one potential way to make support for students intrusive at urban-serving institutions, particularly when we know that students who have access to the support are more successful. One VP described an academic coaching program delivered in a case management format that included academic advising as well as housing, financial, and other assistance, which ultimately led to higher persistence rates among students.

One result of these intrusive, wrap-around approaches is that they create connection for the students to the institution, a sense that they belong at the institution and that someone cares about their success. In addition to eliminating structural silos, these efforts boost continuity and create institutional memory of the student, thereby minimizing the disconnect that students tend to feel, a common difficulty identified in higher education literature as one cause for dampened student success (Burlison, 2015; Hagedorn et al., 2007; Newbold, 2015). In short, students feel connected to schools that connect to them. A related challenge at our largest institutions is creating community among students. As a result, senior leaders are actively strategizing about ways to strengthen a sense of community for students at urban-serving schools. Chapter 5 more extensively discusses ways these leaders increased a sense of belonging, but one VP challenged her staff to provide more individualized support for students instead of treating them like a number. This led to the creation of the university's own version of the case management approach, "school teams," in which groups of faculty and staff from each school at the university are charged with collectively supporting students each from their own specific areas of expertise so that students have an individualized yet connected experience. This approach can also address the lack of consistency, one of the three challenges that Clark (2006) found in her study of urban commuter campuses. Wrap-around advising, in addition to creating a relationship and community for the student, also counteracts the structural challenge of administrative silos discussed earlier in this chapter. Creating community between students and their universities allows students to enter each new phase of their collegiate experience with consistency, a thread that connects them to the college-going experience.

Wellness and Mental Health Programs and Initiatives

Though programs and services that support student wellness and mental health are central to wrap-around support and advising, this area is increasingly critical to student success and requires focused attention. A recent *Chronicle of Higher Education* cover story documented the continuing phenomenon of widespread college student mental health concerns (Lipka, 2018). Students in the article reported feeling the pressure to succeed when they are the first in their family to attend college, and that stress goes beyond the classroom when they experience anxiety about family issues and conflicts with friends. These pressures are exacerbated when students are commuting (sometimes from long distances), working part-time or full-time jobs, or are perhaps parents themselves or taking responsibility for other family members. These circumstances require that we address mental health concerns in the urban-institution setting in a wide variety of ways.

Although some research has shown the increased likelihood and desire among commuter students to seek out and maintain relationships with faculty members and higher levels of academic engagement within this group (Burlison, 2015; Newbold, 2015), the reality is that lonely students, those without peer and family support, are less likely to persist, as these emotional factors have a negative effect on student success (Nicpon et al., 2006). Commuter students, the largest population at urban-serving institutions, are predisposed to not make connections in the collegiate environment, making loneliness a significant risk. According to Clark (2006), urban commuter college students in her study reported that "the peer support systems they relied on prior to enrolling shrank or disappeared during their first year in college" (p. 4) Clark went on to describe the increased role that families assumed in students' lives. Students experienced mixed support from family members, with some family members feeling threatened or challenged by this new influence on the student's life, and others feeling very proud of their students but unable to provide support for the new academic expectations their children were facing. This is important because without that support, students are without resources when there are challenges at college, as demonstrated by students in Clark's study, who endured "chilling behaviors from professors, rude treatment from administrators and poor teaching" (p. 4) in silence. Clark (2006) concluded that these students lacked prior experience or reliable sources of information and, thus, believed that, being a successful college student meant being able to accept, accommodate, and adapt to whatever experience came their way within the college environment. [And] tended to assume that anything they encountered in college was justified and acceptable—or, at the very least, static and nonnegotiable.

(p. 4)

This can lead to students feeling more frustrated and lonelier, and even constructing attributions where they may believe that this treatment is all that they deserve.

Other mental health and wellness challenges described in the literature include high levels of stress attributable to the wide range of school, family, and work responsibilities that these students must fulfill, in addition to general adjustment to college (Newbold, 2015). Clark (2006) pointed to the ongoing need to adjust as new transitions present themselves at each stage of the college experience, despite the inability to establish a common thread that offers stability and support. New classes mean making new friends and encountering faculty with different academic expectations, which require revised approaches from students each term. The complexity of the urban commuter student's life and the wide range of emotions they encounter related to even the act of commuting (parking problems, transportation difficulties, etc.) add to the emotional toll that academic challenges and life circumstances can cause, requiring programs and services that are multifaceted in nature.

As noted elsewhere in this volume, some institutions address the varied social and personal needs of their students by creating relationships with community organizations. Knowing that resources may be scarce within their own university budgets, these schools have sought out local organizations that are established to address the personal needs (e.g., housing, food insecurity, etc.) of their students. This can be an especially effective remedy given that many urban students do not live on or near the campuses they attend. Additionally, given that a large number of students at urban-serving institutions are commuters, many of our institutions are developing relationships with community providers of mental health and social service agencies that can serve our students in their home communities.

One major challenge these institutions face is to provide service when and where students need it. For mental health services and health education, this oftentimes means stepping out of the traditional counseling-center setting and offering assistance in other campus spaces, including academic buildings, student centers, or residence halls, and in other formats, including groups, workshops, themed brown bag lunch meetings, or staffed information tables in campus buildings during peak periods of the day. One vice president described the growth in groups for "survivors" on her campus. These groups, she explained, address a number of serious concerns that accompany students to campus, including sex addiction, drug addiction, and sexual assault, among others, that must be processed in order to eliminate their potential to negatively impact student success. One VP discussed having an anxiety group created for women of color to address the anxiety that is specific to their identity in academia, and a residential recovery program to support students who were seeking sober living environments. Another described an interesting format that engaged the students in their own mental health education. At town-hall style "problem-solving events," this school's students propose projects to teach their peers about the importance of mental health. A growing counseling format that some schools are testing is online counseling. As our 24/7 culture grows, some schools are making access to counseling services available via online modules that students can access through the school's portal at any time of the day or night.

Mental health concerns are just one facet of wellness that many students encounter. Urban-serving institutions must also address the basic needs of students like food insecurity and homelessness, which are realities on some campuses. Several senior leaders in this study described needing to provide emergency housing for students, some of the students having come to school from foster care or homelessness. In some cases, students who were domestic violence victims and, as a result, have experienced unstable access to essential basic resources, also need support to gain access to affordable or free food and housing. As discussed in Chapter 3, some campuses now have food pantries, which are growing in popularity as food insecurity grows and students learn that food and personal items can be obtained from campus facilities.

Other campus services that stive to address the wellness needs of students at urban-serving institutions go well beyond what has previously been seen on college campuses. One vice president talked about legal services and tax filing services, and another mentioned services for undocumented students. A significant consideration in these examples provided by the senior leaders in this study is the need to understand wellness broadly and to devise interventions that are equally broad. Several spoke of taking a comprehensive approach to providing wellness services, understanding that student needs are layered and that no single response will effectively meet the wide variety of needs and concerns that must be addressed. Additionally, broad wellness services are a significant component of wrap-around support and advising. If a student has an academic issue, these senior leaders noted that mental health and wellness issues may be underlying and even exacerbating the academic problem.

Given the major influence that family plays in the lives of students at urban-serving institutions, and the fact that many of these students live with their families, the VPs spoke readily about a variety of parent and family programs at their institutions that are well substantiated by the literature. These programs are largely aimed at including the family in the college experience so that students experience family support and, in turn, academic success. Clark (2006) noted the importance of websites that address parent concerns and provide parents with information and resources, sometimes in several languages, to guide their children through the college experience. Gefen and Fish (2013) specifically suggested that college mental health programming help first-year students in these settings to focus on family dynamics, including understanding conflict and renegotiating relationships as students immerse themselves in the college experience. Barbatis (2010) also pointed to the need to develop programs that include families since, unlike traditional expectations that students separate from their families when they go to college, these families remain integrally involved in their children's lives. In keeping with this reality, one VP offers parent and student orientation together so that the families are not separated at the outset of the college experience. Programs like these enable families to understand the college experience and provide support for students in the process. Family programs also potentially reduce the stress that students experience when family members are unfamiliar with the college environment and the expectations that come along with it.

Career Development and Life Skills

According to the National Association of Colleges and Employers (NACE), first-generation college students and their postgraduate transition represent a significant issue for higher education leaders in general, and career services professionals in particular (Eismann, 2016). With a significant proportion of first-generation students attending urban-serving institutions, a study undertaken by the organization revealed the needs of this population in regard to career readiness and utilization of career services programs on their respective campuses. Given the results of NACE's study, concern for first-generation students' postgraduate transitions into the work force is well founded. Job-search-success rates of first-generation students, at least as measured by the survey, were significantly lower than those of their counterparts. A lower average job-offer rate also exists, but the lower job-acceptance rate—driven largely by a mismatch between compensation expectations and the reality—was cited as an even more troubling concern. The study indicated that first-generation students would benefit from additional support in the job search. It specifically cited their inability to tap into family members for assistance and their greater reliance on online career services as impediments to their advancement. The study also suggested that outreach programs encouraging first-generation students to make use of the on-campus career center and its resources could make a positive difference, while reconfiguring online resources to address first-generation concerns could be beneficial as well. Eismann (2016) also recommended that institutions provide support and encouragement for students to use resources that expand their job success, which ultimately could prove useful to their overall college experience.

One VP spoke of how his institution has adopted the NACE standards (www. naceweb.org) as a framework to guide its career and leadership enhancement program, which is centered on the experiences of the school's student workers. This senior leader stated:

> We're going to do a student employment experience for all—we have hundreds of student employees in the division. We're going to be working with them, educating them that it's more than a job, and

tracking them academically so that we're assisting our own student workers versus just having them come in, do work and leave.

This innovative practice makes on-campus work experiences a vehicle for professional development, an uncommon but useful method of maximizing learning gained as a result of a significant urban-student responsibility, namely work. This practice is also important because the student is at work *on campus*. A common challenge for urban students is the need to create a compatible schedule that accommodates both work and school. Often off-campus jobs or internships compete with the academic schedule and so having an on-campus job that also teaches career readiness can be a true "win-win" for students.

The NACE article examined the issue of career readiness and the experiences of nontraditional students, many of whom have extensive work experience, while others are first-generation college students (NACE Staff, 2016). The population described by NACE mirrors that of students attending urban-serving institutions. While nontraditional students with extensive work experience may have had multiple professional role models, nontraditional, first-generation students may have few professional role models, if any, and in some cases, limited or no experience working in career-oriented jobs. If a student has never seen career readiness skills demonstrated, they may be unable to emulate them. The article goes on to state that these students may have limited knowledge about career management, having seen few others manage their careers or provide mentorship to others. Conversely, NACE noted that many nontraditional students may have life experiences that have helped them build career readiness skills. Equipping them with the tools and strategies to identify the skills they possess and articulate them to employers is cited as important as well. Another area of concern with nontraditional students is managing their expectations. Many nontraditional students commonly expect that a degree alone will guarantee them a professional job without understanding that other skills and experiences may be needed, such as gaining hands-on work experience in addition to classroom knowledge or having networking ability. The observations made by NACE concerning this demographic highlight the importance of the specific career readiness standards that focus on professionalism/work ethic, career management, and oral and written communication.

How students at urban-serving institutions connect with and make use of career services on their campuses to learn the importance of the key workplace competencies cited by NACE is an ongoing concern. This issue was expressed by a VP who voiced the need for her institution to develop a "relationship between the student and career development." What that relationship looks like, how students are brought into that relationship, and how to engage students in discussions about their strengths and areas of development were a few of the questions posed that will guide the implementation of new program strategies at the university.

The Coalition of Urban Serving Universities' (USU) 21st Century Workforce Development initiative was established to examine what makes students more workforce ready, what relationships with employers should look like in the twenty-first century, and how universities must transform themselves to meet the needs of twenty-first-century workforce learners and employers (USU, 2018). Such an initiative underscores the critical need for urban institutions to provide a broad range of career services, with the development of life and soft skills central to this task. The idea of fostering an environment of "inclusive excellence"—in which students can come and study and engage effectively with people that are different from themselves—was discussed by one of our leaders in the context of developing this particular skill set:

> We know, for you to be effective in today's workforce you have to be effective in working with others. . . . We're putting a lot of energy into helping students to understand that your emotional intelligence, your capacity to have empathy, and compassion and respect for others will make you a far more effective employer, or employee. . . . How do we not only provide technically sound professionals but [ones] who have this notion of what we call inclusive excellence, where they can effectively work with different people in different settings?

Another leader is integrating these hard and soft skills in programming no matter the source or focus so that every event,

> has some components of preparation for life after graduation—whether it's public speaking, whether it's managing a budget, whether it's learning to negotiate, whether it's working in teams. . . . Let's think on the front end, "What can I put in this program that will give the students one of these experiences or opportunities to practice one of these skills sets?"

The University of Tampa (UT) is cited by NACE as a best-practices institution for its Spartan Ready Career Readiness Program, the goal of which centers on a focused and intentional strategy to help students develop the high-demand competencies that are relevant to succeed in today's workforce. Career center leaders at UT conducted research on competencies and what employers are seeking. They then worked with the university's employer advisory board to validate the ones that were critical to student success and, from this collaboration, developed a list of competencies for the school. The seven competencies, or pillars, are (1) communication, (2) interpersonal abilities, (3) critical thinking, (4) organization, (5) global engagement, (6) teamwork, and (7) self-awareness (Gray, 2017). Wake Forest University built a campus-wide mentoring culture to support holistic student development and to develop skills and practices valued by employers and graduate schools (McWilliams, 2017). Their newly developed Mentoring

Resource Center uses a decentralized model of mentoring to support mentor- and mentee-skill development with online and in-person tools and strategies.

The Association of Public and Land-Grant Universities (APLU) includes three urban-serving institutions among its winners of the Innovation and Economic Prosperity Universities award program, which highlights institutional efforts to provide novel approaches to increasing career readiness through experiential learning and collaborative partnerships (APLU, 2017). Two are institutions included in this project. The University of Massachusetts (Boston) brings together cross-sector stakeholders from education, industry, and the community to build an education-to-workforce pathway in information technology for students from underrepresented backgrounds. The University of Houston has created novel, cross-disciplinary, and experiential learning programs to help students develop skills that not only support them in whatever career they choose but also help the university drive innovation from lab to market.

Acknowledging the diverse student populations that so often characterize institutions in urban settings, one of our leaders shared,

> I think about it from a Latino/Latina perspective, how career services might offer culturally responsive career services. With Latino and Latina students, career decision-making takes on a different element when they are impacted by the desires of the family and the responsibilities they hold in the family. In my institution, we have a lot of East Asian–American students and their families are like, "There are three occupations you can go into." And if, God forbid, if you don't have academic ability or a desire, then there's a lot of mental health consequences.

These comments reinforce the need for the provision of culturally responsive student services, particularly in USI career services departments where a student's consideration of family involvement may be paramount in their decision-making concerning career choice and life planning.

Culturally Relevant/Responsive Student Services

An overarching theme across every program area discussed in this project was the need to actively incorporate cultural awareness, knowledge, and sensitivity into student programs and services at urban colleges and universities. Though institutional contexts differ, and cultural characteristics vary, the need to acknowledge and, in effect, respond to these characteristics as a contributor to student success resonated in a variety of ways with the vice presidents in this project. Their discussion of cultural responsiveness in their university environments corresponded directly with the discussion of the importance of culture in the literature.

Some senior leaders spoke of cultural responsiveness with respect to culturally specific programming. One acknowledged that while programs aimed solely at underrepresented students seemed outdated or to be challenged by critics, there continues to be a need for cultural identification embedded within the understanding of the needs of students, or as one put it, the need to speak "to each group in a different way." One university started a new multicultural office in the last 3 years to focus specifically on diversity and inclusion. This contradicts the idea held by some that in culturally diverse environments, a functional focus on diversity and inclusion might not be necessary. Two VPs expressed concern about defining culturally responsive student services through a lens that makes it "separate from the core of what we should be doing." One described being in an institutional context that uses cultural responsiveness as its primary frame of reference. In that setting, being culturally responsive is *the way*, not *the other way* of promoting student success. Embedded in their discussions on this topic is a rejection of a deficit framework for understanding and supporting urban students (Garcia & Guerra, 2004; Green, 2006; Nair & Thomas, 2018).

Chapter 3 calls us to consider the broad diversity within our USI student populations and the need to acknowledge the richness of each student's identity along with the personal and life circumstances that they bring with them to the university environment. One VP said, "We have to tailor our services to meet the needs of our students. . . . I think that being culturally relevant allows you to design programs, services, policies, that are relevant and that make sense for the setting you're in." The individuality of students at urban-serving institutions offers us an opportunity to customize our programs and services in a manner that is truly culturally responsive. Acknowledging the need for a greater emphasis in meeting the cultural needs of its diverse student population, a private 4-year institution in New York City opened its Inclusivity Resource Center (IRC) in fall 2018. The IRC was established to provide resources to assist in authentic and informed peer dialogue on topics of equity and inclusion. It provides social justice training for students, hosts equity and inclusion themed workshops, and through a collaboration with the Center for Counseling and Consultation, offers the services of a mental health counselor for both individual and group counseling. Even a mandatory 30-minute online training is required to reserve the community meeting space. The event must support and address the needs of historically minoritized identities and the groups must have missions that are consistent with the university's. This focus represents a broadly envisioned approach to cultural responsiveness utilizing a social justice lens to achieve cultural education and support student success.

Staff who can identify with students has been identified as significant to student success. In one study, the staff who were selected to support the students had come from similar educational backgrounds which shaped their approach to the work. The students in the study noted that "the energy and persistence, the "never give up" attitude, and the loving family-like concern and attention were what got many of them through difficult transitions" (Grutzik & Ramos, 2016, p. 125). This is particularly salient given our earlier discussion of loneliness, silence, isolation, and inconsistency as defining characteristics of the commuter and beginning college student experience at urban-serving institutions. One vice president, while acknowledging that culturally similar backgrounds do not guarantee a trusting mentoring or advising relationship, also recognized that "it's important sometimes that you see someone like yourself that can tell you how to get where they are." Another, who leads at the system level, said that "[staff need] to have an understanding of the culture and individuals they're serving." Because each of the four system campuses are distinctly different, both the culture and individuals was key to providing culturally responsive student services and to avoiding misunderstandings resulting in "individuals feeling that they're left out or not getting services that they really deserve."

Another strategic aspect of providing culturally relevant/responsive student services involves intentional activities to bring about institutional and staff sensitivity. Some leaders described faculty professional development programs to improve cultural competency and address the personal and professional needs of faculty as they relate to equity and inclusion. Another discussed identifying classroom materials and activities that would be culturally relevant in a particular academic discipline's context. The power of faculty sensitivity cannot be underestimated (Yearwood & Jones, 2012) and student affairs is well suited to contribute to this effort. Another spoke of engaging in discussions at the cabinet level of the university about institutional policies and whether they make sense for the student population. This is particularly important since policy is created and supported at this level. A personal awareness of cultural competency at this vice president's institution, and at many, can ultimately impact how decisions are made. As many institutions move toward outcomes-based learning and decision-making, having a culturally responsive lens becomes even more important. As one VP pointed out, the student learning outcomes that we set should encompass student identity and culturally specific programming; in short, we should be able to identify what students are learning in and out of the classroom. Having an understanding of who our students are enables us to better define and meet those outcomes.

Many senior leaders also acknowledged that cultural responsiveness in the university context is a work in progress. While some were intentional, others acknowledged reacting to needs and situations rather than anticipating them. Even though there is work to be done, the fact that the idea of being culturally relevant/responsive resonates in these environments is an important one that undoubtedly results in programs that more directly address what urban students need to succeed.

Much of what we have discussed here ultimately presents hurdles to urban-serving institution students' retention and ultimate graduation. Those students who make the daily commute to urban campuses face academic and nonacademic issues not typically experienced by their suburban or rural counterparts (Clark, 2006). To meet these challenges institutions have implemented a wide range of support services and initiatives designed to promote the academic success of their students and lead them to graduation. These approaches to fostering student success include intentionally utilizing theoretical foundations to ground support services, improving new student orientation and advising practices, providing personal outreach to students, and developing seminar and student success courses to facilitate academic achievement and persistence (Jacoby, 2015; Lovano McCann, 2017).

In their strategic plans, many institutions have incorporated a specific focus on providing a seamless pathway for students from entry to graduation. One leader described a system-wide initiative to improve 4-year graduation rates:

> Graduation 2025, everybody's very, very focused on that. Everything we do is with an eye toward making sure we're going to meet that plan. We're just really trying to strengthen everything from orientation and connection to advising, to student life and engagement.

When asked about institutional priorities, a leader made the statement:

> I would say that student success is number one. So, everything we're doing from the onboarding process of students all the way through to the time that they are ready to graduate is a priority and I'm working very closely with academic affairs and trying to create different initiatives that will help in that regard.

Inadequate funding can often hamper the efforts of an institution to strengthen its academic support program. In an effort to bolster financial resources and support for services that assist students toward graduation, one institution applied for and received external grant funding to support their student success initiative. Another's VP affirmed the urgency to provide graduation initiatives from start to finish and address the need to be attuned to the impact of life events on student progress:

> We do focus on everything from the very beginning experience, to being engaged in student activities. We have a really strong CARE Team[1] out of the Dean of Students Office now. Because we know that life happens to a lot of our students, and we want to make sure that students can pick up and move on with their life no matter what happens. If students are in crisis, if a faculty member notices when a student stops coming to class; we reach out to that student. We had 400 cases last year.

Advising initiatives for commuter students, like CARE Teams, are central to degree completion. While this approach to advising is far from limited to urban-serving colleges and universities, it does however take on particular weight and relevance for these institutions due to their large percentage of commuting students, the diversity, depth, and volume of the issues facing urban students, and the integral relationship between campus and community resources for these teams.

Darling (2015) recommended the creation of an institutional academic advising culture that supports commuter student success and incorporates the development of advising curricula, pedagogies, and learning outcomes. The benefits of an intrusive academic advisement model are outlined by Donaldson, McKinney, Lee, and Pino (2016) and include characteristics of effective advisors and contributions of the practice in promoting student success. More specifically, the benefits cited include helping students to develop a pathway toward their educational goals, students demonstrating more help-seeking behaviors, and their expressing an increased level of confidence in degree planning.

This approach corresponds with that of one community college VP, who discussed an advising model under consideration at their institution:

> A model that we're looking at is completion coaching. The district just finished a 3-year grant. The model includes completion coaches, who work with and try to reengage students who are at that 70-credit marker and have stopped out. Or if students are near the end, coaches just say, "Hey you're almost done, do you know this is what you need to do?" That project has been really successful.

This same VP noted the importance of eliminating the administrative silos, discussed previously in this chapter, as an important contributor to graduation by building stronger working relationships with registration, admissions and financial aid.

The need to create a culture within institutions that supports students is also examined by Grutzik and Ramos (2016). They discussed the use of "student support specialists" as liaisons for students trying to navigate the challenges of the collegiate environment. The initiative they described is specifically designed to address concerns about the transition and success of community college students in transferring to universities and completing teaching credential programs. Conducting an evaluation of one of our institution's existing academic advising program is what one institution did to improve its effectiveness in preparing students for graduation. Inefficient credit tracking protocols were replaced with those utilizing technologies that alert both students and advisors to "red flags" that signal potential threats to timely degree completion.

Students of color compose a significant portion of the student population at many urban-serving institutions. Accordingly, a number of colleges and universities in these settings are addressing the provision of academic services for this population through a cultural lens, an approach informed by theoretical foundations of intellectual, psychosocial, and identity development. One example of this approach is from another institution in this project, the City University of New York's Black Male Initiative (CUNY BMI). CUNY BMI's vision is to create model projects throughout the University that are intended to provide additional layers of academic and social support for students from populations that are severely underrepresented in higher education, particularly African, African American/Black, Caribbean and Latino/Hispanic males. It is expected that BMI program activity will be institutionalized and absorbed into academic departments and student affairs offices throughout the university for the benefit of these students and, ultimately, all CUNY students (CUNY, 2019). The goals of the initiative are to increase the enrollment, matriculation, and retention of underrepresented students; improve the overall grade point average of underrepresented students; and increase the graduation rate of underrepresented students. Of the six strategic areas that form the basis of CUNY BMI, three—culturally competent peer mentoring, academic enhancements, and socioemotional programming—represent the support services provided.

The Division of Student Affairs department at one urban institution in the northeast, where 73 percent of the undergraduate population consists of commuters, created the RISE (Reach, Inspire, Succeed, Empower) Network to proactively tackle the issue of student success. The goal of RISE is to create an environment where successful, high-potential students come together to assist in increasing the retention and graduation rates of the university's Black and Latino students. The program is for first- and second-year students who are dedicated to their academic success and personal and professional development. These students become part of a network of dedicated, committed, and passionate students who support and hold one another accountable for their overall performance and growth within the program. Begun in 2013, the network focuses on the successful completion of the first 2 years of enrollment by assisting with academics, career preparation, spiritual development, and social integration by establishing connections with relevant support services at the institution. Since the program's inception, the institution has seen a steady rise in retention rates for program participants.

Utilizing the framework of critical race theory to examine the success of Black undergraduates at an urban university, Harper, Smith, and Davis (2018) also cited the importance of racial and cultural sensitivity in the design and implementation of support services for this population of students. The expansion of Puente, a Hispanic/Latino themed learning community, described by one of our leaders, is another example of such an initiative. A similar initiative was discussed by another VP whose Urban Experience Program, initially designed as a retention program for African American students, has been broadened to provide intrusive, high-need programming for first-generation students, those with an undocumented status, and those in the foster care system. These examples powerfully demonstrate the ways that urban-serving institutions tailor programs aimed at degree completion so that they are culturally responsive with the intention of recognizing salient identities that significantly impact student success.

Advice for University Leaders

This chapter underscores the fact that promoting student success at urban-serving institutions is an institutionally expansive endeavor. The broad range of concerns that must be addressed in order to promote urban student success requires that higher education leaders examine and adjust the university environment at both the macro and micro levels. Unfortunately, many colleges and universities have come to accept the environmental and cultural norms of their institutions as status quo and most often call upon our students to fit themselves into our existing paradigms. We fervently believe this does not have to be the case. First, we posit that successfully educating students in the urban context requires that we examine our administrative structures, questioning the siloes that have long permeated university settings. Though breaking down walls and truly collaborating across administrative and disciplinary lines can be "messy," by doing so we regularly devise programs, services, and pedagogy that are more suitable to the students we serve.

Structural concerns, however, are just one element of the change that may need to occur at your institution. Although traditional notions of college included the process of separating students from their families to be made anew by a residential college environment and classically tailored education, in the urban setting you cannot responsibly ask students to leave their lives behind, nor expect that you exclusively influence a student's growth, aspirations, and development. Know that your deep knowledge of students, including an understanding of their intersectional identities, their personal journey, and their family backgrounds can imbue you with the needed information and respectful context to create university environments that are compatible with students' lives. Seek that knowledge; it will transform your perspective and support your efforts to help students succeed.

Discussions of urban student needs and how to address them in these instances often lead to questions of tradition, policy, funding, regulations and the limits of our powers as university leaders. Ultimately, degree completion is fully impacted by the characteristics and life circumstances of students attending your institution and it becomes your responsibility to incorporate student needs into the appropriate structures if you seek to fulfill your goal to increase degree attainment and student success. As an institutional leader you have the power to positively affect student success by holistically providing support services that address students' needs and a college environment that is designed to maximize their connection with the university. Your attention to this connection is paramount to supporting student success.

In nearly all significant support service areas, senior student affairs leaders have identified concerns and best practice programs and services that can help colleges and universities to intentionally support student success. In sum, conducting a comprehensive assessment of structures, programs and culture is an important first step in determining whether your institutional environment encourages or inhibits student success. Further, as you endeavor to create seamless pathways for students to graduation, you should be attentive to the quality and nature of the experiences that you design. While your institution may utilize technology to reach large numbers of students in a flexible and accessible format, for students-and for a wide variety of college personnel-this approach should be responsibly balanced with the need to promote positive interpersonal relations with the institution. Technology must be paired with intrusive and, at times, mandatory advising strategies that encourage student accountability and ownership of the academic plan. Additionally, your students' career goals must be assessed, developed, and connected to the overall USI college experience. If the intended life cycle of the relationship between the student and the university extends from recruitment to alumni status, developing career readiness in students contributes to maintaining your students' connection to your institution after graduation.

Perhaps among the most challenging and simultaneously essential elements of promoting student success is your ability to connect with external partners to secure funding opportunities to support student success initiatives. Seek to establish partnerships with city agencies, corporate partners, and philanthropic foundations, among others, to provide eligible students with additional financial and/or personal support, or to generate support for university programs that address basic needs (e.g., food insecurity, housing, childcare, etc.). These efforts can mean the difference between a successful and unsuccessful student.

In a quickly changing world, with constantly emerging student concerns, urban-serving colleges and universities that pay careful attention to student demographics and adopt a willingness to make key cultural shifts, can lead the way in fully educating a group of students who are fast becoming the future of higher education in America.

Discussion Questions

- What structural changes at your institution could be implemented to minimize departmental silos and student runaround, and to strengthen the delivery of student services?
- How would you characterize your institution's overall environment and culture of student support?
- What is the level of cultural competency that exists at your institution? Does your staff understand and do your programs and services address the multifaceted nature and needs of the students you are serving?
- In what ways do your institutional, state, and federal financial aid and enrollment policies affect urban college students?

- What partnerships does your institution currently maintain with external organizations (e.g., city agencies, corporate partners, philanthropic foundations, etc.) to provide support for students? Can you identify additional partnerships that meet their needs?

Note

1 A cross-functional crisis intervention and support system for students experiencing academic or nonacademic concerns that impact their success: www.calstatela.edu/careteam

References

Anderson, C., & Steele, P. (2016). Foiling the drop-out trap: Completion grant practices for retaining and graduating students. *Coalition of Urban Serving Universities and the Association of Public Land Grant Universities.* Retrieved from www.luminafoundation.org/resources/foiling-the-dropout-trap

The Association of Public and Land-Grant Universities (APLU). (2017). 2014 IEP University awardees. Retrieved from www.aplu.org/projects-and-initiatives/economic-development-and-community-engagement/innovation-and-economic-prosperity-universities-designation-and-awards-program/award-winners.html

Barbatis, P. (2010). Underprepared, ethnically diverse community college students: Factors contributing to persistence. *Journal of Developmental Education,* 33(3), 16–26.

Benson, G., & McClendon, S. C. (2008). Engaging in a systemic partnership to increase college access and success. Metropolitan Universities, 19(4), 57–62.

Burlison, M. B. (2015). Nonacademic commitments affecting commuter student involvement and engagement. *New Directions for Student Services,* 150, 27–34.

City University of New York (CUNY). (2019). Black Male Institute overview. Retrieved from www1.cuny.edu/sites/bmi/

Clark, M. R. (2006). Succeeding in the city: Challenges and best practices on urban commuter campuses. *About Campus,* July–August, 2–8.

Association of Public and Land-Grant Universities (2016). *Collaborating for change: Engage faculty for student success.* Retrieved from www.aplu.org/library/recommendations-to-engage-faculty-in-student-success/file

Conway, K. M. (2009). Exploring persistence of immigrant and native students in an urban community college. *The Review of Higher Education,* 3(32), 321–352.

Darling, R. A. (2015). Creating an institutional academic advising culture that supports commuter success. *New Directions for Student Services,* 150, 87–96.

Donaldson, P., McKinney, L., Lee, M., & Pino, D. (2016). First-year community college students' perceptions of and attitudes toward intrusive academic advising. *NACADA Journal,* 36(1), 30–42.

Eismann, L. (2016). First-generation students and job success. *NACE Journal,* November. Retrieved from www.naceweb.org

Flynn, E. E. (2015). It's all about saving face: Working with the urban college student. *College Student Journal,* 49(2), 187–194.

Garcia, S. B., & Guerra, P. L. (2004). Deconstructing deficit thinking: Working with educators to create more equitable learning environments. *Education and Urban Society,* 36(2), 150–168.

Gefen, D. R., & Fish, M. C. (2013). Adjustment to college in non-residential first-year students: The roles of stress, family, and coping. *Journal of the First-Year Experience and Students in Transition*, 25(2), 95–115.

Gray, K. (2017). *Starting a campus-wide competency development program: Different approaches, common ground*. Bethlehem, PA: National Association of Colleges and Employers. Retrieved from www.naceweb.org/career-readiness/best-practices/starting-a-camp us-wide-competency-development-program/

Green, D. (2006). Historically underserved students: What we know, what we still need to know. *New Directions for Community Colleges*, 135, 21–28.

Grutzik, C., & Ramos, S. (2016). The role of the student support specialist: The possibilities and challenges of a long-term, proactive, and scaffolded relationship. *Community College Journal of Research and Practice*, 40(2), 113–132.

Hagedorn, L. S., Perrakis, A. I., & Maxwell, W. (2007). The negative commandments: Ten ways urban community colleges hinder student success. *Florida Journal of Educational Administration & Policy*, 1(1), 25–35.

Harper, S., Smith, E., & Davis III, C. H. F. (2018). A critical race analysis of black undergraduate student success at an urban university. *Urban Education*, 53(1), 3–25. www.naceweb.org/career-readiness/best-practices/addressing-the-career-readiness-of-nontraditional-students/

Jacoby, B. (2015). Enhancing commuter student success: What's theory got to do with it? *New Directions for Student Services*, 150, 3–12.

Kruger, K., Parnell, A., & Wesaw, A. (2016). *Landscape analysis of emergency aid programs*. Washington, DC: National Association of Student Personnel Administrators.

Kuh, G. D., Kinzie, J., Schuh, J. H., & Whitt, E. J. (2005). *Student success in college*. San Francisco, CA: Jossey-Bass.

Lipka, S. (2018, February 13). 'I didn't know how to ask for help': Stories of students with anxiety. *The Chronicle of Higher Education*. Retrieved from www.chronicle.com

Lovano McCann, E. (2017). *First-generation college students: Perceptions, access, and participation at an urban university* (Doctoral dissertation). University of Southern California, Los Angeles, CA.

McWilliams, A. (2017). Wake Forest University: Building a campus-wide mentoring culture. *Metropolitan Universities Journal*, 28(3), 67–79.

NACE Staff. (2016). Addressing the career readiness of nontraditional students. Retrieved from www.naceweb.org/career-readiness/best-practices/addressing-the-career-readines s-of-nontraditional-students/

Nair, A., & Thomas, C. (2018). A social justice approach to building community in higher education today. *Insight into Diversity*. Retrieved from www.insightintodiversity.com/a -social-justice-approach-to-building-community-in-higher-education-today/

Newbold, J. J. (2015). Lifestyle challenges for commuter students. *New Directions for Student Services*, 150, 79–86. doi:10.1002/ss.20129

Nicpon, M. F., Huser, L., Blanks, E. H., Sollenberger, S., Befort, C., & Kurpius, S. E. R. (2006). The relationship of loneliness and social support with college freshmen's academic performance and persistence. *College Student Retention*, 8(3), 345–358.

Potter, M. (2017). Student success for all: Support for low-income students at an urban public university. *Metropolitan Universities*, 28(2), 63–71.

Price, D. V., Roberts, B., Kraemer, S., & Chaplot, P. (2018). *Community college approaches to address basic needs and improve financial stability for low-income students: Lessons from the working students' success network implementation evaluation*. Working Students Success Network. Indianapolis, IN: DVP-Praxis LTD.

Urban Serving Universities (USU). (2018). Coalition of Urban Serving Universities. Retrieved from http://usucoalition.org/initiatives/overview/21st-century-workforce-development

Yearwood, T. L., & Jones, E. A. (2012). Understanding what influences successful black commuter students' engagement in college. *The Journal of General Education, 61*(2), 97–125.

Ziskin, M., Fischer, M. A., Torres, V., Pellicciotti, B., & Player-Sanders, J. (2014). Working students' perceptions for paying for college: Understanding the connections between financial aid and work. *Review of Higher Education, 37*(4), 429–467.

5

PROMOTING ENGAGEMENT AND BELONGING

Michael A. Freeman and Anna M. Ortiz

Engagement and belonging resonated with my experiences as an undergraduate student at the University of Iowa, and with experiences leading to my current role of Vice President at Coppin State University. Long before higher education leaders began promoting the benefits of engagement, I was a fan of retention expert Vincent Tinto and his work imploring university officials to construct avenues that connect students to the institution; creating a sense of belonging. I discovered Tinto working as a peer counselor for students in special services at Iowa. Although the University of Iowa was a beautiful campus and well resourced, as a young man, black and poor, from the urban streets of Chicago I did not always feel like I belonged. Engagement in special services (a TRIO program) and finding a circle of mentors provided the sense of belonging which fueled my success. As a first-generation, low-income student I became a highly involved, respected student leader on campus. Becoming an Iowa Hawkeye required an investment of time, energy and interest. It took a combination of engagement and a sense of belonging to provide an environment for growth for students like me. Looking back, I had early institutional connections as a TRIO student, but never realized them. Through engagement and involvement activities I was also blessed to follow my mentors into the College Student Development graduate program. I will never forget being included on a panel at the American College Personnel Association as a senior in 1980; my very first professional conference. Now, 35 years later as a student affairs professional, 18 as a senior student affairs officer, and currently as Vice President at an HBCU on the west side of Baltimore, Maryland, I continue to engage students by inviting them to participate in programs and activities. Next to academic learning, cultivating belonging and encouraging productive engagement are critical elements of a successful undergraduate experience. In this chapter my colleagues share their experiences with students like me, as they struggle with how to effectively engage all students in an urban context. Students at urban-serving institutions are not always readily available to participate in created activities. Sometimes they lack the sophistication of recognizing and embracing every opportunity before them. There might also be a sense of frustration as university officials try to ascertain if our efforts are effective or even appreciated by students, faculty or other administrators. What

Promoting Engagement and Belonging   85

> *comes across without a doubt is an ethic of care and a willingness to create opportunities for students to feel they belong. We know all too well that a connection, just one, can make the difference between remaining at the institution and deciding to leave. And in the urban context we do not wish to lose a student, not one.*
>
> *— **Michael Freeman**, Ph.D., Vice President for Enrollment Management and Student Affairs, Coppin State University*

Student engagement is widely considered by scholars and practitioners as the critical element in advancing effective student success. The concept of engagement today was made popular largely through the work of George Kuh (1995, 2005) and his research leading to national surveys (e.g., NSSE, BESSE, CESSE, etc). However, the importance of engagement has strong roots in the concept of student involvement previously advanced by Alexander Astin (1984). Here, the quality of involvement was as important as kinds of activities in which students might participate. The more psychological and physical energy students put into their experiences determines the kinds of outcomes we can expect. Additionally, the number of activities (in and out of the classroom) and the amount of time spent makes a difference, where continuous involvement leads to more positive outcomes. The core to this concept is that a variety of academic and psychosocial outcomes result from what students bring to college (inputs), and what they experience while they are there (environment). In essence, Astin focused on the background experiences students bring to campus, how they become involved while enrolled and what students learn as a result of their involvements. Astin cautioned that not all students would experience the same results from their investment of time, because gains are directly proportional to the quality of their involvements. Finally, he assumed, and well over 40 years of research has shown, that academic performance is positively correlated with involvement.

A similar case of early foundations to student engagement could be made for the work of Vincent Tinto (1975, 1993) and reasons why students may leave higher education institutions. He called on practitioners to improve students' sense of belonging by connecting them intentionally to the intellectual and social life of the institution. Tinto (1993) developed a model that identified broad areas: student pre-entry attributes, student goals and commitments, institutional commitments, and student academic and social integration. The model demonstrates that belonging, by students finding places of integration on campus, is important for retention and graduation. The theoretical model actually makes a stronger case for the implications students' failure to integrate (departure) and hypothesizes possible reasons for a lack of engagement.

The work of Tinto and Astin provided important insights to institutions about students, and Kuh (2008) and Kuh and O'Donnell's (2013) student success concepts, especially high-impact practices, extends this by calling for a more active involvement on the part of institutional professionals to create opportunities for meaningful involvement on the part of students. These concepts are interrelated, and empirical research shows a natural link to student success outcomes, such as persistence, academic achievement, satisfaction, and social engagement (Astin, 1984; Berger & Milem, 1999; Chickering & Gamson, 1987; Kuh et al., 2006; Kuh, Pace, & Vesper, 1997; Pascarella & Terenzini, 1991, 2005). More than 40 years of research clearly provides evidence that supports higher education institutions' efforts to have focused programs and initiatives to improve student engagement. More recently, interest in student engagement and belonging has increased significantly as higher education has been called to demonstrate student learning beyond the assignment of course grades and to increase metrics of student success, especially in public institutions where funding is increasingly tied to measured outcomes. This is supported by the many authors (e.g., Hausmann, Schofield, & Woods, 2007, 2009; Thomas, 2012) who found support for student engagement and belonging as positive contributors to degree completion.

The foundational theories of engagement, involvement, and integration work well to guide the work of student affairs in helping students in traditional institutional settings experience positive outcomes. However, the models may not be as applicable in USIs because their largely commuter student populations have fewer opportunities to engage beyond the classroom (Pascarella & Terenzini, 1983). Paradoxically, these students are in greater need for academic and social integration, as their background characteristics and commuting status make retention and, ultimately, graduation more difficult endeavors. Although engagement research deepened to include community colleges, for-profit institutions, public and private institutions, little information is available about student engagement at urban institutions, in particular. Urban institutions have unique challenges developing, implementing and measuring effective student engagement and increasing a sense of belonging. Trowler found that,

> generally, engagement is concerned with the interaction of time and effort and other resources invested by students and institutions intended to promote student experiences, enhancing student learning outcomes, and enhancing development of student performance and the reputation of the institution.
> *(Trowler, 2010, p. 3)*

Key here is the interaction of time and effort on the part of both students and the institution. Effort, often a function of time, is at a premium with students who may work multiple jobs to pay for college and contribute to the family income. Effort, time, and resources are also at issue for institutions who struggle with competing for state funding to provide needed services, staff, and facilities.

Much of the research on student engagement and belonging has been conducted on traditional residential campuses, and with traditional, college-age students. We experience that professionals at urban-serving institutions are expected to report similar patterns of engagement and belonging for students at USIs. We certainly have that expectation of ourselves. We are increasingly concerned about student,

Promoting Engagement and Belonging **87**

family, and community engagement. But there are different challenges for students, faculty, and staff in determining how to be effective in our unique setting. In this chapter, we discuss what urban-serving institutions are doing to foster and enhance engagement. We found that intentionality of effort was paramount and that these efforts could be achieved through partnerships with academic affairs, community involvement and through family activities—all of which could be threatened or enhanced by campus climate. At the close of the chapter strategies to develop a greater sense of belonging are offered.

Engagement and Belonging Must Have Intentionality

Nearly all participants in the project referenced the need to be intentional about student engagement—to have a plan and include student engagement and belonging in strategic planning objectives. Of critical importance among our VPs was the need to be very purposeful about making connections with students and creating environments where students feel they belong. For many, intentionality was a challenge, one mentioned that they do not have a plan for how to engage those students who aren't active on campus. The California State University system has a system-wide initiative, 2025, with the goal to significantly increase the 4-year graduation rate. The senior leaders in our project from that system made it clear that this initiative could be a way to enhance engagement. They are doing this by strengthening orientation, advising, and student life. One senior leader found an opportunity to highlight engagement where it did not exist previously:

> There was nothing related to student belonging, connection, and engagement in the 2025 initiative. And so, we talked a lot about it and now, with our provost and our academic colleagues, we have one bucket and in that we're looking at student belonging and engagement on campuses.

Through consultation with her colleagues, she was able to make belonging and engagement one element of this strategic plan.

Many VPs suggested physical spaces be designed and utilized intentionally to enhance student engagement by using specific locations or specific times that meet the needs of the wider diversity of students attending urban institutions. Intentionality is a critical component in improving engagement. One senior leader explained that,

> if you come to the union, you'll get what you need. But you know, how do we go to where [the students] are? Part of that is pushing the staff to think about the fact that we need to look at where we have events differently, because this campus is not that big. So, if we are going to be intentional about reaching more students, that means we have to be intentional about where we do things.

Here, the simple logistic of choosing spaces to hold events takes on greater importance in the urban setting. Working with academic colleagues to make sure those spaces are "safe spaces where they belong and a healthy place for them to be." Needing more recreational spaces was also an issue, spaces where students can increase their physical activity. The lack of residence hall space also posed a challenge to belonging because it is hard to get students to stay on campus after classes are over for the day. However, even when there was an increase in private student housing adjacent to a campus, changing the way student affairs works continued to be a challenge:

> Now there's more off-campus housing being built adjacent to campus. So these students are walking to campus, I mean they are still in [our] footprint and by all accounts still "on campus" essentially. But there is no intention-ality in how we look at the footprint of students. Where are we advertising? Where are we having events?

Intentionality around a plan's ability to provide connection and belonging for students, a goal of any new building projects or institutional strategic plans, is important for student engagement.

Often, institutions have little immediate control over physical space, but as several of our VPs described, they do have some control in making sure that staff has a disposition to engage students. This VP described combating the mentality that staff wait for students to find them:

> A study I read said students who already feel marginalized, are less likely to access resources. So, there's a, build it and they will come [attitude]. But if you're already feeling like, "This is not my place," even if you know that tutoring is available, or counseling, you still might not seek it.

Mattering and validation are key concepts, discussed in this chapter and expanded elsewhere in this volume. This means that the institution has the responsibility to ensure that programs, structures, and personnel place students at the forefront of their purpose. Another VP stressed that "too often we treat students at our front counters as if they are just one of 30,000 students," and then he posed the ques-tion, "How do we change their experience?" Working with staff so that they know how to engage students and hiring and promoting staff who *want* to engage students is a place to begin.

Ultimately, the priority becomes finding any way for students to connect and create relationships with each other, with staff, and with the institution itself. One senior leader stressed that the goal is always "to create a relationship between the institution and the student, because the ways that students might connect on other campuses don't [work] here." Another, who is a system leader, expanded this notion when he talked about trying to create a "one-college feel" among the community colleges in his district. And that is an urgent matter, he said, "because our students are first-generation; we need to provide these experiences that allow them to connect, because it's really important. And they need that right away." This might also mean that professionals at USIs reassess effective engagement for urban students. For example, is regular classroom attendance every bit as effective an indicator of positive engagement for urban students as participation in a student organization is for traditional residential students?

Place and time will remain critical considerations to engaging urban students. Institutions are rethinking services, co-locating functions not typically placed together in buildings. Coppin State University in Baltimore placed a child-care center and community health center in an academic classroom building. This decision is an example of using physical space planning in consideration of student time. Students with children can choose to engage by enrolling children on the campus close to classroom space, thereby decreasing the need to leave campus and increasing opportunities and time for more campus engagement.

Transforming the Concept of Engagement

As we consider conversations of engagement and belonging, an emerging theme is just how difficult it is to determine what counts as true engagement. The definitions and interpretations vary according to role, functional area, and, indeed, type of institution. It could be that an entirely different definition of student engagement and student belonging is required to define student success on urban-serving campuses. The definition is important because it is so closely related to our ability to assess the quality of student affairs' efforts. The range and scope of perspectives from our senior leaders confirms the difficulty of making progress on student engagement when there is a lack of understanding of what it means and how to measure it—trying hard not to reduce quality to merely counting heads. One senior leader shared that she has a "deep concern" that her campus leadership does not know what engagement means and how to make it work, yet they tell her that "these are the things that need to happen." Another encourages her staff to see "linkages [between] academic success and retention" and engagement. She explained that helping her staff realize that "they're definitely part of that success story" is bringing a new level of quality to their work.

Thinking about engagement differently calls for student affairs to consider that quality engagement can be found when students participate in specialized programs, not necessarily those of traditional functional areas like student activities and residence life. The senior leaders in this project found that these programs, many of which are focused on student sub-populations, were far more prevalent. For example, does being a scholarship athlete count as student engagement? Or is it only more traditional activities that are sponsored by student affairs? One leader mentioned that his scholarship student athletes are "not involved in anything but their sport" because they are too busy. But, how often do we, in student affairs, dismiss this as a legitimate kind of engagement? In our analysis of how the senior leaders talked about ways in which students were successfully engaged, it seemed that they were almost apologetic when students were involved in as little as one activity and when more traditional programs and activities reached few students. For example, one said that "our cross-cultural center does an incredible job and it's really a home, though it does not serve a lot of students." Similarly, another leader highlighted a mentor program: "So you get upperclassmen who are making contact with [new students], checking in on them, doing programs, getting them to campus events. But the number's not as high as I want it to be." Other leaders met the challenge of successful engagement through innovative programs. One gave the example of a partnership created by student affairs and the alumni association to create "Students Today/Alumni Tomorrow," and that has become their largest student organization. On another campus they created a scholarship that required students to be involved in two campus activities in their first year.

Almost universally, the senior leaders in this project contemplated how they could promote levels of engagement for students who commute, hold jobs away from the campus, or are adult learners not interested in the traditional college-student life. Professionals at USIs have to understand that programs need to be customized for their varied population. Time is especially critical for students who commute. Finding parking spaces, getting a meal before or after class, and/or meeting faculty for discussion or assistance can complicate the educational experience for commuting students and affect their success. Earlier, we discussed Astin's 1984 theory of involvement and the importance of time on task to facilitate involvement, making the lack of time a critical factor for commuting students. Because they spend less leisure time on campus, it can appear to others that they are less engaged, less caring about campus programs; and that may be true. But it would be untrue to label commuters as "less engaged" simply because they do not attend sporting events or run for office in the Student Government Association. I (Freeman) have found commuting students much more involved in goal setting and career-related activities. Some institutions represented in this project had commuter student offices, one even having a dean of commuter affairs. One leader described a commuter assistance program for first-year students where "they get a little more special attention than you get in a residence hall." Developing commuter student assistants is an interesting way to mirror the resident assistant attention normally provided to students living on campus. Another leader "put more money into student employment at our campus, whether it is work study or not" because his president believed that was a way to keep students on campus, reducing the need to travel back and forth from home to campus to work. Giving commuting students scholarships to live in residence halls was another way to build belonging and engagement. Two strategies stand out as innovative: a student union with academic classrooms and a fund for students to participate in high-impact practices.

As college-going demographics continue to change, more students who are adult-age, with families, jobs, and seeking career changes, are enrolling in USIs more than residential institutions. Student affairs needs to pay attention to these changes and make sure they know the places students define as most important to their success. Without a doubt, academic departments and colleges are places where students who commute will directly link as places of importance. Places to grab a meal and service centers where students can manage institutional business or transportation hubs will also be important. For students with families, day care centers, schools, and planned activities that involve families will increase levels of engagement for these groups. Most of the examples presented do not include programs or activities that consider students with school-age children. Providing opportunities to engage that consider the whole of students' backgrounds will be increasingly important to persistence and student success.

Thus, our senior leaders questioned whether the expectations for engagement are the same for all kinds of students. Sometimes the frustration these leaders experienced in getting students to attend events or participate in organizations—to engage—led them to wonder how urban-serving institutions could be fairly measured by the same indices as residential or traditional campuses. But they remained committed to creating a sense of belonging among their students and strived to find better, more innovative ways to engage them. Some also realized that it was their responsibility to develop their own definitions of engagement and success, as state agencies or regional accreditation bodies were not going to do this for them. Measuring student success will be difficult for USIs, especially for those students who commute (Newbold, 2015). One recommendation could be to look at student persistence semester by semester as a measure of student success. We might also consider students holding a full-time job and managing a family while obtaining a positive grade point average as a measure of engagement. Perhaps measuring career-involvement activities on and off the campus will reveal a different and more significant level of engagement for commuting students. And the number or the frequency of visits to academic departments, student support services, and faculty office hours could be measured and studied as potential indices of student engagement. Engagement can even be measured as simply a function of regularly attending class, in addition to the academic activities they might require. These methods recognize that for commuting students, belonging—the outcome of engagement—often happens on the academic side of the house.

Engagement Through Academic Affairs

A long-standing conversation within U.S. higher education is connecting academic or in-class activities with those that are normally planned by student affairs outside the classroom. Professional organizations such as NASPA, ACPA, AAC&U and AASC have all authored position papers and devised models to bridge student learning with engagement in and outside the classroom. The senior leaders in this project revealed that urban institutions, by necessity, are closer to a reality of in-and-out-of-classroom activities alignment to improve student learning, engagement, and belonging.

This was accomplished by connecting to academic departments, and more specifically, by supporting programming that emanates directly from departments or courses:

> For programs like Black History Month, you will find here that a lot of the programming is embedded in the academic department, or emanates from the academic department, and is often championed, or owned, however you want to look at it, by a faculty member or faculty group.

Student programming imbedded in academic departments has the potential for enhanced learning that benefits students. Student affairs professionals may be challenged if they perceive no role for themselves in enhancing engagement in the classroom. However, student affairs professionals can prove extremely useful by partnering with the programming coming directly from academic departments and colleges. Furthermore as one senior leader said, "I don't have much control over" what happens in the classroom, "but I can work with academic affairs on what the student experience [is] like, not just outside the classroom, but inside the classroom." This might come in the form of working with faculty on ways to use acquaintance activities at the beginning of the term or in helping them to develop effective active-learning techniques, as those are often the cornerstone to student affairs programming and training.

Another way that the senior leaders discussed partnering with academic affairs was through working with student life to be more supportive and engaged with academically oriented clubs and organizations, as that is "where their [students'] identity is strongest." Participants in the study commented positively on linking traditional student activities programs and collaborations with academic departments or courses. An example of this was:

> One of the things we did with the history department was in a course based on history and environmental sciences that they offer over the summer where they bike, kayak, and canoe. So it's those two departments with our outdoor adventure guys. And that's been a pretty interesting and successful venture.

There are a myriad of ways in which student affairs can become involved with these kind of efforts. One institution in the project has student affairs deans located in each of the academic colleges to advise student organizations, support co-curricular programming, and to provide academic advising to students.

Career-related activities were another prominent topic of interest among the senior leaders. Among these activities were those related to internship opportunities and entrepreneurship, such as demonstrated in the following example:

> We have a lot of students that are really interested in entrepreneurial [activities]. So, we have a guy that was hired from [a college of business] who has kicked off some really cool entrepreneurial opportunities for students. We have lots of students that are creating start-ups and getting some funding or getting that experience. A third of our students, when they come here, say they want to start their own business.

Others work closely with academic units to develop internships. One senior leader requires that any student worker in his unit work on identifying ways that experience connects to the academic major and career goals, as discussed more thoroughly in Chapter 4.

Of course, many senior leaders described how they work with faculty to support students, including making them aware of resources, knowing that it is the faculty that often have the best connections with students. Oftentimes, that effort was "extensive." At one institution, they link student clubs to the college student success teams. Through that communication, "students are connecting student life activities to the school programs." That staff continually asks themselves, "How do we connect all these pieces so they become more coherent for students?"

In discussions about academics many responses showed great promise for engagement in the classroom. Senior leaders cited opportunities and efforts to connect in and out of classroom activities, which bode well for the future of placing students at the center of learning and for instilling feelings of belonging among students. This is critical because urban and commuting students often consider their academic departments as their home base, the core of their institutional identity. The more student affairs, alumni services, and others connect to the departments, the more likely that they will deepen opportunities and open up possibilities for further engagement.

Community Involvement Programs

In higher education today, every institution boasts of being involved in the community. Clearly, the work of higher education scholars (e.g., Boyer, 1990) called on institutions to do more to remind the public that one of the goals of higher education is to create citizens by developing an ethos of citizenship through becoming involved in the community. Now engagement and involvement in communities have become staples, and sometimes requirements, as government officials, state boards, and regional accrediting bodies determined that students being involved in communities is desirable. The involvement programs in various communities might differ due to mission and local community needs. However, this focus was a way to provide service and to model participation in higher education as a means of encouraging community members to consider higher education as a pathway to future success. Often, for urban institutions, involvement in the community was a necessity to secure enrollments and to successfully retain students to graduation. Thus, community service has been an effective way for USIs to engage students and to create a sense of belonging at the institution while also helping the community. Institutions with well-defined missions and institutional-level planning hold the most promise for this kind of effective engagement.

Nearly all of the senior leaders spoke of community service or involvement as both a part of the mission of the institution and a way to engage students. This makes sense, as one of the criteria for an institution's selection for this project was an overt commitment to serve communities where they reside. Often, "community" varies from the campus, to the local area, and to the world community. Community involvement also has overlaps with engagement programs sponsored by academic departments or student affairs' functional areas. Two leaders cited their medical programs as a primary vehicle for supporting their community while training their students. For example:

> We have a lot of pre-health students because we have medical school, nursing school, a dental school, and allied health. And a lot of those students are involved in things like blood pressure clinics. There is a clinic here that does outreach to the Latino community.

Students at all levels participate in these kinds of outreach initiatives, connecting them with each other, to the community, and preparing them for careers. This area is also an example of a high-impact practice—one that is more easily accessible to USI students, as many of those practices may require resources that these students might not have. One institution with a "long history of activism" participates in civic engagement to increase voter participation. That leader even noted, "That's why students, all the time, why students want to come here." Many described mentoring programs in which students mentor in the community. Others were involved in mentoring programs in local schools, one even providing a "bridge" experience where they "provide peer mentors for every single high school graduate who comes here." This effort is supported by a partnership between the local Hispanic Federation, the city's mayor, and the university.

A few urban institutions considered assessing their students to determine students' capacity to for involvement. Often, finances or availability due to schedule affects the time students devote to community involvement, even if the desire is there (Burlison, 2015). It will continue to be important for urban institutions to review their mission and set priorities consistent with the purpose. Some schools may learn the community they intend to serve is not "out there," but the one right on the campus. At one institution, they are preparing to "outreach in the academic departments to identify students in need" so that they can participate in community service. At another, a similar effort funds participation in a range of high-impact practices.

As a final thought on community involvement, consider the numbers of mandates and requirements from federal agencies, state officials, and local/regional governing boards. Higher education institutions are being asked to comply with any number of involvements: Cleary Act, Title IX, opioid training, alcohol awareness, firearms on campus, and mental health awareness. All include some level of time commitment on the part of students. Many schools, in response, now require community involvement or engagement to satisfy the growing numbers of requirements. For example, as a result of a young man being killed at the University of Maryland College Park in an alleged hate crime, all Maryland schools are now required to develop cultural diversity strategic plans and submit reports to the Maryland Higher Education Commission with the numbers of diversity programs and how many campus community members attended. The Maryland governor's office has made training for opioids mandatory, so the expectation is that the entire campus will be trained regardless of their exposure and involvement. Finally, sexual harassment training has become a mandatory responsibility of all colleges and universities. Currently, there is a vigorous debate about what constitutes engagement, with the state making a case that online training programs are not adequate. Many of these new requirements add a layer of complexity for USI students. The mandates are often issued with a traditional college setting in mind, where students have time and resources to comply with mandatory trainings. And while community service at most USIs is not yet required, one leader did describe how it is mandated through the general education and capstone requirements. The question we raise is, would this type of required community service and community involvement engender the spirit in which we intend it for students? Or are we simply complying with the laws and mandates. The challenge for urban-serving institutions is to retain focus on the schools' mission and purpose, and work to understand the needs of the populations who make up the campus community and student body. Urban-serving institutions should regularly review community involvement programs to ensure they are meeting the expressed needs of their students and the local community. As students increasingly choose to remain closer to home and more than 60 percent of the U.S. population is clustered in and around urban areas, real opportunities exist for these institutions to shape the conversations and efforts around what it means to be community involved.

Family Engagement

Family involvement is traditionally thought of as a one-time annual event, often referred to as "parents' weekend." However, at USIs, the consideration of how families are engaged in the institution is more than an annual event, often occurring daily. As a side note, I (Freeman) have made the point with my president that students at Coppin State University are overwhelmingly nontraditional and have families. They place their family life above the education they seek. For example, during registration periods, I have observed that students will register after matters at home are in place, including work schedules, preparation for children's schools, before- and after-school child-care arrangements, live-in parents, and medical matters. How and to what effect urban-serving institutions consider family responsibilities and engage family may determine the extent to which their students will persist semester to semester and indeed to degree completion.

The manner and degree in which students and families are welcomed and made to feel a part of the campus community was important (Guiffrida, 2005). Most leaders in this project placed great significance on orientation, with one describing how an hour at orientation has expanded to an academy:

> We have parent and family academy that we provide for first-year students. Because we know it's not enough to do a parent orientation in the summer. Because parents don't get it; they don't understand what their students need to do outside the classroom.

This leader's campus has realized that one of the impacts of having a majority of students who are first-generation is including the family in education. The academy brings parents on campus three times a year for workshops. During these workshops, they utilize returning parents to speak with new parents, and she reports that "it's just a wonderful thing." The workshops are offered in Spanish as well as English, as this is a Hispanic-serving institution. Creating multiple opportunities to connect with families increases students' comfort level and sense of belonging, provided the individuals involved pay attention to evolving needs. A good example of paying attention is offering the sessions in Spanish as well as English. Family members will feel welcomed and included as a part of the whole. Any features that pay attention to cultural nuances increase the feelings of belonging and the potential for success.

Some institutions are beginning to layer involvements much in the same way we think about adding alumni to events traditionally thought of for students only. When USIs think about families, children, parents, and even extended family members, they broaden the reach of the campus into communities, promoting good will. Also, by extension, other family members may begin to consider pursuing additional education as they feel more connected to the campus. Including family in sporting events is one idea that has been successful at one of our campuses:

> I think it's really important; all the work that we have done, getting our parents to come on campus and stay on campus. We had a great family night at soccer event. Families brought their children, the other siblings too, and we had food and they received free tickets to the soccer game so they can begin to see that there is life here for everyone on campus. But you have to be intentional about the invitation.

Another senior leader described their annual Spring Fling:

> It is one event that lent itself to nontraditional students or students with families. With several blow-up bouncy houses, games, food, music, and prizes, many of our students with children attended, and it was great. I said this is the kind of thing we need to be doing more of—and in different ways.

A sustained focus on family engagement will be important as urban-serving institutions continue to educate more and more first-generation and non-traditional students. Ongoing and regular engagement is important to building relationships and raising awareness, both important factors in promoting student success. Support of family members is critical for many urban students. Family members are in better positions to provide support and encouragement if they understand the institution and feel a part of its community. And especially in communities of color where extended family relationships and their influence play a major role, students are more centered and confident when they have the endorsement of family and community in their activities (Dennis, Phinney, & Chuateco, 2005). Students with engaged families are more likely to succeed.

Provided as follows are a few recommendations of what urban institutions can do to encourage effective family engagement:

Parenting—Assist families with information to set home conditions to support their students. Provide a calendar of important dates, useful resources, and family-friendly events. This also includes helping campus personnel understand the families of our students, especially students who are first-generation.

Communicating—Develop multiple types of communications between campus and families and from families to campus about important information and activities. Recognize the importance of two-way communication to families and from families. Ensure the messages are consistent and inclusive.

Volunteering—Organize opportunities for families to support the school and its students. Provide family volunteer opportunities in various locations, at various times, on and off the campus, and in varied formats.

Decision-Making—Include family members, when possible, as participants in community-related institutional decisions and develop parent leaders and representatives. Collaborating with Community—Urban institutions can coordinate campus resources and services with other community agencies and partner with others to provide services to families, students and the local community.

Important to recognize with any advice or list of recommendations is that institutions must think through their campus cultures to decide which initiatives fit best with the students they serve. Institutions may want to review campus messages, values statements, traditions, and symbols to ensure they are sending family-friendly signals.

Campus Climate and Its Relationship to Belonging

To a certain extent, promoting campus engagement and belonging for students is about campus climate. Prospective students, current students, faculty, staff, family members, and community agents must feel a sense of welcome, safety, comfort, and support. However, the feeling of belonging also extends to matters of race, ethnicity, citizenship status, gender expression, age, and ability (Harper & Hurtado, 2007). The campus must exhibit and practice an ethic of inclusion beyond the occasional seminar or annual program series. Our senior leaders expressed concern for addressing issues of climate and how best to demonstrate support, particularly from an urban-serving-institutional context. The range of needs these leaders are working to manage is demonstrated in these varied examples:

> Our Dreamers feel very insecure, unsafe; they distrust our campus police, for good reason. But trying to rebuild those bridges is very important.
>
> Our Black students feel marginalized, right? Because they're such a small proportion of our student body.
>
> This past year we established services for our transgender student population . . . [by asking,] what do we need in the health center? What do we need to do in counseling? What do we need to do in campus buildings? How do we make sure our trans students are comfortable and welcomed and integrated into our community?
>
> We have conservative students on campus who want to make sure their voice is heard. We have Young Americans for Freedom who regularly bring speakers to campus through a well-funded national organization that gives them a lot of money.

These are examples of why it is so difficult to improve campus climates, which is critical to developing a sense of belonging among such diverse students. Each of these exemplifies something different, from legal issues and first amendment rights to shrinking numbers of some demographic groups, and health needs for students experiencing significant transition.

Therefore, a part of improving campus climate has to include educating and training the campus community. This requires intentionality, which is sometimes missing when "diversity" programming has become routine and stale. One senior leader reminds us, "There is an opportunity for us to be a bit more intentional in how we train the campus community, in how we educate and engage the campus community around issues of diversity and difference." Many campuses have now adopted "inclusive excellence" as a part of their institutional mission statements and strategic plans, which has brought to the forefront efforts historically confined to student affairs, making an excellent opportunity for cross-divisional collaborations. One of our leaders told a story that reveals how complex the challenge to improve the climate for racial diversity might be. He said that what he sees among his faculty is a "deficit framework." This has hampered their ability to improve campus climate. Correcting this is difficult because those using this framework "can be well intentioned," but in reality, he questions if "it is just racist." He gave the example of a faculty member who referred student for being disruptive in class. Here is that exchange:

FACULTY MEMBER: "I'm scared."
SENIOR LEADER: "Well, what are you scared of?"
FACULTY MEMBER: "Well, he raised his voice, I felt threatened."
SENIOR LEADER: "Okay, well did he threaten you?"
FACULTY MEMBER: "No, it was the way he was looking at me."

The senior leader then went on to explain that the student was an African American male, a common occurrence, in his experience. The student told the senior leader that he felt that the faculty member disrespected him, and he was standing up for himself. This is in no way unique and is probably much more common than we care to admit, but it demonstrates the scope and impact of a negative campus climate and how it becomes a barrier to belonging.

University campuses have been featured in the headlines of major news stories with disturbing stories: nooses hung on trees at American University; a student stabbed to death at the University of Maryland by a student associated with White supremacy rhetoric; fraternities and sororities with racist chants at the University of Oklahoma; denials of conservative speakers; questions about undocumented persons; and how to handle transgender students and restrooms. These are but a few of the incidents in the last 5 years. Campus climate issues will continue to manifest as the United States' formerly minority populations increase in number. Predominantly or traditionally White institutions are paying close attention to minority populations with the hopes of increasing minority enrollments on their campuses in the future. As these institutions work to improve their campus climates to improve the experiences of their underrepresented students, there is a potential outcome that threatens the unique role USIs have played, especially those that are minority-serving institutions. For example, historically Black colleges and universities (HBCUs) are also concerned as larger universities commit vast resources to recruit minority and first-year students. HBCUs are now experiencing significant enrollment declines as larger and predominantly White institutions attempt to immolate support features of belonging on their campus that initially drew students to HBCU campuses for decades.

Urban-serving institutions are beset with new issues and difficult decisions about how to best serve students. Many urban institutions have a history rooted in providing access and have developed campus climates that considered the needs of first-generation, ethnic minority, adult learner, and commuting students. With declining enrollments attributable to a shortage of high school graduates, traditional residential urban and nonurban institutions are seeking populations they previously ignored. Many colleges and universities are attempting to remake themselves to appeal to nontraditional and urban populations. Comprehensive urban institutions, especially smaller ones, will have a difficult time competing with larger institutions due to inequity of resources. Urban institutions have the historical experience and expertise in providing a welcoming campus climate and sense of belonging, and all in this project are working to build on this, as this leader explained:

> Last year was the first year we actually did a huge homecoming. All these years ASI tried to do their own, little approach to homecoming. And now we have whole new approach. We have a new basketball coach, so we are really trying to strengthen the athletics program itself. Along with that we want to capitalize on that and build more school spirit and get more students involved. We had this huge turnout for homecoming, it filled the gym in a way we'd never done before and we had alumni come back.

Another institution took a different approach to improving its campus climate:

> We created a new AVP for community, equity, and diversity—the first of its kind for the college. We mobilized an inclusive excellence commission made up of 25 community leaders, industry leaders, and government officials. Also, [we had] community-based organizers from across the state to guide us in helping us to become a regional leader [in improving campus climate].

This is a large initiative and it requires resources that USIs with smaller enrollments may not have. They will struggle to match campus climate investments made by larger institutions. For example, Coppin State University in Baltimore is diverting resources needed in core areas to match institutions now interested in first-generation and ethnic-minority students. One concern is that 100 years of providing a safe welcoming climate for students could be eclipsed by the spending of larger institutions who are sincere about a welcoming climate but do not have the practice or expertise.

If there is any confidence moving forward about creating supportive campus climates on urban campuses, it resides in the role student affairs will play in facilitating conversations, enacting plans, creating policy, and implementing programs. Student affairs should be called upon more in the future as urban-serving campuses grapple with increasingly complex climate issues, as this leader makes clear:

> I think if you do student affairs work, [you should be] highly cognizant of how the work we do mitigates issues that students encounter. Some of it ameliorates the conditions that get in the way of people being academically successful. I think our staff feels like one of things that promotes success is that students feel a sense of belonging. And there's this sense that campus is inclusive. So, a lot of our offices work really hard on that.

Strategies to Develop a Sense of Belonging

Throughout this chapter participants shared thoughts about engagement and belonging. As we discovered, the terms are sometimes used interchangeably. We have learned over time and through research that sense of belonging is essential to physical, emotional, and mental well-being (Maslow, 1968) and leads directly to engagement (Goodenow, 1993; Osterman, 2000). We observed that engagement must be intentional. Also important is that engagement should happen both inside and outside the classroom. Some institutions acknowledge the role of families as an important element of engagement, probably more so for urban students. Campus climate was also cited as a key to engagement and, without a doubt, influences any sense of belonging.

Campuses are taking new approaches to encouraging engagement, as this leader described:

> I think a lot of urban institutions don't necessarily have the residential experience, where things are kind of served up to you programmatically. You're engaged from Day 1 with floor programs, floor meetings; everyone kind of does things together oftentimes in these residential settings. I think a unique need of urban students are creative strategies for engagement. We're, for example, looking at using game theory to incentivize student engagement towards things we know will benefit them on a points system.

Taking advantage of the resources of the city to increase engagement is also a way that our senior leaders made their engagement experiences unique, where "the city becomes the campus and social experience." Doing that requires the intentionality we spoke about earlier. One leader explained:

> Sometimes many of our flagship institutions are in the middle of places where there isn't anything else to do. The [leads students] to do whatever's on campus. In urban settings, it's very different here. There are many, many options to get engaged off campus. The challenge is how do campuses engage students in a meaningful way that actually involves the urban setting?

New definitions of successful student engagement are needed as participants from USIs offered strategies that mirror those of residential and rural campuses. These strategies included technology to count student participation effectively and creating programs and activities targeted at minoritized populations:

> We're embarking on a new engagement platform where we'll be using some technology in the next year or so. We're going to start implementing that very soon. That will help, the communication between us and the students. . . . but it's

through the communication piece that's probably more important. And maybe with a better enhanced communication, we can then get more engagement or more involvement in that regard.

This campus built-in rewards that students could use at campus bookstores or eateries when they "checked in" to designated events. Others have used similar technologies, such as QR codes, to offer similar benefits for participation.

Data from student experiences at research universities (Pascarella, Martin, Hanson, & Trolian, 2014) confirmed links between measures of student satisfaction and belonging and their experiences with diverse peers and their sense of campus climate. Given the population at USIs, this is an opportunity to build on what research has shown to work. In my experience, we can consider a wider range of diversity in an urban setting, since students likely already interact frequently with diverse peers. One's peer group isn't always made up of the same ethnicity or national background. Sometimes interest affinity, career interest, or hobbies work just as well. A second strategy is connecting students with members of the faculty. Important in attempting to establish this connection is that the faculty members believe the students belong. How many times have you heard faculty long for more qualified students? These seemingly minor suggestions are of critical importance to urban students who are often first-generation, low income, ethnic minorities, returning adult learners, or fit multiple categories. Negative comments, low expectations, and a lack of interest by the faculty suggest to students that they do not belong.

Another effective strategy is the use of learning communities. Urban institutions without student residences will need to rethink and reconfigure the delivery learning communities. Perhaps the communities are housed within the academic department offices, or space is created within student centers clearly identifying the program group. It is important the learning communities are guided by faculty with a sense that all the students belong and matter to the institution. Students' perception of those within the campus milieu directly affects students' sense of belonging and whether they feel like they matter.

The role of family and friends matters and their support is needed in developing a sense of belonging among urban students. At Coppin State University we are reminded often of the multigenerational makeup of our enrollments. And we are consistently surprised that in 2019 we are still receiving significant numbers of first-generation college students, often the first in their extended families. The ideals of family and welcoming them are reinforced from application to orientation to first classroom experience. Belonging is about knowing enough to know when to care, when to help, and when to challenge. The implied understanding is that we were with you all the way and we knew all the time that you could do it.

Discussion Questions

1. If we agree that different strategies for engagement and belonging are required at USIs, what are the differentiating characteristics? What constitutes effective practice?
2. How will you assess the needs of urban students to design effective student engagement programs and services? What will be your approach for evaluation?
3. Who should be involved in critical conversations about developing a sense of belonging?
4. What does a sense of belonging look like on your campuses? Will your students agree?

References

Astin, A. W. (1984). Student involvement: A developmental theory for higher education. *Journal of College Student Personnel*, 25(4), 297–308.

Berger, J. B., & Milem, J. F. (1999). The role of student involvement and perceptions of integration in a causal model of student persistence. *Research in Higher Education*, 40(6), 641–664.

Boyer, E. (1990). *Scholarship reconsidered: Priorities of the professoriate.* Lawrenceville, NJ: Princeton University Press.

Burlison, M. B. (2015). Nonacademic commitments affecting commuter student involvement and engagement. *New Directions for Student Services*, 150, 27–34.

Chickering, A. W., & Gamson, Z. F. (1987). Seven principles for good practice in undergraduate education. *American Association of Higher Education Bulletin*, 39(7), 3–7.

Dennis, J. M., Phinney, J. S., & Chuateco, L. I. (2005). The role of motivation, parental support, and peer support in the academic success of ethnic minority first generation college students. *Journal of College Student Development*, 46(3), 223–236.

Goodenow, C. (1993). Classroom belonging among earl adolescent students: Relationships to motivation and achievement. *Journal of Early Adolescence*, 13(1), 21–43.

Guiffrida, D. A. (2005). To break way or strengthen ties to home: A complex issues for African American college students attending a predominately white institution. *Equity & Excellence in Education*, 38, 49–60.

Harper, S. R., & Hurtado, S. (2007). Nine themes in campus racial climates and implications for institutional transformation. *New Directions for Student Services*, 120, 7–24.

Hausmann, L. R. M., Schofield, J. W., & Woods, R. L. (2007). Sense of belonging as a predictor of intentions to persist among African American and white first-year college students. *Research in Higher Education*, 48, 803–839.

Hausmann, L. R. M., Ye, F., Schofield, J. W., & Woods, R. L. (2009). Sense of belonging and persistence in White and African American first-year students. *Research in Higher Education*, 50, 649–669.

Kuh, G. D. (1995). The other curriculum: Out-of-class experiences associated with student learning and personal development. *Journal of Higher Education*, 66(2), 123–155.

Kuh, G. D. (2005). What student engagement data tell us about college readiness. *Peer Review*, 9(1). Retrieved from www.aacu.org/publications-research/periodicals/what-stu dent-engagement-data-tell-us-about-college-readiness

Kuh, G. D. (2008). *High-impact educational practices: What they are, who has access to them, and why they matter.* Washington, DC: Association of American Colleges and Universities.

Kuh, G. D., & O'Donnell, K. (2013). *Ensuring quality and taking high-impact practices to scale.* Washington, DC: Association of American Colleges and Universities.

Kuh, G. D., Pace, C. R., & Vesper, N. (1997). The development of process indicators to estimate student gains associated with good practices in undergraduate education. *Research in Higher Education*, 38(4), 235–454.

Kuh, G. D., Kinzie, J., Buckley, J. A., Bridges, B. K., & Havek, J. C. (2006). *Commissioned report for the national symposium on postsecondary student success: Spearheading a dialog on student success.* Washington, DC: National Postsecondary Education Cooperative.

Maslow, A. H. (1968). *Toward a psychology of being.* New York: D. Van Nostrand.

Newbold, J. J. (2015). Lifestyle challenges for commuter students. *New Directions for Student Services*, 150, 79–86.

Osterman, K. F. (2000). Students' need for belonging in the school community. *Review of Educational Research*, 70(3), 323–367.

Pascarella, E. T., & Terenzini, P. T. (1983). Predicting voluntary freshman year persistence/withdrawal behavior in a residential university: A path analytic validation of Tinto's model. *Journal of Educational Psychology*, 75(2), 215–226.

Pascarella, E. T., & Terenzini, P. T. (1991). *How college affects students.* San Francisco, CA: Jossey-Bass.

Pascarella, E. T., & Terenzini, P. T. (2005). *How college affects students: A third decade of research.* San Francisco, CA: Jossey-Bass.

Pascarella, E. T., Martin, G. L., Hanson, J. M., & Trolian, T. L. (2014). Effects of diversity experiences on critical thinking skills over four years of college. *Journal of College Student Development*, 55(1), 86–92.

Thomas, L. (2012). *Building student engagement and belonging in higher education at a time of change.* London: Paul Hamlyn Foundation.

Tinto, V. (1975). Dropout from higher education: A theoretical synthesis of recent research. *Review of Educational Research*, 45(1), 89–125.

Tinto, V. (1993). *Leaving college.* Chicago, IL: University of Chicago Press.

Trowler, V. (2010). *Student engagement literature review.* New York: Higher Education Academy.

6

LEADING IN AN URBAN INSTITUTION

Larry W. Lunsford and Edward G. Whipple

Urban-serving institutions are unique in almost every facet; thus, the leadership at USIs should also be unique. This chapter's authors learned from experience that it is not only valuable but important that leadership at USIs be educated to work with students typical to those that matriculate at a USI. Student demographics, needs, and values at USIs are different from those at other institutions. Understanding these specific needs enable USI leadership to help students succeed. When filling leadership vacancies, attempt to recruit individuals who have experience at USIs or have worked with first-generation and minoritized students. New staff, regardless of background, should attend an orientation and training program that will better prepare them to work with and advise students at the institution. It is important to invest in staff the same as investing in students. The role of the senior student affairs officer (SSAO) varies greatly from institution to institution, and the SSAO should be prepared to deal with the intricacies and politics of the university; be able to work with and possibly meditate with unions; be adept at important management skills, including personnel and fiscal management; develop collaborative efforts with faculty and other campus and community entities; implement change and innovation; make data driven decisions as part of the change process, implement assessment; and handle crisis management. Developing a plan and successfully handling crises may be the most important part of the SSAO's job. It takes special caring to work with students that attend USIs. It takes knowledge. It takes patience. It ultimately is worth the effort, because each success story makes it worthwhile. Watching the students with whom we've spent infinite hours advising, counseling, and merely listening to, walk across the stage at commencement while parents cheer with pride from the audience is the epitome of why we do what we do.

— **Edward G. Whipple**, Ph.D., Vice President for Student Affairs,
Williamette University and
Larry W. Lunsford, Ph.D., Vice President for Student
Affairs, Florida International University-

Leading in an urban-serving institution (USI) presents unique challenges not faced by administrators in other institutions. Like all institutions, there are characteristics that differentiate those senior student affairs officers (SSAOs) who are successful from those who are not. These include specific training and experiences that help these SSAOs support student learning in the institution. However, working at a USI requires a keen understanding of student demographics, needs, and values. In addition, the SSAO must have strong relationships outside of student affairs with faculty and staff to provide needed support to students, as courses, majors, and academic departments are the primary places of engagement for urban students.

Just as important as programs and services are the characteristics that the SSAO must embody to ensure students' needs are met and learning occurs. While both USI and non-USI SSAOs should embody these characteristics, it is especially important that the USI SSAO understands the unique characteristics of the institution, many of which were discussed at more length in Chapter 2 and are reflected throughout this volume. Leaders need to have (a) a full understanding of the institutional mission and commitment to supporting it, (b) knowledge of the ever-changing urban demographics,(c) a keen sense of academic programs and student support services available to meet the needs of the student population, and (d) an awareness of both the local community's resources that support students' needs and an enthusiasm for supporting the needs of the community. As had been made clear, an appreciation for and commitment to student success are critical. For example, Florida International University's Student Affairs adopted the following motto to define its relationship with students. The student is:

- The most important person on the campus. Without students, there would be no need for the institution;
- Not a cold enrollment statistic, but a flesh and blood human being with feelings and emotions like our own;
- Not someone to be tolerated so that we can do our thing. They are our thing;
- Not dependent on us; rather, we are dependent on them;
- Not an interruption of our work, but the purpose of it;
- We are not doing them a favor by serving them; they are doing us a favor by giving us the opportunity to do so.

Like Florida International University, this ethos was held by nearly every leader who worked on this project, with one simply stating, "We want to make sure that this is an environment where people feel welcomed and included by our staff." For students to be successful at a USI, the staff must be well educated regarding the needs of and issues pertaining to these students. How the staff is managed; the educational preparation; the sensitivity to diversity, inclusion, and equity; and ongoing professional and personal development are critically important issues.

Establishing and Maintaining a Dynamic Team

Managing and empowering staff is one of the most important responsibilities for any senior student affairs officer. As Jackson, Moneta, and Nelson (2009) explained,

> the process of finding, hiring, and keeping competent managers of the overall entity is quite daunting. As we look beyond the "top-down" staffing needs of Student Affairs, we discover a far more challenging environment. Are the human resource approaches identical for career centers and women's centers, for religious life programs and student activities offices, for judicial affairs and enrollment management? All of these are commonly found within student affairs portfolios, as are quite often units distinctive to one campus or another.
> *(p. 358)*

Hiring individuals, providing solid orientation, offering ongoing training and development, and regularly evaluating performance will result in successful staff that can address the myriad issues that USI students face. Hiring an individual who has a strong desire to work at an urban institution is also important. The USI SSAO and staff need experience in working with differing populations on campus. The campus dynamics on an urban campus are much different because of the range of student ages, socioeconomic levels, and academic needs. The most effective student affairs staff understand these differences, can effectively work in a fluid and diverse environment, and consistently strive to build a campus community of learners. All of this is much more challenging than working on a campus that draws a homogenous student body.

Training and experience that can aid in an SSAO's success in a leadership role include (a) a degree in higher education, student affairs, or related field; (b) previous work in areas such as nonprofits, social service agencies, or programs supporting children and families; and (c) experience with various technological applications and programs/software that support student learning, diverse populations, and state and federal financial aid programs. Other staff in USI institutions would benefit from similar training and experience but obviously to a lesser degree. With the differences among students, the need for a staff member to be flexible, open to ideas, and quickly responsive to students' concerns is vital. Regular discussions with staff through one-on-one meetings or in-service programs can reinforce the expectations for helping USI students be successful.

The SSAO ultimately is responsible for the hiring of staff at all levels, regardless of whether there is direct supervision involved. Whether it be a position involving secretarial work or the SSAO's associate, there are basic expectations for all staff at all levels. These expectations include understanding of (a) the institution's mission, (b) the role of student affairs at the institution, (c) the student demographics, and (d) the role of all members of the community in helping the USI's students achieve success.

Professional Experiences and Preparation Necessary to Work at a USI

Past experience in varied work environments is important. As one urban-serving SSAO stated, "I think we need people who have experiences in other institutional types, educational backgrounds, and trainings [because they] bring different perspectives to the table." Not only is it important for students to have different staff with varied expertise, but it is also beneficial for the student affairs staff to learn from their colleagues. The synergy that comes from a staff with varied skill sets allows for professional growth and, ultimately, a better learning environment for the students.

Varied perspectives are critically important given the demographics on a USI campus and the programs and service approaches to support a wide range of populations. The balance of diverse expertise, skills, and perspectives is important to attend to when SSAOs make hiring decisions, as one explained:

> I have to be mindful of who we have on staff and who else we need to have on staff. I think one of the best things about being in this position is that I have the power to make sure that we have a diverse staff [with people who] are bringing in skills that complement each other.

The demographic make-up of the student population requires that staff must be sensitive to and cognizant of issues surrounding diversity, equity, and multiculturalism. For example, one may be dealing with an international Muslim student from the Middle East concerning the lack of prayer space on campus and then minutes later be talking to a residence hall student about a roommate conflict. Both situations require sensitivity, understanding, and effective problem solving. As one SSAO stated:

> My expectation for our staff members is cultural competence. Cultural competence, [or at least a complete openness and understanding of what it means], and an awareness of what our students are bringing to the table [is important] because I don't want students to have to get past [cultural incompetence] to get to our services. [We] should be providing services in the context of the diversity of our students. So, I think that's very important, that you arrive with that [competence or openness].

The SSAO provides leadership to educate a new generation of students, and, often at the same time, to re-educate and reinvigorate staff. Competent and active leadership in an urban institution is crucial to student success. Urban-serving institutions are unique in their mission, the communities in which they are located, and the students they attract and enroll. Thus, administrators at USIs should have skills and personalities that can help those students succeed. When recruiting staff, experience at USIs or previous work with students typical to USIs is not necessarily a requirement, yet it is beneficial. The importance of staff with a keen sense and understanding of what it means to be "multiculturally competent" cannot be overemphasized.

Hiring a Diverse Staff

The SSAO, in hiring staff, must be attuned to the past experience, commitment, and passion that candidates bring to the workplace. As the higher education student-demographic landscape continues to change rapidly, those staff who embrace this change will be successful both personally and professionally. One SSAO noted, "We tend to look for diversity. We're committed to having a workforce that is reflective of our community. But when I say 'diversity' we are looking for those who are comfortable with a broad range of experiences and perceptions." She went on to emphasize that in a big city, one can expect a range of backgrounds and experiences. Staff diversity also is important for coaching and mentoring students. McClellan and Larimore (2009) explained:

> The needs and experiences of first-generation and lower-income students are likely to require intensive and intentional efforts to help them understand and navigate the culture and systems of any campus. Engage faculty, staff, and junior/senior/graduate students from low-income and first-generation backgrounds in developing strategies to support and mentor new students as they negotiate the transition to college life.
>
> (p. 237)

These students often require more specialized support, personally and academically; thus, varied staff and faculty specialties can be of great help in assisting the students to resolve issues. Another SSAO articulated the importance of hiring for diversity, stating:

> I want to hire staff who have worked with a diverse population of students, and that diversity could be in any kind of diversity. It doesn't have to be race and ethnicity; it could be all kinds of diversity. I think that when individuals have had that experience, they are more likely to be more comfortable in any urban institution. Secondly, many of them have brought with them best practices and other qualities that make them much more valuable to the institution and much more effective with students.

Diversity in hiring does not only mean understanding issues related to ethnicity, socioeconomic levels, or personal circumstances. In this case, diversity embraces the range of human differences in our society.

Staff Orientation, Training, and Professional Development

The SSAO has a responsibility to lay a strong foundation when staff are hired. The new employee orientation program at both the institution and in student affairs at all levels will set a positive start for one's work. Part of this orientation should include specific job training with expectations for one's performance clearly articulated. This training could range from several weeks to several months, or up to a year, depending on the position. Finally, "job honing" is vitally important for all staff through regular professional development programs. These programs can be campus-based or part of a regional or national association's offerings.

Orientation and Training

When bringing on a new staff member, the SSAO has an obligation to ensure there is a well-planned orientation to the division and the institution. Significant time discussing the culture of the institution and the characteristics of the students is important, along with an ongoing dialogue about the culture and how it promotes, or does not promote, student learning. Additionally, a detailed initial orientation to a new position—including information about what the job entails, criteria for success, and evaluative measures used—is important for the employee. One urban-serving SSAO said:

> The kind of patterns I noticed, prior even to being here, have been that maybe someone was a coordinator or an advisor and then they get into the director position, but we haven't given them any training on things like how you run a budget, how you build and run a team, how you handle conflict—interoffice conflicts between staff. Or we're not even training people on the contracts. So, they don't even know what their responsibilities are or how they can hold people accountable. They just don't do anything, because they're scared and they're super busy.

When this occurs not only do staff became frustrated and demoralized but the ability to help the student also diminishes considerably. Training programs tailored to working in urban environments will prepare staff for job duties and responsibilities that may vary from their past experiences or graduate preparation work. For example, director-level positions entail both significant work with students as well as substantive administrative responsibilities. These responsibilities might include budgeting, preparing reports, supervising other staff, and dealing with faculty. For staff moving into a director's role for the first time, the SSAO may need to be more instructive, directive, and nurturing. The same holds true for staff who advance internally in the student affairs organization—the SSAO needs to work with the senior staff to help them understand staff member learning curves.

As one SSAO indicated, professional student affairs staff may find that the variety of students and the changing demographics provide unique challenges:

> More and more—particularly at urban settings where you have diverse students with various backgrounds of languages, challenges, and issues—I think that's important [to think about] how you help staff to be versed in those issues [and] to be responsive and to not shy away from or be [un]responsive to some of those challenges.

For staff new to the USI, training on student background characteristics and their unique needs helps to prevent "shying away." Chapter 3 provided an in-depth discussion of USI student characteristics, but it is important to further emphasize here. While many USI campuses do have residential students, the commuter student population far out-numbers those who live on campus. While some literature has not found differences in outcomes between residential and commuter students, family demands, finances, work demands, and transportation can affect academic success. Training on the impact of intersecting identities is also important for new USI staff. For example, commuter students with disabilities require services different from their residential peers. The same is true for non-traditionally-aged students, students from minoritized groups, first-generation students, veterans, and returning students. Any of these students can also experience life events that are not typical to the non-USI student population, such as job loss, divorce, chronic disease, or caring for aging parents. These institutions may also have a greater number of online students. Online students who pay the various student fees—health, activity, service, technology, and the like—should be provided the services offered by these fees. Staff in the areas covered by the fees should develop a means to provide these services. Online counseling, assistance for students with disabilities, and access to programs and activities are examples of services and opportunities that should be available for online students. SSAOs at a predominantly commuter campus must have staff trained to meet the specific needs of all these students, in addition to providing different programs and services, as discussed in Chapter 4. Continued professional development—both on and off campus—is important to refresh staff's skills as the demographics and issues evolve and change.

Urban-serving SSAOs speak to the fast-paced work life on a campus attributable to students' increasing personal and academic issues:

> We have to train our team very quickly to work as a team, to network, to really identify resources in the community, and to think in a certain way, to think in [terms of appropriate] scale. I think that's one of our biggest conflicts that we struggle with, especially with student services, is how do we scale up and provide the services that all of our students need, while at the same time not losing the individual? There's a lot of work, we have a lot of [conflicts] around that—trying to figure that out.

112 Lunsford and Whipple

Continued discussion on who our students are and how we best serve them is important within the context of an institution's mission and current priorities.

Professional Development.

Resources must be directed to professional development, even when budgets are tight. Investing in staff is just as important as investing in students. As one SSAO pointed out:

> This next year, I'm going to spend a lot of time on cultivating that sense of belonging . . . for the students and from a staffing end, through cross training, so that people feel like they actually can answer the question and feel empowered even if it's not their area. Working with directors and managers to support their staff to get up and leave the desk and take a student to the next space if they need to. And not feel like the messaging is "you have to be sitting at the front desk."

The days of student affairs staff focused on a specific program with set responsibilities are over. Due to shrinking budgets and the ever-changing student, staff must come to work with an almost generalist approach and be ready to move between and among different program areas. Thus, the SSAO has an obligation to look at ways to best cross-train staff to work in this fast-paced environment.

Changing federal and state mandates and funding, coupled with the ever-changing demographic diversity requires ongoing staff development. Scott (2000) cautioned that continual education on these issues is critical for staff to provide quality services and programs for student success, and that couldn't be truer today, as these factors have multiplied in recent years. Professional development does not have to be expensive nor does it have to mean sending the staff member to an expensive conference. Bringing over institutional faculty from relevant disciplines to talk about managing time, setting priorities, understanding student demographics, providing excellent service, communicating, and so on can be extremely beneficial. Also, utilizing local community resources such as business leaders, community health personnel, and alumni can offer perspectives sometimes not found on campus.

Staff Morale

In any institution, positive staff morale is important in helping students and making them feel they are part of the community. That becomes increasingly challenging as resources—both human and fiscal—dwindle. However, if staff believe they are part of a team, the ability to manage the resource issues becomes easier. The SSAO we quoted earlier did this by empowering staff using cross-training. The SSAO continually must articulate the importance of job roles, including programs and services, especially when the working with long-term staff who perhaps have a bit of burn out or with those who may not be well-trained or prepared in student affairs work. As one SSAO said:

> People have embraced—truly embraced—some of the concepts that I have brought to the table about care and concern, about putting protocols in place about being a 24/7 operation. Because students are our students 24-hours-a-day for our institution. And so, I'm feeling very good about the direction that we are headed but it has not been the norm, at all.

Most student affairs staff enjoy their work and making a difference in students' lives, even though their salaries are sometimes the lowest among campus administrators. Staff can better serve students and are more likely to be the final stop in a student's effort in solving a problem if they are in the right positions. Staff who believe their job is only 9 to 5 are in the wrong profession, or at the least, the wrong position. Clark (2006) noted that a contributing factor to meeting student needs at USIs is that often staff are from the area in which the university or college is located and have been at the institution for a long time. They have grown into a routine that may not be conducive to the demands of their positions. Many of our SSAOs found this to be the case at their institutions, and the ones who had arrived recently to their positions were strategizing on how to reinvigorate these staff members or counsel them into other positions or retirement.

Supervising a Motivated Staff

Student affairs staff's characteristics significantly influence the student experience. Staff new to the institution may need an indoctrination period to learn the unique characteristics of their students. Staff attitude is important to making sure that students are encouraged and challenged. First-generation students, particularly, often require more attention and follow-up on concerns and issues. Working with students requires patience and understanding; however, not all students are cooperative, and some may be downright rude. The same is true for staff; thus, the SSAO is sometimes faced with challenges from both staff and students. One USI administrator said, "The student culture is what it is, but it's changing staff culture and the staff delivery. They almost have a survivalist mentality where students just have to survive the institution." Understanding the campus culture and institutional mission are also important. If the campus culture reflects the institution's mission, the student culture will most likely be aligned. As new students enter the institution, faculty and staff will have an easier time developing the student culture to be reflective of the institution's mission. If the campus culture, though, does not reflect the institution's mission, there will be challenges working with developing a student culture that aligns with the mission.

Most importantly, when there is mission alignment, the learning environment becomes much richer. As Harper (2011) wrote:

Intentional student affairs educators read and routinely revisit mission statements to reacquaint themselves with the aims, purposes, and educational philosophies that supposedly govern their institutions. Their own practices are then juxtaposed with these ideals to determine the extent to which personal and collaborative efforts lead to mission enactment. Such examination is important, especially as evidence of educational effectiveness is being increasingly demanded.

(pp. 293–294)

Keeping the job "exciting" for some staff is a challenge the SSAO could encounter. Staff may become bored with the same daily routine. For example, one USI has 36 orientation sessions for new freshmen and family members each summer. The director constantly reminds staff that as August nears and only a few orientations remain, they must remain as motivated as they were for the first orientation sessions in May, because even though they have repeated the same information dozens of times, it is the first time for those attending the last orientations. Possible remedies for boredom include varying job responsibilities, utilizing more staff for repetitive programs so the burden doesn't fall on one or two individuals, and watching carefully for signs of burnout. A perceptive SSAO knows when staff have challenges in their jobs and works to remedy the situations. These remedies may entail time off, responsibility changes, counseling, or simply visiting with the staff member to be supportive.

Continually learning about the changing students' characteristics is important. One USI leader agrees that staff not knowledgeable about student characteristics may easily miss critical opportunities in responding to student needs. These staff need to be intentional about what they do. For example, first-generation students are particularly vulnerable to the academic process. This is why so many of them merely accept things as they are because there has been no previous guidance about collegiate expectations, and they trust that the advice they receive is accurate. Motivating staff to remain diligent when working with students is key to their successful progress. This may mean that SSAOs set standards and expectations that advisors meet with students on a regular basis and set systems in place to ensure this happens for all staff. Intervening early helps to ensure that students get tutoring before mid-terms so that poor grades don't prevent later registration and financial aid difficulties. When SSAOs reward forward-thinking and prevention measures, staff members are motivated to continue or enhance their outreach.

Working With Unions

Challenges for the SSAO may increase if staff is unionized. One administrator whose staff is unionized said:

This has been very difficult to work with because the people who have been around for a while have adopted this union mentality of, "I work 37.5 hours a week . . ." Just, trying to give people feedback, and you've got a grievance against you immediately.

The number of unions on a campus may vary from a few to the majority of workers. Regardless of the number, relationships with personnel are crucial to maintaining a healthy learning environment for students—a major priority for every college or university. The SSAO should articulate with those who are members of a union, such as support staff, other administrative staff, or faculty the importance of the educational mission and the goal for student success, regardless of where one works. In giving feedback, it is helpful to remind unionized staff that they are important in the work with students. For example, oftentimes contract negotiation time can become quite tense, particularly toward the end. Staff may feel tensions in an office. The SSAO must take a leadership role in letting all staff know that their jobs are important. If, by chance, a strike occurs, the SSAO must emphasize that relationships are important regardless of what role a person has. For example, if a secretary is walking the picket line, when that secretary returns to the office, "business as usual" must go on.

SSAOs should be cognizant of key points regarding the institution's work with unions even though they most likely will not be involved in negotiations. Their colleagues will be, though, and they'll need support. The key points include understanding the (a) principle of seniority; (b) role of union leadership in any decision; (c) contract negotiation time; (d) challenges with a win–lose approach; (e) importance of a collaborative approach in negotiations; (f) focus on mutual gains bargaining benefiting all parties; and (g) importance of continually building a collaborative, trust-based, transparent management relationship (Kello, 2014). While all these points are important, the last one provides for a campus that ensures a focus on the student and supports students' learning and success. However, this will not occur unless both sides understand and support the institution's mission and have a shared understanding about the institution's role in educating students.

Unions have increased dramatically on college campuses, "both private and public, have been a hot spot of union organizing and solidarity in recent years" moving from the more expected areas of facilities management to "the recent spate of organizing victories by student workers," with even student groups supporting their efforts (Wood & Gruenberg, 2017, p. 4). Not only does this add one more layer to campuses as a site of struggle for social and economic justice, but it also means that SSAOs may be working with more categories of unionized workers than ever before. Working with unions is challenging for any SSAO. Knowing the union leadership and developing a relationship based on the institution's mission and values are extremely important. Also, student affairs leadership should be aware of the various union contracts' conditions, endeavour to honor those conditions, and make sure their staff does the same. Finally, the SSAO must be knowledgeable about the grievance procedures if there are problems involving an employee.

Executive Leadership

The SSAO should avoid taking sides publicly during contract negotiations and maintain a stance of neutrality. There will be parties on both sides who will pressure the SSAO to take one side over another. This could impede the SSAO's effectiveness, relationships with others and negatively affect work with students.

Executive Leadership

Executive leadership is the major role of the SSAO. Personnel management has been discussed previously. As a part of the senior leadership team at the institution, the SSAO also has major fiscal responsibilities, focuses on policy development or institutional change, provides input into important decisions, and coordinates student crises responses.

Fiscal Management

Fiscal competence is a necessary quality for any SSAO to be successful. USI SSAOs not only have campus financial issues with which to deal, but also often find themselves in a business community in which there are fundraising and partnering opportunities. "If Student Affairs leaders are to achieve their goals on campus, it is essential that they become expert fiscal managers, articulate advocates for their programs, creative resource procurers, and knowledgeable contributors to their institution's overall budget processes" (Sandeen & Barr, 2006, p. 106). One of the closest relationships an SSAO can have on campus is with the chief fiscal officer. In addition, the SSAO must understand not only the division's budget but also the institution's budget and how the division budget aligns with it and the institution's priorities.

The urban campus lends itself, most often, to working with business leaders to procure sponsorships for programs and services. This might be supporting work in a career center, providing internships in the community, or helping fund a speaker on campus. One SSAO stated, "We've done a lot around getting sponsorship from corporate partners, working with corporate partners on fundraising. So, I'm trying to build capacity intentionally, and some people are jumping on to that very quickly because they want it, too."

Fundraising is increasingly important to student affairs and given dwindling resources and increased demands, it behooves the USI SSAO to work closely with the institution's development vice president to seek support dollars. This urban-serving SSAO spoke for many in saying:

> I don't know if this is just a point in time at this institution, or if it's reflective of other MSIs [minority-serving institutions], but the lack of sophistication in fundraising is apparent to me. I do believe that this is the type of place where you can really go after big money; it's often there. This is the kind of place that [private donors, and then corporations and foundations] want to invest in, and [accessing them is] definitely not our strength right now.

Furthermore, pressures on personnel and time can hinder the fundraising effectiveness: "It's a total disconnect and now it's piecing [things] together. Do we have the capacity to do it, or where can we start building that capacity?" Thus, time management and the establishment of priorities are very important, as Schuh (2009) wrote:

> Developing relationships with prospective donors can take a substantial amount of time. In many respects, fundraising is a process by which the interests of potential benefactors must be matched with institutional needs. That does not occur overnight; rather, it is the result of a process that can take an extended period.
>
> *(p. 100)*

The SSAO must understand the institution's fundraising issues, both short and long term, and work to ensure that student affairs priorities, such as specific program, capital, and scholarship needs, are part of overall institution's goals.

The SSAO as Change Agent

Planning is a critical function for the USI SSAO. Effective planning most often results in some degree of change, either minor or major. This may simply be a program change or it may include something more substantive, such as adding or eliminating a major service to students. For the USI SSAO, this function becomes even more important with the changing dynamics of student population, program focus, and environmental demands. Cuyjet and Weitz (2009) stated that "the components of context, goal, plan, and implementation apply to the planning process whether a new program is being created, an existing program is being enhanced, or a program is being eliminated" (p. 546). USI SSAOs can get caught up in the day-to-day operations of leading a staff and fail to spend the time reflecting on these planning components. As one SSAO noted:

> The type of partners, whether it's government, community-based organizations, foundations, not-for-profit—how do you partner with those folks not just to do great programs but to scale up programs? We all can have 50–100 students in a program that do very, very well. That's no longer the question. The question is, how do you have 100% of your students go through something with great success? How do you scale it? And it's going to require bringing others to the table because we'll never have enough resources to do it by ourselves.

This SSAO shows how difficult it can be to take successful experiments to the university level—an important skill of being a change agent. The pressure is compounded when time enters the picture, as this kind of scenario highlights.

One SSAO described that her president expected that change needs to happen faster: "We don't have the luxury of 'Let's talk about this, let's see how the year goes, let's see how we can move to that'; instead we're told, 'This is going to happen, effective immediately.'"

For planning to be effective, the SSAO must ensure that communication is clear and staff is aware of the rationale behind the change, because there isn't often the opportunity for deep discussion about the change, as this SSAO explained:

> We are the practical version of the university, so we don't [get to] benefit from the theoretical conversations. We look at research, we look at data, we'll have a quick conversation about it, then we'll start talking about what do we do with it. And we don't spend a lot of time talking about what it means and what else we should consider, so [theoretical conversations] are spaces that we can benefit from.

He clearly knows they can benefit from theoretical conversations to make sure that all the pieces to connect with one another and that staff will more likely buy into the change, as Feldblum (2015) advised:

> Even if perfect alignment is not possible, take the time to understand the gaps and engage in planning to help foster buy-in and identify leaders among your team. Buy-in often involves individuals across departments of the division. Collaborating across departmental lines is essential, but as you plan to "switch" lanes, you must mind the rules of the road. Staff members and colleagues appreciate understanding your intentions, and as we know, they are invested in change when they can own it and see the results of their labor. Everyone has different commitments; what you may experience as resistance may be a manifestation of someone's active adherence to another priority or responsibility. Understanding competing commitments can be the critical first step to successful change.
>
> *(p. 23)*

Effective program planning that can result in positive changes is dependent on ensuring the student affairs administrative areas and each unit have intentional and strategic goals that align with the institution's strategic plan and mission. Cuyjet and Weitz (2009) provided valuable advice pertaining to successful program planning:

- Do not underestimate the importance of both time and process;
- Involve students in planning programs and listen to them;
- Communicate with other concerned constituents early in the planning process;
- Identify the individual with responsibility for leading the initiative and provide support for that person;

Leading in an Urban Institution **119**

- Do everything possible to succeed, but be willing to fail and to learn from that experience;
- Be prepared to make adjustments in the plan as needed;
- Try to engage as many people as possible in the planning and implementation of the programs—there is a great deal of expertise on any campus;
- Enjoy the process of planning and implementing programs and use the process and opportunity to teach students and staff; and
- Remember that the contest, goal, and plan are important, but that the most important element is a committed and interested staff member.

(p. 563)

Leading a change process that encompasses these elements also contributes to morale as staff then are involved in the program. This helps staff understand the reasons for change and makes it easier to gain support. The Council for Adult and Experiential Learning (Flint, 1999) recommended many of these same actions, but they added the importance of proceeding with caution and patience.

Using Data Driven Decision-Making

Assessment is an important part of work at an urban-serving institution, especially with the myriad of programs serving the many different student communities. Unfortunately, as is the case on nonurban serving campuses, assessment often is not a priority, done poorly, or not done at all. One SSAO declared:

> There's no consistency in terms of how things are assessed. There is some assessment going on to varying levels, but not necessarily across-the-board consistency. There's room to be more intentional, to share our case. The president has some very clear edicts of what he wants to see happen in terms of change. All of them are very manageable and all of them are actually very simple but they're all very new.

This SSAO demonstrates the need for data driven decision-making as a part of the change process to meet the edicts of his president. This aligns with the need to benchmark by reviewing "best practices with institutions across the country," a part of the change process recommended by the Council for Adult and Experiential Education (Flint, 1999, p. 15). Another SSAO indicated:

> We've done a good job anecdotally of telling our story, but not with data. So, how does the data complement the story that we're telling? For instance, we know that our students that live on campus, their 6-year graduate rate is better than students who live off, their first- to second-year retention's better, things like that.

Here she rightly connects data with developing credible messages to advance goals of student affairs, in this case to support the argument for more residence halls. But we can also imagine that the same might be said for the use of data in fundraising campaigns.

It is important that the SSAO develop an assessment program, if one is not in place. An important partner in this process is the senior academic officer and the staff member responsible for institutional research. As Keeling and DeSantos-Jones (2016) noted, there are three primary types of assessment: student academic performance, focusing on the student; operational/institutional effectiveness, pertaining to the institution or some part of it; and student learning, which assesses learning experiences. They stated that the role of the SSAO is to:

- Prioritize assessment;
- Establish and communicate expectations for assessment;
- Hold staff accountable for conducting, reporting, and using assessments;
- Ensure that assessment is objective and free from bias; and
- Communicate and partner with colleagues outside of Student Affairs to share and use assessment to support student learning and organizational effectiveness.

(Keeling & DeSantos-Jones, 2016, pp. 509–510)

Many SSAOs approach assessment skeptically and apprehensively. Bresciani (2011) provided practical suggestions for addressing student affairs practitioners' concerns by asking questions such as:

- What are we trying to do?
- What do I want students to be to do or know as a result of this program or service?
- How well are we doing it?
- How do we know?
- How do we use the information to improve or celebrate successes?
- Do the improvements we make contribute to our intended results?

(p. 323)

At a minimum, the SSAO should develop an assessment plan as part of the overall student affairs planning process and work closely with campus partners to further develop measures that will enhance the programs and their outcomes.

Crisis Management

Crisis management has become essential for leadership at universities and colleges since the tragic shootings at Virginia Tech on April 16, 2007. Not only did this shock the nation but it also touched deeply those who work in student affairs.

Along with campus shootings, other risk factors include sexual assault, drug and alcohol abuse, suicide, mental health, and hazing. These major campus issues have led to federal legislation and state laws requiring better due diligence by campus administrators and the addition of new staff who handle compliance and Title IX. Administrators spend more time on prevention and mitigation versus response.

Student affairs plays a leading role in developing and presenting training opportunities related to campus violence for students, families, faculty, and staff. Students should be considered part of prevention and training to recognize signs of distress. Staff should develop plans and train personnel to respond to a variety of crisis events. New faculty orientation should be utilized to clarify roles and expectations. Specific resources for faculty to identify troubled students and refer them appropriately should be provided. Involve faculty in developing crisis response procedures. Similarly, beginning at orientation, students should be taught that if they see something, say something. Use top student leadership in discussions about crisis management.

Mental health issues on the college campus have risen dramatically in the last 15 years. Leadership at USIs faces various challenges not encountered by their residential counterparts. Students bring concerns and demands that staff must be prepared to meet. Mental health issues and affordability have risen to the top of higher education concerns. Initially, the president and other campus leaders may look to the SSAO for handling these matters. SSAOs must be resourceful in the use of multiple options, on and off campus, to meet these demands. Severe mental health disorders affect the academic progress and retention of students, making a strategic way to address them important for a division of student affairs to develop. Student suicidal behavior is on the rise, making this a personal tragedy and one that affects the campus community. When a tragedy occurs on campus, no matter its source, students are often left struggling to understand how and why it occurred. They should be encouraged to talk about it with staff and faculty. Receiving care and support can be comforting and reassuring. They should reestablish daily routines, while at the same time realizing that dealing with shock and trauma takes time.

Faculty should be educated about dealing with disruptive behavior in the classroom. Offering a means to report behavior issues, anonymously or not, is essential to quickly addressing them. McKinney (1999) wrote, "Instructors have the right to tell a student who is disrupting the class to leave for THAT particular class period. In extreme cases, campus security can be called to remove the student" (p. 8). More attention and safety procedures have been added to the classroom. The quality of mental health services has improved, including expanding and improving federal privacy regulations. Campuses have seen that by having faculty and student affairs staff working together regarding problems, student issues are resolved more quickly and in the best interests of the students.

Despite improvements, challenges still exist on most campuses. With increasing student and parent concerns and legislators demanding action, risk management is taken more seriously and has become a priority. Administrators should constantly reassess their responses to crises and risk management matters so that they are prepared to respond to any situation that may occur on their campus. Regular communication with an institution's general counsel is important, in addition to keeping abreast of changes in higher education policy and law, as well as risk management best practices. The national higher education associations plus *The Chronicle of Higher Education* are excellent resources for the most up-to-date information.

Student affairs, on most campuses, takes the lead in a student crisis. It is the responsibility of the SSAO to have a plan ready and be able to support its execution. In addition, the SSAO must ensure that the plan is aligned with institution policies; has conferred with key campus and external stakeholders to ensure coordination of the plan's implementation and communication; and has integrated the most current technology, such as mass notification, including text messaging, to notify and update the campus community about critical situations. Important, but sometimes overlooked, is to incorporate follow-up and evaluation measures in the plan.

Few universities and colleges deal with a campus-wide crisis; however, Florida International University, where Lunsford is the SSAO, dealt with two major crises within an academic year. On September 10, 2017, Hurricane Irma hit Miami as a Category 3 storm. The university has an emergency response team that operates in a fortified command center once activated. Several "table-top exercises" are held throughout the year so that university leadership can be prepared for almost any type of disaster. The response team is divided into several departments, including facilities, media and public relations, student affairs, human resources, finance, food service, transportation, police, and others. Each area's personnel are familiar with expected duties and responsibilities. In-person and conference-call meetings are held daily. Designated leaders are required to remain at the center for 24 hours until the crisis has officially ended. Doing as much advanced preparation as possible when a potential crisis is known makes for a much better outcome during and after the crisis. Unpreparedness can lead to further confusion and delay of return to normal university activities.

FIU's Biscayne Bay Campus (BBC) is located in North Miami Beach on the shore and is in the first evacuation zone when a mandatory evacuation order is issued. The university houses 410 students at BBC. Students who have no other place to go are transported 30 miles to the main campus. They are housed in an Enhanced Hurricane Protection Area–designated residence hall. Campus police are stationed at the residence hall, and food is provided by the university's food service provider. Resident assistants and area coordinators are required to remain on duty during the evacuation period. Leadership must lead by example. Students, faculty, and staff should be informed regularly of the status of the emergency. They should be informed of when the crisis has ended and it is safe to return to campus.

After the hurricane hit, classes were cancelled for 10 days because of damage at several of the university's satellite locations as well as in the surrounding area. The residence hall at BBC was damaged and could not reopen when the university resumed operations. Students were temporarily housed in the ballroom of the student center at BBC. Counseling services were provided for students, faculty, and staff who were affected by the hurricane. Emergency funds were provided through human resources, and students with other problems caused by the crisis were assisted on an individual basis.

A mere 6 months later, March 15, 2018, the university faced a second major crisis. A $14-million pedestrian bridge being constructed across a busy eight-lane highway between FIU and its neighboring city, Sweetwater, collapsed. Several cars had stopped underneath the bridge for a red light, and the collapsed bridge killed five individuals in their cars, including one FIU student. A construction worker at the site also died.

A stunned FIU community went into emergency response action. The university's emergency management team was immediately activated. Though every institution has some form of an emergency response plan ready to implement, there is no one plan that covers every situation. Undoubtedly a bridge collapse is not in any institution's plans. The university did not cancel classes, as it was on Spring Break, but cancelled social, academic, and athletic competitions for a designated period. Student affairs staff provided counseling and psychological services to affected students. The university ombudsman worked with students who requested short or long-term leave or had other problems. Transportation was arranged for students who lived in the area where the bridge collapsed and could not cross the street to campus. Student affairs and the student government association held a vigil to honor those killed and injured in the collapse. The division's staff from counseling and psychological services and the student union staffed a "family" center created on campus where loved ones could wait during recovery efforts. Privacy, food and beverages, and sleeping arrangements were provided.

Working Across the Institution—Developing Partnerships

Divisions of student affairs sometimes are the least appreciated or understood areas on campus. The role they play in assisting with student retention and timely graduation rates sometimes goes unnoticed or is not appreciated. As one SSAO explained, "We're just not good at telling our story because we're just everything to everybody. And I just think we need to be really explicit about who we are and what we do." One USI administrator said that he found it necessary to meet with other campus administrators, particularly in academics, to educate them on the role of his division, noting:

> I learned that we were in a silo and people didn't know what we were doing. Someone said, "Oh, you are the ones that stuff teddy bears in the

student union on Valentine's Day and throw dances and parties at Homecoming." And I went, "Well, we do, but let me tell you a little bit more that we do."

Student affairs can provide to the campus community updates on programs and services through an email newsletter, regular campus update program, new employee orientation, and of course (and most importantly) development of relationships across campus.

Developing key partnerships with all members of the campus community is essential, especially with faculty. In most cases, the SSAO will need to initiate the relationship and hold steady while it develops. One SSAO suggested reaching out to certain disciplines or faculty members whose interests or backgrounds might align with programmatic efforts. Involving student affairs in the work of faculty is also a way to build relationships. One SSAO is involved with its campus faculty development programs said:

> One way we're [working with faculty is] with our teaching and learning program, which basically prepares faculty with different tools that they use inside and outside the classroom. That's headed by academic affairs. And so, we're working with them in many regards, particularly now with things like Title IX and student conduct. Trying to get training and information to faculty [is best done] through a faculty run system or organization and engaging them in that way.

There are multiple benefits to student affairs staff being involved in faculty development. Not only are important relationships developed but also student affairs staff learn about the some of the challenges facing faculty in working with students, develop a better understanding of the faculty enterprise, and discover areas of mutual concern where resources can be combined and programs developed.

Involving faculty on various student affairs committees and work groups is important. Not only do these faculty learn more about programs and services offered, but they have the opportunity to meet staff and students. A SSAO noted, "We have faculty on our advisory boards like the Center for Leadership and Service, and the Women's Center and we have 35 student affairs folks who teach, which I believe is excellent." There is great benefit also in working with specific academic programs on campus due to the close alignment with an institution's co-curricular offerings. Often student organizations related to an academic area such as a biology club or performing arts group are advised by faculty and work with student organizations staff. This SSAO also teaches graduate courses in the College of Education and a First-Year Experience course. When student affairs staff teach, especially the SSAO, it sends a message to the campus community that student affairs staff are educators and are just as concerned about academic success as are faculty.

The SSAO should work closely with the senior academic affairs officer to discuss the possibility of attending appropriate academic meetings to develop relationships and find ways to collaborate on programs and services for students. One SSAO stated:

> I go to the council of deans' meetings, so I have a relationship with those folks. I'm on the president's cabinet so I have access to vice presidents and we do a lot in conjunction with [them]. . . . We work with campus police around safety and security issues.

How does one develop these partnerships? The most effective approach is strategic and intentional. Certainly, the SSAO must have a partnership with colleagues at the vice-presidential level. Often, depending on the institution, these relationships begin as work—dealing with common issues. Again, depending on the institution and culture, these relationships turn into friendships through problem solving and idea sharing. The partnership evolves into one of mutual respect and trust. While that certainly doesn't happen all the time, it should be a goal. An SSAO wrote:

> When we hired [a new Vice President for Academic Affairs], [the president] sat us down and said, "You two will be best friends." My expectation is that we are integrating academic affairs and student services because to the student experience, they're all on in the same. And it's been bumpy, but I think we've made a lot more progress in the integration over the last 2 years than we had previously.

When academic and student affairs leaders work together and are seen as collaborators it sends a message to the community about the importance everyone's role in the educational mission. Problems are more easily resolved when there is a relationship between the academic and student affairs senior officers. The two leaders also are role models regarding how everyone should work together.

Leadership can further promote the division by not only allowing but encouraging employees to become involved on campus through university-wide committees and activities, and teaching. In addition, simply attending events not sponsored by student affairs, such as a concert or an IT update session, will let others see staff out of their offices. While this promotion is important for helping the campus better understand the role of student affairs, more importantly, it allows for the building of those important relationships as previously discussed.

Words of Advice

Urban-serving institution SSAOs are faced with a quickly changing environment and student population. Key leadership characteristics are important for success, along with awareness of the priorities needed to best serve students. Blixt and Smith (2015) wrote that the SSAO must be cognizant of national trends creating opportunities for student affairs, including new needs and expectations of students, preparing students for a work that expects more than academic skills, new technologies, accountability for student engagement outcomes, and continued focus on helping students find meaning and purpose. USI leaders must be aware of these trends as they evaluate and assess their programs and services and establish new ones to meet the ever-changing student. A keen sense of management and operational issues, and the ability to handle these successfully, are important. Develop and implement a recruitment plan to attract individuals with experience at USIs or in working with demographically diverse student populations. Recognize that investing in your staff is as important as investing in students. Remember that people support what they help create. Involve individuals, including students, affected by your decisions in the decision-making process. They will have ownership and are more likely to support the decisions and outcomes.

Additionally, in our experience, the USI senior student affairs officers must be prepared for all that comes their way. Develop a plan for crisis management, perform table-top exercises for various scenarios, and ensure all staff are prepared for any emergency. Implement a behavior intervention team that meets regularly and discusses students of concern. Understand the importance and value of relationships on campus—faculty, staff, and students. Work to obtain a sense of others' issues and challenges and where you may be able to be of support.

Finally, students are best served by staff who support the college and university's mission and work with all members of the institution's community to promote student success. Be familiar with your student demographics, needs, and values and how they are different than those at non-USIs. Understanding these will enable you to help students succeed. Give additional efforts to first-generation and lower income students. They face challenges not encountered by other students.

Discussion Questions

1. How does leadership at a USI differ from leadership at a non-USI? What additional qualities may be needed at a USI?
2. What topics should be included in staff orientation and training at a USI?
3. What are ways to maintain a dynamic staff? How do you invigorate those who have become burnt out on their jobs?
4. Discuss ways the SSAO can collaborate with faculty and develop community partnerships.
5. What are your greatest concerns in managing a crisis?

References

Blixt, A. B., & Smith, L. N. (2015). Five megatrends creating opportunities for leaders in Student Affairs. *Leadership Exchange*, 13(2), 24–25. Retrieved from www.leadership exchange-digital.com/leadershipexchange/2015summer/MobilePagedReplica.action?pm=2&folio=24#pg26

Bresciani, M. J. (2011). Assessment and evaluation. In J. H. Schuh, S. R. Jones, S. R. Harper, & Associates (Eds.), *Student services: A handbook for the profession* (5th ed., pp. 321–334). San Francisco, CA: Jossey-Bass.

Clark, M. R. (2006). Succeeding in the city: Challenges and best practices on urban commuter campuses. *About Campus*, 11(3), 2–8. doi:10.1002/abc.166

Cuyjet, M. J., & Weitz, S. (2009). Program planning and implementation. In G. S. McClellan, J. Stringer, & Associates (Eds.), *The handbook of student affairs administration* (3rd ed., pp. 545–564). San Francisco, CA: Jossey-Bass.

Feldblum, M. (2015). Making the case: VPSA's as agents of change. *Leadership Exchange*, 13 (2), 22–25. Retrieved from www.leadershipexchange-digital.com/lexmail/2015summ er/MobilePagedArticle.action?articleId=1144046#articleId1144046

Flint, T. A. (1999). *Best practices in adult learning: A CAEL/APQC benchmarking study*. Chicago, IL: Council for Adult and Experiential Learning.

Harper, S. R. (2011). Strategy and intentionality in practice. In J. H. Schuh, S. R. Jones, S. R. Harper, & Associates (Eds.), *Student services: A handbook for the profession* (5th ed., pp. 287–302). San Francisco, CA: Jossey-Bass.

Jackson, M., Moneta, L., & Nelson, K. A. (2009). Effective management of human capital in student affairs. In G. S. McClellan, J. Stringer, & Associates (Eds.), *The handbook of student affairs administration* (3rd ed., pp. 333–354). San Francisco, CA: Jossey-Bass.

Keeling, R. P., & DeSantos-Jones, J. (2016). Student learning assessment. In N. Zhang, & Associates (Eds.), *Rentz's student affairs practice in higher education* (5th ed., pp. 493–523). San Francisco, CA: Jossey-Bass.

Kello, J. (2014, January 2). 10 points for working with unions. *Industrial Safety & Hygiene News*. Retrieved from www.ishn.com/articles/97667-points-for-working-with-unions.

McClellan, G. S., & Larimore, J. (2009). The changing student population. In G. S. McClellan, J. Stringer, & Associates (Eds.), *The handbook of student affairs administration* (3rd ed., pp. 225–241). San Francisco, CA: Jossey-Bass.

McKinney, K. (1999). Dealing with disruptive behavior in the classroom. *VEUS*, 28(2), 8–9, 12.

Sandeen, A., & Barr, M. J. (2006). *Critical issues for student affairs: Challenges and opportunities*. San Francisco, CA: Jossey-Bass.

Schuh, J. (2009). Fiscal pressures on higher education and student affairs. In G. S. McClellan, J. Stringer, & Associates (Eds.), *The handbook of student affairs administration* (3rd ed., pp. 81–104). San Francisco, CA: Jossey-Bass.

Scott, J. (2000). Creating effective staff development programs. In M. J. Barr, M. K. Desler, & Associates (Eds.), *The handbook of student affairs administration* (pp. 477–491). San Francisco, CA: Jossey-Bass.

Wood, R., & Gruenberg, M. (2017, June 2). Union organizing takes off on college campuses across nation. *People's World*. Retrieved from http://peoplesworld.org/article/union-organizing-take-off-on-college-campuses-across-nation/

7

PREPARING STUDENT AFFAIRS PROFESSIONALS TO SERVE IN URBAN INSTITUTIONS

Darrell C. Ray and Scott Radimer

When considering taking the leap to seek my first vice presidency, a host of questions arose. With educational and professional experiences all situated at Research I (R1), flagship institutions, the initial question was whether I could thrive as an African American male chief student affairs officer in that space. Informational interviews and conversations with mentors reinforced my desire to be in an environment serving a more diverse student body and with diversity in leadership. Urban institutions seem to primarily align with those desires. My two previous positions included an adjunct faculty appointment in the graduate preparation program. That was a role I knew I wanted to continue. Assuming that instruction would be the same across environments, I was not fully prepared for the differences and how the approach to instruction needed to be modified based on being in an urban setting. This chapter and the voices therein bring attention to the critical role of faculty and instruction to consider how practice operationalizes in various campus settings.

*— **Darrell C. Ray**, Ph.D., Vice President for Student Affairs and Clinical Assistant Professor, Higher Education Administration, University of Memphis*

As discussed in the previous chapters, urban-serving institutions share qualitatively different relationships with their local communities and students compared with the more traditionally conceived higher education institutions that have largely monopolized the attention of researchers and educators in graduate higher education programs. This gap in the research then results in a mismatch between the what is taught to the student affairs professionals who will be working at urban institutions and the skills and knowledge they will need to succeed and flourish there. Building from the interviews with senior student affairs officers (SSAOs), this chapter explores the skills and knowledge provided by master's- and doctoral-level graduate preparation programs that these administrators have found most useful for their staff and the gaps that currently exist in these programs, and then makes recommendations for the areas in which these programs could

Preparing Student Affairs Professionals   **129**

improve to better address the needs of urban institutions and their constituents. We also discuss necessary professional development for those looking to transition from traditional institutions to urban institutions. The senior leader perspectives on graduate preparation are bolstered by the fact that 75 percent of the group have taught or currently teach in graduate programs, making them uniquely situated to comment on programs and curricula.

The Usefulness of Student Development Theory Applied to the Urban Context

Across the interviews, senior leaders spoke about the usefulness of student development theories to the work of urban institutions. A common critique of early student development theories, voiced by the senior leaders, was that the samples on which they were based are not representative of college students today, especially college students at urban institutions:

> The theories upon which we are operating as a profession are dated, outmoded, and were statistically insignificant in terms of sample size and things of that nature. So, if Kohlberg's work was published now, it would be dismissed because it was a sample size of all White men. . . . At a certain time where things like access, affordability, were just different.

Not only does the higher education landscape look very different nationally in terms of access, enrollment, and cost compared to 50 years ago but it also looks even more different at urban institutions, which have more adult learners, more students of color, more low-income students, and fewer residential students than the type of "traditional" institutions where these theories were developed, as discussed more thoroughly in Chapter 3.

With these differences between the environments in which many theories were developed and the spaces where senior leaders are employing them, it is not surprising that the theories that were found the most useful were the ones that were either focused on individuals or were more sensitive to the urban context. Theories that the senior leaders found useful included Chickering and Reisser's (1993) vectors of student development, Sanford's (1967) concept of challenge and support, Stanton-Salazar et al.'s (Stanton-Salazar, Marcias, Bensimon, & Dowd, 2010) work on institutional agents, critical race theory (Bell, 1995), Vygotskian's (1978) zones of proximal development, and Nancy Schlossberg's (Goodman, Schlossberg, & Anderson, 2006; Schlossberg, 1989) theories on transitions and mattering.

The Value of Individually Focused Theories

Individually focused theories include those of Chickering and Reisser (1993), Sanford (1967), and Schlossberg (1989; , Schlossberg, & Anderson, 2006). They are more useful to student affairs practitioners at urban-serving institutions than many other theories of development because they are not predicated on a specific type of collegiate environment (e.g., rural or suburban, predominately White, residential, etc.), regardless of where they were first developed. Models such as Fassinger's (1998) model of sexual identity development, Kohlberg's (1981) cognitive-developmental model of moral development, or Cross's (1991) theory of Black identity development are built on a foundation that assumes that certain patterns of development are universal and cannot be separated from the environment and cultural values of the places and people who composed the study. Each of these models ignored the ways in which individuals have multiple identities that intersect and impact each other (e.g., Crenshaw, 1989). This concept of intersectionality is especially important to keep in mind for students at USIs, not only because they tend to come from more diverse backgrounds, but also because they are more likely to have multiple identities that embed them within the community (whether it is at their work, with their families, their place of worship, etc.) and not solely existing as full-time college students.

These theories are also very much products of their time, and so the challenges facing individuals in the United States regarding race, ethnicity, sexual identity, and what constitutes ethical behavior have changed dramatically since 1998, let alone 1981. Over time, many larger group-focused theories have been revised to account for the multiple ways in which different individuals from the same group can develop (e.g., Dillon, Worthington, & Moradi, 2011; Rest, Narvaez, Thoma, & Bebeau, 2000; Cross & Fhagen-Smith, 2001); they have necessarily also become more individually focused and are much less predictive than earlier stage models.

The theories of Sanford (1967), Schlossberg (1989; Goodman, Schlossberg, & Anderson, 2006), and Chickering and Reisser (1993) are all particularly well situated to informing practice at urban institutions because of the ways in which they inform student affairs practice. Sanford's concept of challenge and support reminds student affairs professionals that students are most successful when they are experiencing optimal dissonance—that they are neither too overwhelmed and in survival mode, nor so coddled that they never have to test their limits or challenge previous ways of thinking. This necessitates thinking of the different challenges (or lack of challenges) that students at an urban institution are likely to experience, challenges that are often different from those at more traditional institutions. This can include interactions with a more diverse student body, differences in how students are engaged in campus activities, or the influence of the urban area on the campus.

Similarly, theories from Schlossberg around transitions and mattering remind student affairs professionals that the ways in which people successfully navigate transitions are dependent on the different resources and expectations that they hold, as well as the degree to which they feel they matter to others at that institution. This means that student affairs professionals need to be aware of the different ways in which students at USIs have support networks that may or may not meet the typical challenges experienced in college, as well as the ways in which individuals at the institution can signal to students that they are important and matter to other students, as well as to the faculty and staff at that institution.

In her transitions theory, Schlossberg (Goodman et al., 2006) explained how individuals change through the transitions they experience and the ways in which they navigate those transitions. *Transitions* are "any event, or non-event, [which] results in changed relationships, routines, assumptions, and roles" (Goodman et al., 2006, p. 33). In this model, a transition only occurs if it is perceived as such by the individual experiencing it (Goodman et al., 2006), and so, in this way, the theory is adaptable to students from diverse backgrounds and life experiences as it considers the individual and their varying contexts. Contexts likely to be present in urban settings can include higher percentages of adult/nontraditional, veterans, and part-time students. This theory also highlights the importance of the expectations, resources, and networks of the individual student as the student's ability to cope with transition is influenced by the 4 Ss: situation, self, support, and strategies (Goodman et al., 2006).

As part of the *situation*, students are appraising whether this transition is expected or unexpected, something under their control or not, a positive or negative change, and whether this is a permanent or temporary change. If students appraise the situation as a positive change, something they are in control of, and something in which they are ultimately experiencing a permanent change, they are better able to cope with the transition and grow developmentally. If, however, they view the situation as out of their control, resulting in diminished status, unusual, and/or permanent, they may be less likely to be able to cope with the change. In this way, simply helping students to reframe the situation they find themselves in as normative and/or something they have power over can serve to dramatically reduce anxiety and increase a student's sense of self-efficacy.

As part of the *self*, factors such as the individual's demographic characteristics and psychological resources affect the perception of transitions. Demographic characteristics such as gender, race/ethnicity, and socioeconomic status can differently impact whether students experience transitions as normative or deviant. For example, students from middle-class socioeconomic backgrounds with parents who attended college may be less likely to worry about taking out student loans to pay for their college education, while students from lower socioeconomic backgrounds may be more likely to view taking out student loans as a very stressful and negative life event. Similarly, depending on the psychological resources of students, the same situation can be experienced very differently. Psychological resources include how optimistic or pessimistic they are, how much self-efficacy they have developed, how strongly they have committed to a set of values, and how resilient they are naturally (Patton, Renn, Guido, & Quaye, 2016). Through better understanding students, their backgrounds, and their instigative characteristics, an administrator can help students better identify tactics that will work for them and their situation rather than attempting to utilize methods they have seen work for their friends or what they think they are "supposed" to do.

Support refers to the kinds of social support that an individual has from their intimate relationships, families, networks of friends, and from their communities. These different groups can provide emotional comfort, positive reinforcement, financial or physical/intellectual assistance, or provide important feedback to help an individual better navigate a transition. The difference in kinds of support an individual has access to helps explain some of the differences in success between first-generation college students and their continuing-generation peers. The family members of continuing-generation college students have a familiarity with the structures and norms of higher education and can help their students more successfully navigate the challenges they experience, whereas first-generation students do not have access to the same knowledge within their families. Through conversations with students in distress, administrators can help both by making students aware of institutional supports that they may not have been aware of as well as helping to normalizing utilizing supports (whether it is family, community, or institutional supports) that they may have been hesitant to use.

The fourth and final S is for *strategies*. Strategies are the ways in which an individual can modify a situation, control the meaning of the problem, or manage the stress of a transition. Methods of coping with a transition include information seeking, taking action, stopping action, and changing the way one thinks about or views a problem (Patton et al., 2016). The effectiveness of different strategies is impacted by the extent to which they complement the personality traits of the individual employing them, as well as if they are reinforced or counteracted by other important people in the individual's support network. Individuals who are most effective at coping are able to be flexible in their approach and use multiple methods (Goodman et al., 2006). It is this final S where the different methods highlighted for each prior S all come together. Working through the prior 3 Ss with students can then help them work out their strategy for coping with a crisis, and help them transition from feeling overwhelmed and helpless to feeling empowered and capable in navigating the current problem as well as positioning them to be better equipped for any future crisis that emerges.

Finally, the vectors of development from Chickering and Reisser (1993) remind student affairs professionals that while there are multiple dimensions of development that college students go through that colleges should help to facilitate, individuals find themselves at different positions along those vectors. Not only are there meaningful differences between students at urban institutions compared with more traditional institutions, but there are also meaningful differences between students in their developmental journeys within urban institutions. Chickering and Reisser's theory helps to remind professionals that the heterogeneous student populations of urban-serving institutions mean that the developmental needs of students will not only differ compared with students at other institutions but also that there will be significant differences in the types of developmental needs within the institution as well. For example, older students coming back to college to earn a degree so they can make a career change likely are in very different places along the vectors of developing purpose and moving through autonomy toward interdependence than are students who are fresh out of high school.

Environmentally Focused Theories

Other theories that senior leaders found were more appropriate to the urban institution included Stanton-Salazar's concept of institutional agents, critical race theory by various authors, Vygotskian's work on zones of proximal development, and Yosso's types of community cultural wealth. These theories provide frameworks that can account for how institutions are part of environments that privilege or oppress students' learning and development. All of these theoretical frameworks are important to higher education in the urban context, as they make salient the ways in which urban institutions are part of social and structural environments that disadvantage a majority of their students in different ways and must be attended to if the institutions are to serve their students effectively.

Stanton-Salazar's (Stanton-Salazar et al., 2010) work on institutional agents focuses on how high-status agents within universities provide access to social capital and how working-class minority youth have differential access to that social capital. *Social capital* was defined by Bourdieu (1986) as "the aggregate of the actual or potential resources which are linked to possession of a durable network of more or less institutionalized relationships of mutual acquaintance and recognition" (p. 248), and is made up of both bonding and bridging capital. *Bonding capital* generally refers to the social capital and support from close ties (family, friends, other similar individuals that provide support), while *bridging capital* comes from weaker ties and individuals who are more heterogeneous and is generally more important for economic advancement (Zhang, Anderson, & Zhan, 2011). Examples of bridging capital in the college setting could include learning about work–study opportunities from someone who lives in the same residence hall or getting help on how to write a literature review from someone in the same academic course. Student affairs administrators and student workers typically play a role in providing bridging capital to students by referring students to resources and opportunities.

Stanton-Salazar et al. (2010) defined an *institutional agent* as an "individual who occupies one or more hierarchical positions of relatively high status and authority" (p. 5). Because of institutional agents' connections to a variety of resources and knowledge of how to navigate the system of higher education, they are uniquely positioned to be able to provide bridging capital to working-class minority youth. In proactively providing students with bridging capital, institutional agents can become empowerment agents. This helps disadvantaged students to not only improve their own economic status but also gain the knowledge and tools to alter the systems that work to systematically disadvantage their home communities by passing on their newly acquired capital to family and community members. This is critically important at urban-serving institutions because of both who their students are and where they are located.

Stanton-Salazar's work reminds administrators that the reason students from disadvantaged backgrounds are often less successful in college is not because there is something wrong with them or their communities. Rather the problem is that these students are not given the same access to social capital that individuals from more privileged backgrounds have, and it is up institutional agents to use their networks and social capital to empower these students to develop or identify their capital and access it, ultimately becoming agents of change. In this way, urban institutions are not only contributing to the success of their students, but also providing tools to students to help positively transform the communities they come from and the institutions located there.

Yosso's (2005) community cultural wealth model provides a framework for both administrators and students alike to better understand the different kinds of capital students from disadvantaged backgrounds likely possess. Yosso employed critical race theory to challenge the racism embedded in many assumptions about the culture from which students of color come, and the idea that these students are lacking cultural capital. Rather than seeing students of color through a deficit lens, Yosso created a model that expands the conception of cultural wealth to describe the many kinds of capital that communities of color possess. These different kinds of cultural capital include the following: *aspirational capital*, the ability to remain optimistic despite obstacles; *linguistic capital*, the ability to communicate in one or more language; *familial capital*, knowledge gained through interactions with family; *social capital*, the networks of people and community resources; *navigational capital*, the skills used to traverse different institutional (and sometimes hostile) settings; and *resistant capital*, the knowledge/skills fostered through oppositional behavior and challenges to inequity. Operating through this lens, student affairs professionals empower students to embrace the knowledge, experiences, and support they already possess and use it in their college environments.

While Stanton-Salazar et al. (2010) utilized a framework from critical social work theories and Yosso's work derives from Latina/o/x critical race (LatCrit) theory, both have roots in critical race theory (CRT), another theory recommended by our senior leaders (Delgado & Stefancic, 2017). CRT is part of the family of critical theories (like Marxism, feminism, and critical legal studies) and also draws from law, history, and ethnic studies. CRT specifically investigates how power has historically shaped an environment and continues to shape the opportunities of people of color, and works to dismantle systems that oppress these racial groups. CRT has been criticized for having too narrow a focus on Black/White issues (Yosso, 2005), and so just as it grew in response to deficiencies in prior critical theories, CRT has been expanded to examine the ways other nonWhite and nonprivileged groups have been affected by racism, such as Latino/a/x critical theory (LatCrit; e.g., Trucios-Haynes, 2000), Native American critical theory (TribalCrit; e.g., Brayboy, 2005), and Asian critical theory (AsianCrit; e.g., Chang, 1993). Together, these and other branches of CRT make up a more intersectional family of theories that interrogate how race, ethnicity, gender, and immigration history impact the lives of nonWhite individuals and often limit the opportunities and privileges these individuals are afforded. This is necessary for urban institutions to keep in mind not only because so many students at these institutions are not White but also because these institutions were created in ways that systematically reproduce the oppression suffered by these groups. CRT tasks administrators to not just be aware of this oppression, but to take proactive steps to dismantle it.

Likewise, Vygotsky's (1978) zone of proximal development is useful across institutional types, and it is particularly helpful at urban institutions. The *zone of proximal development* is "the distance between the actual developmental level [of a student] . . . and the level of potential development . . . under adult guidance or in collaboration with more capable peers" (p. 86). This is an important framework to keep in mind, as the students at urban institutions are more likely to be first-generation college students, as discussed in earlier chapters, making it more likely that parents are unable to offer important insider information on college and the important developmental tasks that are germane to the college years. In thinking about capital differently, as Yosso encourages us to do, we realize that the urban environment often provides access to different community resources that might not be available at more suburban or rural colleges (e.g., easier access to internships, professional sports teams, museums, etc.). Through better understanding the needs of students and the available community resources at urban institutions, the zone of proximal development can help student affairs professionals match these needs and resources in a way that would not be possible at other types of institutions.

Schlossberg's Work on Marginality and Mattering

Lastly, multiple senior leaders identified Nancy Schlossberg's theory of mattering and marginality as guiding their work and goals of the divisions they led and "speaks to where higher education is right now . . . none of this matters if we don't make sure that the students are in a [good] space." One of the VPs described:

> I'm a fan of Nancy Scholssberg, of mattering and marginality, because I think that really sets a good foundation for us to remind ourselves that these are important. When students feel marginalized, what do we do in response to that? How can we, bring them in so they feel like they matter? Because we know that mattering is important to graduation.

Whether students feel like they matter or they have been marginalized has a meaningful effect on their ability to succeed in college. Schlossberg described *marginality* as a feeling of not belonging or fitting in, and that can leave individuals feeling self-conscious, irritable, and depressed. Feeling marginalized is a compounded, continual condition for students from minoritized backgrounds, while for other students it can be a temporary condition that results from finding oneself in a new environment, like being a first-year college student (Patton et al., 2016). Feeling marginalized leads individuals to ask whether they matter to others, or even at the university at all. Some of the ways in which student affairs administrators create feelings of marginalization can include using higher education jargon (like the term *first generation*), widely promoting activities that require students to have disposable income (like attending retreats or take an unpaid internship), or having a staff that does not understand or reflect the diversity of the student body.

Having a sense of mattering means that an individual believes "whether right[ly] or wrong[ly], that [they] matter to anyone" (Schlossberg, 1989, p. 9). Schlossberg, building on the work of Rosenberg and McCullough (1981), described *mattering* as composed of five dimensions: attention, importance, ego-extension, dependence, and appreciation. *Attention* is the feeling that someone is noticed; *importance* is the belief that someone is cared about; *ego-extension* is the feeling that others are proud of an individual's accomplishments or sympathizes with their failures; *dependence* means that an individual feels needed by others; and *appreciation* is the feeling that others appreciate the individual's efforts. Before students can fully engage with their college community, both academically and socially, they need to feel like they matter to other people at their institution.

Schlossberg's mattering is very closely related to Rendón's (1994) validation theory. Rendón found that students from nonprivileged backgrounds often doubted their abilities in college and needed to be actively validated to become involved in college and enhance their self-esteem. Rendón defined *validation* as "an enabling, confirming and supportive process initiated by in- and out-of-class agents that foster academic and interpersonal development" (p. 46). Validation is a continuous process rather than an achieved state for students, as "the more students get validated, the richer the academic and interpersonal experience" (p. 44).

Validation of students can come from both institutional and noninstitutional agents. From both groups, messages that reaffirm the student's decision to attend college and normalize experiencing challenges are ways these agents can promote feelings of validation and student success. From institutional agents, it is especially important that when encouraging help-seeking behavior for students experiencing difficulties, that it is done so in a way that avoids a deficit lens and instead illustrates the different strengths and perspectives the student already has, and highlights the many ways students from more privileged backgrounds are also helped by systems and networks of people that have helped them succeed in college. This then helps students to avoid feeling like there is something wrong with them individually, normalizes help seeking behavior, and should help them more effectively navigate institutions in the future. When highlighting the strengths and resources that students at urban serving institutions already possess, Yosso's (2005) model of cultural community wealth is a useful and important framework.

Needs and Gaps in Preparation Programs

American higher education is experiencing unprecedented diversity at all levels. Major shifts in enrollment over the past 3 decades have altered the fabric of many campuses. Morphing demographic profiles is substantially shifting variables such as race, ethnicity, and nationality of students. Beyond those factors, explosions of subfactors in the demographic profile are deeply altering campus ethos and student expectation. First-generation status, age, gender and gender expressions, and socioeconomic status are just a few of the additional demographic factors adding to higher education diversity. Future projections of the diversification of the American population give way to the expectation that higher education will become more representative of society in general, no matter where college or universities are located. The complexity of where all of these elements merge are repositioning the demands on student affairs practitioners.

Access to higher education, expanded financial aid, and multiple delivery points have opened the doors of education to larger segments of the populations. The role urban-serving institutions have played in creating pockets of accessibility positioned a generation of students to either remain in city-centers and/or closer to home to pursue degrees. Initially designed to serve the needs of specific populations such as nontraditional, part- or full-time employed, or career changers, many urban-serving campuses have evolved into full-serving institutions. Many USIs have seen the average age of the student profile decline with traditional-age enrollment growth. This major shift altered the operational definition of *student services* and led to full-student affairs division offerings that mirror offerings of their traditional counterparts, while having to customize all of these functional areas to serve different student populations.

Senior leaders shared that they felt that graduate preparation programs lacked intentional curricular focus on urban environments and the variety of institutions there:

> I don't think we prepare student affairs folks with much versatility. What I mean [is that] we've given them the competencies to be effective in traditional residential type experiences, and, well, that's students affairs. I don't think we expose students well to the diversity of institutions that you can potentially work in.

This VP noted that not only are we preparing students for work in limited institutional types but that we also tend to best prepare them for careers in residence life—a functional area that has less prominence in urban-serving institutions.

Another VP did acknowledge that some programs are starting to recognize the need for more diverse preparation:

> Now we're seeing preparation programs that focus on community college leadership, because if you were working in that setting, there was nothing for you. You just had to take what you got and then try to morph it to your environment. I think there needs to be a different level of segmentation in how we are operating preparation programs.

When there are gaps in preparation, this often speaks to the missed opportunities for graduate students to be aware of and better prepared for employment at different institutional types. It also suggests a level of stagnation in the curricula being offered when programs fail to fully prepare students for the range of opportunities and responsibilities of serving the needs of all students.

This paradigm shift has reshaped student affairs practice and illuminated a need for practitioners with the ability to operationalize their knowledge and competencies in various institutional settings, further illustrating the need for curricula to be more encompassing and to delve into the diversity of practice based on institutional type. Many preparation programs emerged in traditional, primarily residential campus settings, serving the needs of the traditional-age undergraduate. While the locations of graduate preparation programs have expanded to all types of 4-year settings, the curricula may not reflect diversity in understanding student needs and the interplay of institutional type.

Sheer variance of curricula across the country removes an opportunity to ensure standardization of knowledge for those entering the profession. Although the Council for Advancement of Standards in Higher Education (CAS) standards for graduate preparation programs and the shared professional competencies from NASPA and ACPA (National Association of Student Personnel Administrators and American College Personnel Association, respectively) are meant to ensure that all graduate students are prepared for work in the field, these largely miss the impact of institutional type. When preparation misses the point, it is often a function of the faculty, culture, or history of the program and less of the course offered, because more generic course names can reflect a range of content. As a result, gaps in the curricula generate limitations to students' understanding and exposure. Preparation programs must seek to intentionally expose students to research on and experiences in urban-serving campuses to either build affinity for seeking employment or an honest self-selection out of positions in these institutions, because, as mentioned throughout this book, a desire to serve is a critical disposition in those working in USIs. Student affairs professionals can damage students when there is misalignment of the practitioner's values and competencies and the institutional mission.

When our senior leaders hired, they wondered if candidates truly understood what it meant to work in an urban environment. There may have been a

Preparing Student Affairs Professionals **139**

willingness to live in that city, but not a full understanding that the students and the job would be different from what they had been prepared for. They were also concerned about candidates' ability to engage in culturally responsive student services.

> Part of what I've been very interested in is trying to make sure that we are going to find the best candidates for the job who can work in this urban setting. Because it's very different. And sometimes, you know what I would see—I would get candidates who on paper would look great, but they're coming from good institutions or good graduate programs but they're coming from [a rural area]. And nothing against [that state] but I say to myself, can they transition? And I ask them this question, I say, so you've been living in [that state] these many years of your life, have you really thought about moving to [the city]? And moving to this institution, understanding the demographics of our student population? So, it's always pretty interesting to see because part of what I'm looking at is there's a fit; certain people will thrive here and certain people won't, and actually we've seen that happen.

Senior leaders want to hear practitioners operationalize an emphasis on understanding the needs of diverse students across many spectrums, and those coming out of traditional graduate preparation programs are at risk of being effective in only traditional settings.

Urban-serving institutions have played a significant role in addressing increasing access and opening opportunity gaps for historically underrepresented students. Identity-conscious practices to meet the needs of the range of diverse students, positions urban-serving campuses to be economic engines and level the playing field for employment and advancement. As a result, many USIs show greater success in the retention and completion of traditionally underserved populations (Mata & Bobb, 2016). Immense diversity among the student body in USIs requires that practitioners have unique skills and knowledge bases that have been highlighted throughout this volume—more intrusive advising, working with families and communities, building community, and engaging in different ways are all examples of what senior leaders expect of those they hire.

Increases in the number of graduate preparation programs over the past 20 years has placed student affairs practitioners in a variety of institutional types, but it has not assured a curriculum or specific courses to focus on the urban setting. Programs have addressed this by way of special topics seminars or electives, but key courses must have elements of institutional type woven into the fabric to ensure more holistic professional preparation. The educational background and research of faculty play a key role in framing the educational experience and providing an understanding for students. Some senior leaders cited faculty as the change agents needed to refresh curricula. One said that the problem was that faculty may not have been in professional practice for a long period of time:

I think they're all still very traditional in their mindset and in their focus, still very stagnant. And then I think there is still a lot faculty who, again, have not practiced in the past decades or even 20 years, so the shifts in what today's students look like is not necessarily reflected in instruction.

Another senior leader reflected on his graduate program, noting that it was more than the curriculum and the experience of the faculty; it was also the climate in the classroom:

I don't think that there were a lot of honest conversations [in the classroom], when it came to faculty and the things we experienced. They followed the curriculum, but the curriculum really didn't address the types of issues that I think are really the ones that are more challenging in these types of positions.

Without a concerted effort to instruct on urban settings, misalignments can occur as students seek first or new positions. Aspiring practitioners without exposure to urban educational environments may seek positions in the setting, bringing preconceived notions about how students should be. Misalignment can lead to poor fit and job dissatisfaction on one extreme, and disservice and harm to students on the other extreme. Application of one-dimensional approaches rooted in assumptions or misinformation can lead to deficit thinking, which unnecessarily problematizes students in urban environments—not being supported and, eventually, becoming disengaged from student affairs services and staff being the unfortunate result.

Expanding the research that more fully contextualizes the student experience across institutional types and understanding that there is not *one* student experience is critical. Faculty must intentionally prepare graduate students to understand how USIs operate and serve diverse populations. Graduate program curricula must intentionally address and provide context for future practitioners to understand elements of campus environments to consider as they seek employment. The use of internship and practicum experiences can set the stage for students to understand the work environment in the urban setting. While most internships and practicum experiences focus on core job elements (e.g., programming, budgeting, advising students, etc.), one critical element that needs to be included is exposure to the institutional dynamics that differentiate urban settings. Since many placements occur in the summer, students are not exposed to the full operational aspects. This can lead students to a false perception. Faculty should direct students to have specific conversations to compare and contrast campus environments.

These applied experiences are important opportunities for graduate students to see first-hand how many assumptions are built into student affairs at traditional 4-year residential institutions. At urban-serving institutions students are less likely to be living on campus, more likely to work while attending school, and more likely to be nontraditionally aged, which means that the types of services that are typically delivered to students and the ways in which those services are delivered need to be reconsidered. It is one thing to understand those aspects after reading a chapter in a textbook; it is quite another thing to experience them first-hand.

Doctoral Preparation

Doctoral preparation has followed a scripted and prescribed path for centuries, preparing scholars for teaching and conducting research at research institutions. Lack of change could be rooted in multiple factors, primary of which is the fear of the unknown and varying ideas on suitable alternatives—and then knowing how to enact change. Disruptions to traditional methods of classroom instruction (online and distance learning) have increased the number of institutions offering doctoral programs, and competition in the global marketplace squarely places American doctoral education at a fork in the road. Once seen as a dominant world power afforded elite status, doctoral education is now accessible to the broadest populations (Crow & Dabars, 2015), in a variety of formats and content, especially in professional fields like education. This requires a paradigm shift for faculty who may not be equipped to facilitate the seismic transition from preparing researchers to preparing practitioners and leaders. One VP was concerned that the sheer increase in the number of practitioners completing doctorates affects the workforce and the competitiveness for positions:

> I think at the doctoral level, we're giving them out like candy because it's the notion of "we need to produce more PhDs," but I think we're going to get to a point where the market is going to be saturated. And you will start to see more Associate Director—and Assistant Director–level positions that will want a terminal degree verses at the Director level because there are so many people going straight through.

Underlying this is the concern that candidates may be overeducated and under-experienced if they go straight from a master's to a doctoral program. Although he mentions PhDs in particular, the tremendous growth of Doctor of Education (EdD) programs further exacerbates this problem.

A shift in doctoral education is essential in order to have a culturally and environmentally conscious workforce for USIs. The need has to be addressed at all program types. For students who complete doctoral programs in more traditional settings, exposure to understanding urban-serving student affairs can not only open employment opportunities, especially for aspiring vice presidents, but also can lead to informed supervision practices when supervising staff coming from urban campuses. Additionally, as the demographic profile of the country changes, it is only a matter of time before more traditional universities find themselves serving increasingly nontraditional student populations. Like master's-level work, this also draws attention to the need for expansion of coursework offered in doctoral curricula. While core courses on premises, history, and theoretical foundations are paramount, they may not need to be a repeat of master's education. Doctoral programs must accept a role in preparing students to become savvy managers with solid business acumen. Workforce transition to mid and senior levels requires preparation on budgets, finance, fundraising, understanding politics, and, most importantly, human resources. One VP talked about the importance of learning human resource management in doctoral programs:

> The other [area] is actually supervisory skills. You're supervising staff of different backgrounds . . . courses in human resources would be good. There's something in supervision because when I came here, one of the first things I had to do was fire someone. They told me, "Oh, we waited for you to do this once you got here." And I was like, "Thanks."

As discussed in Chapter 6, there is a range of competencies and knowledge that is important for any vice president, but many tend to be more critical at USIs.

Equipping leaders to navigate the operational aspects of administration requires intentionality. If not addressed in the curriculum, professionals can be blindsided by the daily responsibilities of running an enterprise. Early exposure can also assist professionals in honest self-assessment to determine fit for senior-level leadership and identify environments that are best aligned with their skill set. Course content of programs must also be higher education specific. Some programs have "lumped" facets of educational administration together, diluting course content for higher education students, in favor of PreK–12 administration. This is problematic, as the content and curricula do not support higher education leadership, but it is also likely that the faculty lack experience in higher education. This VP explained the dilemma:

> Right now, I probably have 20 people in my division in the EdD program, but it's somewhat geared toward general leadership. I mean of lot of the people in the program are K–12 folks. . . . pursuing different [administrative positions] or principalships.

This creates a greater deficit for practitioners expected to operate at full capacity upon entry. The learning experience must offer both theoretical support and practical experiences that engage learners in meaningful ways.

Course content to prepare professionals may be difficult to develop for some campus environments. Curricular creativity is a platform to address this, which can include cross-institutional courses from USIs. Traditional settings can infuse course content and utilize peers from urban settings for expanding research, as well. Intentional efforts to include institution type and its role in classroom discourse can also expose students to different thinking.

The diversity of American higher education is challenging the traditional hierarchical system of race-situated privilege. Caliber coupled with the diversity of USIs is also challenging the notion that less selective institutions are somehow educationally inferior (Crow & Dabars, 2015). If faculty in traditional settings lack experience and exposure to the urban setting, the USI may be devalued. Faculty must be willing to engage in reflection to identify internal biases. Biases can manifest in what is spoken and what is omitted from the discussion. If students are not receiving instruction that gives them the broadest perspective, they can carry biases into their professional career.

The success of students in urban settings and the rise of urban campuses in the marketplace has created a disruption that must also translate into the professional literature, practitioner preparation, and faculty training. Levels of innovation must be infused in doctoral preparation. Pathways for intentionally focused research require a sense of urgency to maintain pace with the changing higher education landscape. One example of this is offered by Davis (2010) when they found that the very definition of *achievement* may need to be varied on the basis of the institutional setting. For many in USIs, attending college may be an outcome, one that affects future college-going in the family and community, and completion may be, understandably, far on the horizon. Doctoral education must factor in the richness of students' backgrounds that they bring to the various academic environments and not simply instruct from a historically traditional perspective. This can lead practitioners in the urban settings that offer a broader frame and approach to practice differently as their students navigate the environment (Grutzik & Ramos, 2016).

Competencies and Dispositions Critical in the Preparation of Urban-Institution Professionals

Advice from the senior leaders on the skills and information needed to succeed at urban-serving institutions covered a variety of topics and depth, some of which are reminiscent of those highlighted in Chapter 6. They range from the very specific to more broadly generalizable. The themes that emerged repeatedly, however, concerned the issues of greater understanding and communication.

As already discussed in this and earlier chapters, one of the hallmarks of urban-serving institutions is their student diversity. This means that whether someone is a master's student in a graduate preparation program or an experienced professional going back to school to get an advanced degree, a complex understanding of the diversity and the different life experiences and perspectives that students bring with them to college is a foundational competency, and the enthusiasm for learning about and serving in this environment is an important disposition. One of our VPs summed this up:

> I think the dynamics of understanding urban institutions, understanding community colleges, understanding diversity and some of the challenges the students face is critical for somebody [in this field] to really like what they're doing, and to be very effective with the student population that we serve.

144 Ray and Radimer

In addition to requiring knowledge of issues facing different racial and ethnic groups, professionals need to be able to understand and relate to students from a variety of backgrounds and identities, and enjoy doing so. Another VP points out in the following that emotional agility is needed to balance one's subjectivity in this work:

> More and more, I think, having staff that are skilled at working with diversity—diverse religions and the complexities of religion, diverse ability, LGBTQI—is needed. There's a whole vernacular of diversity and it takes training and understanding and then engagement with it. It isn't an annual training, then you're up to speed, you may be in a foundational way, but to really be effective and serving our diverse population— again I alluded to it earlier—I think our staff members need a certain cultural or emotional agility to weigh their own beliefs and their own values, their own background, but then at the same time deliver high-quality services and support with students, and sometimes families that are different from themselves.

Having a strong understanding of the different perspectives and lived experiences of the various student constituencies at USIs is crucial for a variety of reasons. Without this, the programmatic recommendations to promote student success that were presented in Chapter 4 are impossible. Without this, the ability to lead the creation of more inclusive and more just educational environments that lead to a strong sense of belonging—key to retaining and graduating students—is difficult. A strong understanding of diversity is the only way to respond effectively to students and to help professional staff thrive within an urban-serving institution—all necessary for USI leaders.

While there are no measures to fully understand the cultural competency of students, graduate programs must take intentional steps to equip students with an understanding of how to navigate the workplace. Programs must also help students construct operational definitions for diversity that can be malleable and situated in the context of not only the campus setting but also the functional area. Students must enter the workforce knowing how not to impose their beliefs in this area, but to help students they are serving construct and contextualize what diversity can mean for them. Graduate programs must also equip students with the tools to work with and serve those who will have beliefs and viewpoints counter to their own.

One way in which a strong understanding of diverse populations is necessary is being able to unpack how cultural differences can manifest as conflicts between students and university policies or norms. A senior leader described a situation in which cultural conflicts were being exposed through the student conduct system:

> I always say "Relationships precede learning, relationships precede learning." You've got to invest in building that relationship. It can't just be a White,

Western model. So, when I first became a conduct officer, I would [have] students of color sent in for disrupting teaching and learning. [I'd get a] report from the faculty member [and they said the student] kept asking questions. And I said, "Well I think you can [ask questions]." The faculty member said, "Well, it was the *way* they were asking questions, they were too challenging, they stood up." And what the students would say to me, especially my Black and Latino students, was, "I don't give a beep who you are, you can't talk to me any and all kinds of ways." For them there was no relationship, they were thinking "He doesn't even know my name. How dare he correct [me]? How dare he tell me to sit down, or leave the class?"

Without understanding that various groups of people can have different cultural expectations for how respect is demonstrated and how people are supposed to communicate with each other, it would have been easy for this senior leader to conclude that these students were simply "problem" students. However, understanding that these situations were not the result of character deficiencies but, rather, different cultural norms and expectations creates the possibility of being able to bridge these gaps in understanding and expectations, and be able to move the relationship between students and faculty/staff to a place where they can more successfully feel included and respected, and can fully participate in the university life. While this example was undergraduate-specific, as our graduate preparation programs become more diverse, we can imagine that a student from an urban area might experience similar dynamics in a graduate classroom at a more traditional university.

Relationship building was mentioned by many senior leaders as something that they were constantly doing in and outside the university. Thus, like building relationships with students that are respectful and inclusive, it is also important that leaders be skilled at doing this with their staff, as this VP explained:

> My most successful directors are the one that can build strong relationships. They've built enough capital with their staff that when those ruptures happen they can step in. And it doesn't mean the whole relationship goes to crap, you know. Because they've cultivated some trust.

The capacity to build trust is essential to successful leadership, but how often is this stressed or even discussed in graduate programs? As more graduate programs move away from counseling-based programs—some without even requiring one counseling class—"soft skills" such as building trust, communication, or relationship building seldom find a formal place in the curriculum. Developing these soft skills is highlighted by the next VP who framed them in the larger contexts that VPs often find themselves in:

I think the fact that, in my role in student affairs, I've had to become cognizant of how you build partnerships, and I think that's more important than anything else. Having a certain level of emotional intelligence, of empathy, compassion, being able to engage with people on a variety of topics whether or not there's a crisis or not involved. . . . I think those have been the most valuable skills as a student affairs practitioner, because they allow you to go into a conversation. Maybe you haven't been exposed to collective bargaining or building relationships around fundraising and foundation work, but you still have a set of portable skills that allows you to navigate those unfamiliar experiences in a somewhat familiar way.

Portable skills that professionals use throughout their careers are a part of graduate education; those skills need to stretch beyond the day-to-day routine of one functional area or another. Doctoral education is a way to bolster those skills and prepare to use them in more complex ways.

The ability to understand institutional type and associated campus climates and their effects strongly contributes to the success of new professionals and aspiring student affairs leaders. Without understanding how urban institutions are different from more traditional institutions, there is a greater chance that staff members will choose to work at institutions in which they are not equipped to succeed. As an example, this VP talks about just such a case:

I lost a good guy who came in here from [the Midwest]. They loved him in his interview, I liked him. He fell apart. Even mentally fell apart. He sold himself so well and then he got here and [realized] "I don't fit in here, I can't do this." Part of what I'm getting at is you really have to think about the type of institution that we are, the city we're located in. I think it's for some people and not for some others. And while you may look good on paper, are you the kind of person who can thrive in this environment?

Another VP echoed this when he discussed how competency in issues of diversity and inclusion is important not only as part of making the right hires but also of helping to respond to student needs and reduce the likelihood of burnout from professional staff:

What happens when you get a Black Lives Matter [incident] or a tragedy happens in your state, or in your city, or on your campus; and how do you prepare staff to still be able to balance all of those feelings and emotions and serve your student body? That's the emotional agility part because, our staff will get beat up, they get exhausted, right? And how do you help them navigate those waters?

The rapidly changing societal landscape requires a curriculum that can prepare practitioners to navigate, and respond effectively, while maintaining emotional equilibrium. Most curricula focus on giving students skills to execute but not to apply internally. Faculty must identify places in existing courses or create venues for discussions on self-care. This can include special-topic seminars, guest speakers, or discussion groups.

In addition to being knowledgeable about issues of diversity and multiculturalism, the senior leaders repeatedly stressed the importance of strong communication skills as a way to navigate institutional politics and get things done:

> Another thing that I've had to learn along the way is to be a better communicator, [and] it's not just with the students. I think that when you try to advocate for different things at an institution, especially large institutions, whether I've been at the executive level or dean's level or even before that, I've had to learn how to be a better communicator with individuals at my same level as well as individuals across other divisions. And, that's something that I don't think developed through my doctoral or my other education. I didn't really get that sense of how important communication is and how to communicate with others. That's something that I've had to learn along the way.

The senior leaders stressed that not only is good communication important at the vice president of student affairs level but also throughout the division, across campus, and within the local community. Effective communication and relationships not only help you partner with others but help you resolve potential conflicts and help you learn and advance your career, as well. While there may not be specific coursework to address this challenge, conversations can occur on maximizing professional development and skill enhancement post-graduation.

Becoming a Life-Long Learner

> The important thing is, we [thrive] on learning. You don't get into senior-level administrator jobs, or even mid-level administrator jobs and thrive without begin a person who is willing to (1) have a mentor and receive critical feedback on your journey, (2) be focused and energetic about where you want to end up, and then (3) just be interested in being a good communicator and team builder.

The most important aspects a doctoral program can provide a student are the tools to continue their learning throughout their career. The curriculum is limited and will only address some aspects needed for success. Faculty must engage students in the discussions about how to be intentional in their growth. Challenge students to develop growth/professional development plans while in the doctoral program that will address skill gaps in the future. Help students understand the wide variety of professional development methods that can enhance their skill set. The role of professional conferences must also be contextualized. Many practitioners view development as attending a conference and returning to campus. The expanding roles of educators and practitioners require that future professionals have the ability to integrate knowledge from multiple disciplines and interpret and apply that knowledge in a broad and practical method. This may require attending development opportunities outside of traditional higher education conferences.

There is also a need for faculty to help students think about development beyond gaining knowledge of a specific content or focus area. Students must be challenged to think about how they develop broad skills that are not bound to a specific function area. These skills can include communication, supervision, public speaking, critical thinking, and the like. Professional development and knowledge acquisition will also be required based on the broad institutional perspective for such areas as government relations, legal issues, fundraising and development, grant-writing, research, and others. One critical area for growth and development is to produce practitioners that can tell the story through conducting and publishing research and giving conference presentations.

Concluding Considerations

This chapter only scratches the surface of the roles that faculty and curricula must play in contextualizing various institutional settings. National scrutiny around the cost of higher education has elevated the conversations around retention and graduation. To that end, campuses of all types are expanding the support mechanisms and services available. A by-product is the creation of different and sometimes additional employment opportunities across all institutional types. The shifting landscape will require graduates who can be agile, adaptable, and able to operationalize practice in settings that may vary from their institutions of instruction.

While every institution has its own culture and feel, crossing institutional types brings with it a completely unique perspective. Students are often not fully engaged in conversations about what it means to work in different institutional types. Even if one was educated in that type, being an employee brings nuances that are rarely discussed with students. Academic and professional work experiences provide the lens for instruction for most faculty. For those faculty who have not worked in multiple institutional types, it may be difficult to direct students on how to navigate different spaces. Faculty must take intentional steps to expand classroom discussions, include readings, and seek placement opportunities for students at different types of institutions. It must be woven into the curriculum so that future student affairs practitioners understand how to serve students across a spectrum. This could also prompt students to consider places of employment that they may not have considered or reaffirm the environments that they do want.

Faculty can also engage any administrative staff who have come from other settings in the classroom as instructors or guest lecturers. They can give context for differences in practice and how some things may manifest differently. Most importantly, they can discuss where similarities and differences exist. Expanding the literature on institutional type is also critical. Collaborative research and student projects that require researching comparisons add to the knowledge base and expose future student affairs practitioners to a deeper level of understanding.

Discussion Questions

1. What are the ways in which your graduate program prepared you or is preparing you to work in urban-serving institutions?
2. What institutional factors do you consider when you explore career opportunities?
3. How can student affairs leaders better prepare entry-level professionals to support the urban college student?
4. What messages did you/do you receive in your graduate program about community colleges and other urban-serving institutions?

References

Bell, D. A. (1995). Who's afraid of critical race theory? *University of Illinois Law Review*, 893.

Bourdieu, P. (1986). The forms of capital. In J. G. Richardson (Ed.), *Handbook of theory and research for the sociology of education*. New York: Greenwood Press.

Brayboy, B. M. J. (2005). Toward a tribal critical race theory in education. *The Urban Review*, 37(5), 425–446.

Chang, R. S. (1993). Toward an Asian American legal scholarship: Critical race theory, post-structuralism, and narrative space. *California Law Review*, 81, 1241.

Chickering, A. W., & Reisser, L. (1993). *Education and identity (2nd edition)*. San Francisco, CA: Jossey-Bass.

Crenshaw, K. (1989). Demarginalizing the intersection of race and sex: A Black feminist critique of antidiscrimination doctrine, feminist theory and antiracist politics. *University of Chicago Legal Forum*, 139.

Cross, W. E. (1991). *Shades of Black: Diversity in African American identity*. Philadelphia, PA: Temple University Press.

Cross, W. E., & Fhagen-Smith, P. (2001). Patterns of African American identity development: A lifespan perspective. In C. L. Wijeyesinghe, & B. W. Jackson III (Eds.), *New perspectives on racial identity development: A theoretical and practical anthology* (pp. 243–270). New York: New York University Press.

Crow, M. M., & Dabars, W. B. (2015). *Designing the new American university*. Baltimore, MD: Johns Hopkins University Press.

Davis, J. (2010). *The first-generation student experience: Implications for campus practice, and strategies for improving persistence and success*. Sterling, VA: Stylus.

Delgado, R., & Stefancic, J. (2017). *Critical race theory: An introduction* (3rd ed.). New York: New York University Press.

Dillon, F., Worthington, R. L., & Moradi, B. (2011). Sexual identity as a universal process. In K. Bussey (Ed.), *Handbook of identity theory and research* (pp. 649–670). New York: Springer.

Fassinger, R. E. (1998). Lesbian, gay, and bisexual identity and student development theory. In R. L. Sanlo (Ed.), *Working with lesbian, gay, bisexual, and transgender students: A handbook for faculty and administrators* (pp. 13–32). Westport, CT: Greenwood Press.

Goodman, J., Schlossberg, N. K., & Anderson, M. L. (2006). *Counseling adults in transition: Linking practice with theory* (3rd ed.). New York: Springer.

Grutzik, C., & Ramos, S. (2016). The role of the student support specialist: The possibilities and challenges of long-term, practice, and scaffolded relationship. *Community College Journal of Research and Practice*, 40(2), 113–132.

Kohlberg, L. (1981). *Essays on moral development: The philosophy of moral development* (Vol. 1). San Francisco, CA: Harper & Row.

Mata, E., & Bobb, A. (2016). Retaining and graduating empowered men of color. In V. Pendakur (Ed.), *Closing the opportunity gap: Identity-conscious strategies for retention and student success* (pp. 25–41). Sterling, VA: Stylus.

Patton, L. D., Renn, K. A., Guido, F. M., & Quaye, S. J. (2016). *Student development in college: Theory, research, and practice*. Hoboken, NJ: John Wiley & Sons.

Rendón, L. I. (1994). Validating culturally diverse students: Toward a new model of learning and student development. *Innovative Higher Education*, 19(1), 33–51.

Rest, J. R., Narvaez, D., Thoma, S. J., & Bebeau, M. J. (2000). A neo-Kohlbergian approach to morality research. *Journal of Moral Education*, 29(4), 381–395.

Rosenberg, M., & McCullough, B. C. (1981). Mattering: Inferred significance to parents and mental health among adolescents. In R. Simmons (Ed.), *Research in community and mental health* (Vol. 2). Greenwich, CT: JAI Press.

Sanford, N. (1967). *Where colleges fail: A study of the student as a person*. San Francisco, CA: Jossey-Bass.

Schlossberg, N. (1989). Marginality and mattering: Key issues in building community. *New Directions for Student Services*, 48, 5–15.

Stanton-Salazar, R., Macias, R., Bensimon, E., & Dowd, A. (2010). The role of institutional agents in providing institutional support to Latino students in STEM. Paper presented at the 35th Annual Conference for the Association for the Study of Higher Education, Indianapolis, IN.

Trucios-Haynes, E. (2000). Why race matters: LatCrit theory and Latina/o racial identity. *Berkeley La Raza Law Journal*, 12, 1.

Vygotsky, L. (1978). *Mind in society: The development of higher mental process*. Boston, MA: Harvard University Press.

Yosso, T. J. (2005). Whose culture has capital? A critical race theory discussion of community cultural wealth. *Race Ethnicity and Education*, 8(1), 69–91.

Zhang, S., Anderson, S. G., & Zhan, M. (2011). The differentiated impact of bridging and bonding social capital on economic well-being: An individual level perspective. *Journal of Sociology and Social Welfare*, 38, 119.

8

THE VICE PRESIDENT EXPERIENCE

Gail DiSabatino and Mariette Bien-Aime Ayala

After 30-plus years of working in student affairs, I found myself "in transition." I was no longer working and wondered what would come next. The next 18 months were a journey that led me to a place I where I never imagined working. This was not the first time in my career where I landed in an environment that I had not considered for myself. However, despite all the apprehension I had, I believe I have truly finally found my calling. My trepidation revolved around my own experience of being a White woman of privilege. I was not sure I would be accepted by the students at my urban-serving institution since my experience was so different. What I have found is that while I have had to prove myself, the students were welcoming and gave me the chance to serve them. Working at an urban-serving institution has allowed me to be my most authentic self and has ignited my passion for making a difference in ways that are hard to explain. Serving as Vice Chancellor for Student Affairs at the University of Massachusetts Boston has fostered in me a deeper level of understanding the meaning of public higher education.

My story is just one of the many that are represented in this chapter. I invited my colleague, Mariette, a doctoral student in Urban Education, Leadership, and Policy, to join me in sharing the stories of the vice presidents of student affairs in urban-serving institutions. Her insight as a graduate student and as a first-generation student has aided in bringing a perspective that we both hope will be illuminating for all graduate students in student affairs preparation programs.

*– **Gail DiSabatino**, Ed.D., Vice Chancellor for Student Affairs,*
University of Massachusetts, Boston

The VPs in this study share a common passion for student access and success—and yet actualize their passions in different ways, based on their backgrounds, values, career journeys, and experiences as leaders. Yet they actualize their passion in different ways. For young professionals, we hope that you may find yourself in the stories and in turn, possibly aspire to serve as a VP at an urban-serving institution. For those of you who serve as current VPs, we hope that you will find affirmation in these stories and consider contributing to the field by sharing your own. And to the faculty in higher education student affairs preparation programs, we hope you will share these stories as a way to ignite your student's personal passion.

The Effect of Personal Heritage on Passion for Student Success

The stories of each of the VPs and their individual personal heritage is a rich tapestry of diversity—like the student populations whom we serve. A combination of family background and personal lived experiences shaped the motivation of the VPs to go to college, work in higher education, and serve students in USIs.

Family Educational Background

Most VPs talked about the educational heritage of their families. Many of the VPs said that one or both of their parents had some college while others were the first to go to college. This vice president spoke in depth of his parents' educational background:

> While I'm not a first-generation college student, my parents really broke that barrier. My mother was born in Mexico, one of nine children, a migrant child. [Her] parents had a third-grade education and settled in Fort Collins, CO [where my mother] was able to get an Associate's Degree—I don't know really how, based on her family and income—and then raised four children; all of us have college degrees, three of us have advanced degrees. My dad was born and raised in Cheyenne, WY [where] he was one of six children. [His] parents had a sixth-grade education, he dropped out of high school, went into the military, was a Marine, and was able to get his GED. [He] used that GED to go to a community college after leaving the Marines, and then transferred to a 4-year, and went on to get his bachelor's and two master's degrees.

This description gives a glimpse to the impact that this VP's parents had on his path to college and pursing further degrees, which have enabled him to lead at a USI. It also reveals that each generation achieved higher levels of education than the one before, much like the students they now serve. Other vice presidents revealed similar strides over previous generations of their families. Not surprising was that some of the VPs' parents and/or grandparents were immigrants. Educational mobility is often found in immigrant families, each generation leap-frogging over the previous one in order to pursue the American dream of economic stability and enhance the quality of their lives. It was not uncommon to hear that family expectations were clear from the beginning—college was essential:

So, it was not a situation of "Oh, I wonder if I'll go to college, I hope I get a chance to go to college." It was, "Have you decided where you're going?" So, I think that familial mindset—I didn't realize certain things because there were some things that were just not options, in the space I occupied.

The messaging from families and peers permeated the stories of the VPs. While not all families had the same degree of knowledge about how to access college, most were well aware of the transformative power of a college education. For some, peers with degreed parents or a high school counselor helped them navigate getting in the door and seeking financial aid. For one VP, starting at a community college provided the bridge to a 4-year education. Regardless of background or family knowledge, almost all of VPs in this study knew nothing other than that they were headed for college.

Early Lived Experiences

The hometown setting was part of the background descriptions that our VPs discussed as related to the drive to overcome the oppressive environment in which they were raised, get a college education, and make a difference. Two distinct geographical areas were specifically identified: rural and urban. As we heard from two vice presidents, we could see the juxtaposition of the shared experience of hardship in contrasting areas—one in Chicago and one in a small town in Colorado. A VP from an urban setting discussed the challenge of her environment and its influence:

I found that because of my family upbringing, in Chicago, [with a] single mom of four, [and] not enough resources to do anything, going to school, often times hungry, cold, and poor . . . that was clearly an oppressed way in which I grew up. I lived in four of the most often cited neighborhoods to be the worst in the city of Chicago, and there was lots of gang culture, drugs, and violence around me regularly.

The vice president from a rural area of the country and discussed how his parents' struggle influenced him and others:

Their example really allowed me to be a witness to what education can do not just for individuals, like my mom and dad but also for their family, generations, their community. Because that's what happened to us. Their work, their effort, their struggle, particularly in the Rocky Mountains and early '60s when, growing up there [it] wasn't uncommon to see "No Dogs or Mexicans Allowed." They didn't have much of a critical mass of Latinos in the Rocky Mountains during those times, certainly not educated or in the political arena. And so, it really wasn't the easiest, but they somehow made it and set the stage for their children and now their grandchildren to continue that legacy.

Despite the contrast of settings, both of these vice presidents talked of the challenging family environments in which they were raised. The combination of oppression—both racial and socioeconomic—and parental struggle seemed to have inspired or pushed them to work hard, leading them to further their education and pursue careers that led them to their current positions at urban-serving institutions.

It is important to note that for other VPs, their hometown setting provided a very different lived experience that was full of encouragement and direction. One VP discussed how highly educated his rural community was, and that although his own parents did not go to college, the community's culture of going to college was important in his own development. Another vice president who grew up in a blue-collar community attended a high school where there were many affluent families. This VP's parents did not go to college and perceived that the family could not afford to send him to college, yet since all his friends applied to college and teachers expected him to go to college, he followed suit.

While the hometown experience of the VPs differs, it was clear from their interviews that the environment and culture in which the VPs in this study were raised had an influence on their individual aspirations to achieve. Their stories reflect the rich and deep stories of the students they serve. This led to a passion for ensuring the success of students—many of whom likely have a story similar to the VPs' themselves.

From becoming students to later supporting them, the vice-president experience showcases the role that personal and professional circumstances play in motivating their career paths. For some participants, their family background motivated them to work in student affairs. For others, the early lived experience that they share with their institutions' population allows them to better understand and serve urban students. The VPs' responses indicated that students are at the center of their motivation for serving at a USI where they could advocate for student access to higher education and welcome their students' success.

Career Purpose

While few VPs grow up always dreaming to be Vice President of Student Affairs, most find their way to the field through their personal sense of purpose. One participant explained how her undergraduate and graduate experiences gave her the motivation to begin her career in higher education. She stated, "Graduate school completely, particularly college, really changed my life. And so, it's been a major motivator for me in terms of having selected the field for my career and the work that I do, every day, with our students." Other VPs found their motivation in their own background experiences:

I think a lot of my passion around working with students and helping students achieve their goals comes a lot from my personal background as a first-generation college student, as well as the fact that my parents were immigrants to the United States. Then sharing their experience, and also just living through them what they experienced as brand-new individuals to the country and the things that they went through, have always put me in the situation where I try to help others reach their goals and obtain whatever their goal or objective is in their life.

Like this VP, others were motivated to work in higher education because they identified with students' backgrounds and circumstances. By identifying with their students, they can authentically serve their students working in a career that is self-fulfilling.

Finding the Right Fit

The family and educational backgrounds of the vice presidents inspired their personal missions to serve urban college students. Whether it was a defining moment in their lives during their formative years or early in the career, their experiences shaped their choice to work at an urban-serving institution. A VP who was a first-generation college student and whose parents were immigrants explained how her own background was a driving factor in the kind of institution she chose to work:

And, of course, it was a great experience working at an Ivy League. I worked with the best of the best. But the students who gravitated towards me and the students who I really resonated with were students who didn't fit the typical profile. . . . I wanted to go somewhere where students needed me. And I think that's what drew me back to—very intentionally—seeking out a different kind of student population, because the United States doesn't look like [the Ivy Leagues].

Some of the VPs sought to work in urban institutions because they saw that the students had more of a need, and others could identify with the experiences of the student population:

I think that's one of the reasons I chose to work in community college because nothing really surprises me, well, that I hear from students, because a lot of it was in my own family. Either in my parental unit, my immediate unit, or beyond. So, students talking about drug addiction or incarceration or violence. . . . I haven't had many moments where I've been shocked.

The VP just quoted decided to work at a community college because she can understand the everyday struggle that students have to face just to be present in class each day. As is evident from this discussion, many of our vice presidents draw from their own hardships and families to connect with students. For each trial, they see a student face; they are able to connect with it because they have shared similar experiences in their own families and communities.

The urban-student population not only helped VPs find the right institutional fit but it also continues to serve a motivating factor for staying at USIs. The student population of urban institutions reveals to them that their work is much bigger than they see each day. By serving urban populations, their work not only touches the students but also their families and surrounding communities, as conveyed by this VP:

> Probably mid-way through and certainly early on in my career, I've always been attracted to and have worked at institutions where there were large diverse populations, first-generation, low income. For example, for our incoming class this fall, 45% will be the first in their family to get a college degree, 50% will be Pell recipients. And that's really where I find a lot of inspiration and motivation to do this work.

For some of these students, a college degree is the one difference that can help elevate them and inspire others. One VP noted, "I realize I had access to something that a lot of people did not." As a result, he reported that working in a private college or religiously affiliated institution would not suffice his personal mission to provide better access and opportunities to urban, diverse students.

Commitment to Student Success

The VPs have shown in their responses that working in urban institutions is about more than personal values or an institutional fit; it is also about seeing the students succeed. Degree completion is a major concern and it comes at an urgent time. The 2010 Lumina Foundation for Education report showed the retention rates for vulnerable populations are lower than those of White and Asian American students (Price & Tovar, 2014). Urban students who enter higher education often come in after overcoming several nonacademic and social barriers (Knaggs, Sondergeld, & Schardt, 2015). One VP expressed a sincere concern about the importance of completion:

> I tend to be a little bit more serious about obtaining a degree, and students finishing, and less interested in the fun and frivolity that they want to engage in, and even more so the older I get. I'm watching myself getting less patient with students who I think are squandering opportunities. And, I guess—kind of, being born just after the civil rights movement, where education meant so much to people of color and low-income people [makes me more sensitive to this].

It is evident that these VPs have made it their personal mission to serve the students from orientation to graduation. They have a strong passion to serve urban students and see each of them succeed. Despite the complexities that come with working with diverse and sometimes vulnerable populations, their passion comes from deep with their personal and professional backgrounds. Therefore, they have made it their personal mission to authentically serve these students.

A Rich Professional Journey

The VPs in this project worked at a wide array of institutions of higher education over the course of their careers, spending time in public and private, Catholic, STEM, master's level, large, small, proprietary, and flagship 4-year institutions. Most worked at over three different universities and different types of institutions. The variations in institutional type were described by one VP who was intentional in finding her path "back" to an urban setting:

> I worked at [another urban institution] a long time ago. We traveled to the Midwest, . . . so, I was at a public university, a Research I [for 10 years]. . . . Then I went to [an urban Ivy League] for 2 years. . . . I spent 4 years at [an]art institute before I was here. And the population was very similar to this one. So they were a bunch of art students but they were mostly first-generation, low-income students. And it was a very diverse population. So, I think that was a good introduction to coming here.

This VP seemed to build a career portfolio that provided opportunities for growth and learning. Other VPs who also had worked at multiple institutional types seemed to have drawn from those opportunities in order to serve in their current role:

> I think that it also gives me quite a breadth and depth of the difference in leadership models, difference in governance models, the difference in funding models, and so I am very grateful for the different experiences that I've had.

This sentiment of diversity of experience was echoed by all of the VPs in this study. Some stayed within the 4-year college path throughout their careers. A few VPs started at a 4-year college and then moved to a community college, and one spent their entire career in the community-college setting. All of the VPs are currently serving at a different institution from where they began their careers.

Career Influences

The VPs in this project were influenced by people, places, and things. For some, it was a person who gave advice or challenged them; for others, it was the location not being a good fit; some talked about their academic discipline or family as being an influence. For some VPs in this project, faculty had a profound impact on their career path. One participant talked about his time in a master's program where the department chair encouraged him to consider a full-time opportunity, unlike what his peers were doing. The department chair was knowledgeable of their student's undergraduate background and had information on an internship at another institution:

> I developed a relationship with my department chair and she asked me to come in one day and she said, "I have a unique opportunity that, rather than spend your second year in classes, you go on a year internship at [another university]. And even though it was considered as an internship, it was actually a full-time job. I was Assistant Dean of Students. With my [under-graduate] communications degree, I advised yearbook, student newspaper. I had a fraternity background, so I worked with inter-fraternity counsel. I was also a head resident over four apartment complexes of students.

He thought that this opportunity gave him a jump on the job market, over peers who were coming out of grad school at the time. The influence of the department chair's knowledge of the position and the background of the student provided a strong launching pad for this VP's career.

In contrast, another VP discussed how an advisor discouraged her from moving through their path of choice:

> When I was in grad school, I remember telling my advisor that I wanted to work in community college—and I wanted to work in multicultural services—and he said to me, "Oh, it would be very difficult to become a vice president, through that route." The messaging then was that you need to start out in admissions or residence life. Like that's the training ground, and if you end up at a community college, okay, but your start should be at a 4-year institution.

Starting in multicultural affairs and in a community college could be considered an unconventional path at the time this VP was in graduate school. Her advisor's advice may have been well intended, but it reveals an elitist attitude that graduate faculty sometimes have about working in community colleges. She went on to say, "Looking back, I was really offended at the time. I was like, here's this White dude, he doesn't know what he's talking about." Ultimately, this VP stayed true to her hopes and dreams and has spent her entire career in community colleges.

Not everyone was as clear in what kind of institution was right for them. A professor's experiential approach to teaching, taking their students on field trips to different types of campuses, had a significant impact on one of the VPs. An introductory course in graduate school helped him see the vast landscape of opportunities for working in student affairs:

> One of the best classes I had in my [master's] program [was] the very first semester in an introduction to student affairs. [The professor] took us [to a community college and] we sat down with the dean of students at the community college, sat down with the student affairs VP at a state college, we sat down with the VP of student affairs at the university, and then he took us to a technical school. And at some point, we went to a rural institution, more of a community college in a rural setting. But it really gave you exposure to envision yourself in different settings.

This VP, like so many others in the project, worked at a wide array of institutions along his career path—large and small, urban and rural, even a private institution. Undoubtedly, the early introduction to the field of student affairs helped to make a number of the VPs see opportunities for career success in a variety of settings.

Sometimes an individual can discover their career path through recognition of not being at the right place at a point in time. For one of the VPs in this project, it was the 2 years he spent in a proprietary setting that confirmed this was not the setting where he belonged. Another VP mentioned how his institution changed over time to become more of a public honors college. For that individual, the change meant that the institution was attracting richer and more privileged students, and therefore, he decided it was time to make a change. One VP mentioned that a change in leadership at the top resulted in him moving on with his career:

> One of the other artifacts of HBCUs is that when a president changes, it's more like a monarchy move than an organizational move. So, you're thinking Game of Thrones, when you kill the king or the queen, all of their people go out and a whole new group of people come in with the new king or queen. And so that's what happened.

Each of these VPs who found themselves in places and times that were not the right fit found new opportunities and appear to be prospering in their careers. One other VP seemed content at a 4-year university, yet discovered that the community college may have been a better fit:

> I started my career working at the 4-year institution, but found, when I started working there, that I started interacting with students at community colleges because some of my work was recruiting students from the community colleges. And that really felt like that's where I should be.

One of the more unique stories came from a VP who appears to have serendipitously found himself getting into to student affairs work:

> When I came back from a year of teaching English as a second language in Germany, I found a job as a classified staff at a community college, working

in their food stamp education program. I decided to go back and get my master's degree in adult ed at that point. So, I was working at the community college with a real interest to actually teach English as a second language at a community-college level.

This VP started his own education at the community-college level, eventually became that ESL teacher, and is currently a president of a community college. While student affairs may not have been his career intention, the greatest influence in moving into this role may have been his overall community-college experiences, as a student, staff member, and faculty member.

Family and parenting were mentioned for some VPs as an influence on where their career path led them. This VP followed her husband's career, which took her to a large Midwest university:

> The good thing about being [there] was, people from all over the country studied and worked there. It was a predominantly White campus, so my [Asian American] family and I were very used to really not being anonymous. I mean, everyone knew who I was or mistook me for somebody else who looked like me. That sort of thing, so it was a good place to raise my children, but we as a family didn't want to stay there forever because we wanted our children to have a more cosmopolitan, urban experience—that's what we were used to, so.

For this VP, it was important to ensure that her children had the opportunity to live in diverse environments; it was a motivator for moving on with her career. Like the students with whom we work, teachers, advisors, timing, fit, and family all appear to have an influence on the career path of a VP. And like our students, each of their stories is unique.

Pathways to the Vice Presidency

The pathway to the title of Vice President has twists and turns and many steps along the way. Almost half of the participants in this project started their professional careers as a coordinator while others started in a variety of other roles, such as program specialist, advisor, or counselor. The average time at this level was 1.5 to 2.5 years. The title of Director/Program Director/Manager was held for 3 to 4 years as the next step for about 83 percent of the VPs. From that point, we saw that around 75 percent of the VPs held a faculty appointment for 6 to 6.5 years. The faculty role often overlapped with another position. Around 57 percent of the participants served as an assistant or associate dean, with another 36 percent holding the title of Dean. These positions were held for 2 to 3 years and 3.5 to 4 years on average, respectively. Seventy-five percent of the project participants served as an assistant or associate vice president for about 5 years. And finally, 75 percent have held the position of vice president/interim vice president/vice chancellor for 5 years on average. Some of the outlier positions were associate and assistant vice provost, grants facilitator, research associate, therapist/psychologist, university ombudsman. Two individuals currently hold the title of President.

All of the participants in the project have a doctorate degree—with most being either counseling or higher education related. There was an even split between the PhD and the EdD. The master's degrees were primarily in counseling or higher education related fields. As one might expect, the bachelor's degrees ran the spectrum: sociology, English, math, elementary education, child study, history, political science, business, public administration, and communications. One individual also held an Associate of Arts in General Studies degree. So, while the VPs all landed with the doctoral degree in related areas, their starts as undergraduates were quite diverse.

The Experience of Leading

Leading within the academy is one of the most important roles of the vice president. How professionals see themselves as leaders, how others impact their leadership, and the impact that this leadership role has on these individuals is important to understand for those aspiring to this executive level. The VPs at these USIs tell a story of authenticity, outside influences, and unique challenges.

In starting this chapter, I indicated that in coming to UMass Boston, I had found my most authentic self as a leader. Friends and colleagues have even noticed, as they have mentioned that this is a good fit for me. The institutional urban-serving mission and our student affairs' stated purpose to transform lives parallels my personal values and passion to serve others by providing the best experience for all of our students. There is something that just fits, just feels right. As with other VPs who found their leadership style aligning with their USI, it is the institutional fit that allows me to bring my true self to the leadership role.

One VP in the project talked more specifically about the ways in which she leads that are consistent with who she is:

> No matter what I had, I worked really hard, but I always felt like I didn't have enough. And I was always proving myself. So, I think I kind of lead sometimes from that mode of operation. . . . And I find that I'm always the hardest worker in the group and that I'm willing to acquiesce and take more from people's point of view or opinion of whatever it may be, my own or the division, or the organization, and I think that comes from being oppressed, that you're willing to take those things.

This VP demonstrated a way of leading that was based on working hard and being accepting of others' points of view that came from an experience of being oppressed. Being authentic, being natural for this VP, meant striving for personal best and embracing the needs and perspectives of others. This is what she did as a poor child growing up in Chicago, and this is what she does today. And still another VP talked about how the principles that have guided him in his student affairs work seem to be more readily accepted at his USI. Alignment of one's guiding principles allows us to be our most authentic selves.

How VPs express their leadership on their campuses can be the result of current and past influences. For example, one vice president commented on the effect that the president had on the direction of her leadership and how she set up goals for her department:

> My president is extremely invested in us being a team. We do a lot of retreat work with a consultant that works for the system, very helpful. I have a 10-day [Multicultural Leadership Institute], executive leadership training, and a few other programs. I have a tendency at the beginning of the academic year to outline my professional development goals as requested by my president and then go about achieving them.

For this VP, it is evident that the leadership of the president has a positive impact on her leadership. Through training and guidance, the president structures the goals and expectations of their VPs.

Some of the experiences that the VPs mentioned were closely connected with leadership theory. One specifically spoke about how her parents modeled servant leadership. Her mother was a third-grade teacher for 30 years, and her father was a commissioner of a health department. As a result, the commitment of her parents influenced her leadership style:

> Both of them were servant leaders all of my life and very active in the community, in our church that we grew up in, and very connected to civil and civic service on all sides. I think that a lot of my commitment to serving my students, particularly my first-generation students and my students from underrepresented populations and underrepresented socioeconomic statuses, has a lot to do with my family background.

The influence of a president or parents can be profound, especially when you have found yourself at a place that's the right fit where you can express your most authentic leadership style.

No matter where you serve as a VP, there will be challenges. It was not uncommon to hear VPs mention isolation in their role as a senior leader. They felt disconnected from their staffs, especially when they were working within a framework of districts or multiple campuses in a system:

> I wasn't prepared for that level of isolation. I always tell folks interested in vice president or [leadership] roles that it can be really isolating. And then if you layer in race or gender, or sexual orientation, it's further isolating.

The Vice President Experience   **163**

For some, this isolation came as a result of spending so much time off-campus. As one VP pointed out, the role in an USI is complex with many opportunities to be engaged outside of the division: "Public-governmental partnerships, leveraging large resources across the city to serve a half a million students . . . exposure to city government, grant-raising, and fundraising through nontraditional resources."

When your role calls for you to be in many places, wear numerous hats, juggle all different kinds of balls, you can wake up in the morning feeling lonely in this journey. Your president will count on you to be independent, solve problems on your own, and get the job done. At an earlier time in your career, you might have been able to turn to your boss for guidance and support to decide. As VP, it is you and, often, you alone! As a VP at a USI, the added responsibility of external engagement or district offices can further isolate you.

Another VP suggested that you have to be ready to be firm and to the point with your directors, deal with problems, and have the thick skin necessary to do the job:

> I have three bargaining units, and I'm like, look, if you're in administration, they're going to grieve everything and they should. I mean, that's their job, so abide by the contract and just expect you're going to get a grievance. I tell folks who are interested in manager/director positions, "If you're uncomfortable with conflict, with resolving conflict, you shouldn't go into management." Because it's personnel, policy, and budget, and that's problems, problems, problems.

And yet, as one VP pointed out, even if we don't come to the table with the experience of dealing with some of the challenges of unions and external work, we bring, "portable skills that allow you to navigate those unfamiliar experiences in a somewhat familiar way." Furthermore, as you will later read, there are networks that exist to support you and help address the isolation.

Every role, position, and job has its trials and opportunities. VPs at USIs certainly have theirs. If you find that a USI is the right fit, and you remember why you are there each and every day, the intrinsic rewards will far exceed the challenges that will likely transpire throughout your journey.

Critical Skills for the Senior Student Affairs Officer

As the vice presidents advanced their careers, there were many critical skills they learned that supported their growth in the field of higher education. The lessons they learned derived from campus stakeholders as well as experiences within their positions as VPs in urban-serving institutions. When working with campus stakeholders, they spoke of the numerous skills they gained from working with students, their parents, and staff. On the opposite side, there were also skills learned from experiences working in new functional areas, making decisions for crises, and personal acclimation to the position. Each of them developed a new outlook because of the lessons they learned.

Connecting With and Learning From Students

There were three VPs who expressed how they learned lessons from students with whom they interacted. One spoke about her experiences working as Director of Multicultural Services before becoming a VP. She spoke in detail about how she enjoyed seeing students on campus for events and activities. What eventually brought a challenge to her, however, was working with the students on a one-to-one level, where she was concerned that everything about the student was a problem. In those cases, the VP spoke about her bias when working with students: "I try to be mindful that my lens is even skewed, like, everything's not a problem." In her experience working with students, she had to eventually learn that each student experience was not necessarily a problem, but sometimes it was just an opportunity to connect with the student. Another VP spoke about his learning curve in working with students from diverse backgrounds:

> I feel like it took me awhile to understand, for example, the Cambodian community and the dynamics in [the city] around the African American community. And through all of the churches in that community and dynamics there as they're related to the growing Latino community. And then how the Cambodian community fit into this.

In this example, although the VP did not have trouble working with the Cambodian community or helping them, he had trouble understanding the Cambodian culture and how that culture fit into the greater community. Other VPs made similar observations with other student populations. For example, one VP spoke about how he was challenged in his first experience working with a transgender student and how he learned how to take a more personalized approach when working with vulnerable student populations. When learning how to support students who were dealing with trials that were personal to them, he also learned how to apply that to the rest of the student population. In this example, the student taught him the importance of looking at all students from a holistic viewpoint. The passion for working with vulnerable students like the one discussed previously was common among our participants.

Changing institutions provides for another opportunity to learn about working with diverse students, such as moving from 2-year to 4-year institutions or by changing geographic regions. This VP's story is rich in telling of how one professional's learning has positioned them to be successful as a VP at a USI:

> I'd worked most of my career at that point at Hispanic-serving institutions and I came to the Midwest and it was a very different place, where Hispanics were only about 2% of the student population, but nonetheless, it had students that were underserved as well. I probably saw more issues related to

students having issues with homelessness and hunger and other issues that I really hadn't faced so directly when I was in south Florida. . . . I think the transition from the 4-year to 2-year institution was pretty easy because that's where my passion was and where I felt I should be. I think the biggest change for me was when I was at [the 4-year], most of my concern was, okay, I'm here to advise you, I'm here to work with you, and there it was more about what classes, what things, and any kind of services [they needed]. Even when I did recruitment, I didn't see the student challenges as much. I'm sure they were there, challenges students would face, but I really didn't see them. When I got to [my last community college], I started seeing discipline and student conduct issues there. As I started working with students there I also started seeing issues that I had really never seen before. I knew that there were students who were homeless, students who were hungry, and I know that students had other issues, other family issues, or even mental health issues. But when I got [there], those things became much more apparent to me. And I had a lot to do with the student body and the mission of the college. . . . I saw even more issues with students that had trouble with the law, and coming back to school, and the conduct issues just became greater and greater. I see that as a reflection of some of the struggles the students were going through because some of the issues I addressed through the conduct process, a lot of them had to do with miscommunication or generational differences between the students and the faculty or the staff. But talking through those things with the students, many times I began to learn a lot more about student issues that I had never dealt with before.

The voices of the VPs in this project echoed each other in the insights they drew from their unique student populations, which led them to better meet the needs of the students they served. And while these VPs had excellent experiences in working with students throughout their career, the learning continued into and throughout their careers.

Interpersonal Relationships Across the Institution

Leading a student affairs division comes with many challenges. One of the challenges that was identified by VPs was learning how to be an effective communicator and relationship builder in various settings. A VP explained his journey in his past three positions and how he had to learn to be a better communicator with individuals at the same level, as well as with other individuals across different divisions. This idea was shared by four other VPs as they spoke about lessons they learned from building consensus and working with bargaining units:

Building consensus is very difficult, but even building awareness of issues is something that more individuals should be made aware of. I think whether you're talking about the budgeting process or talking about initiating a new student program, or you're doing something else at the institution. All these things, I think, have that political nature in them. And I've learned that the hard way—and I'm still learning, that's an ongoing process. But I've learned it through just working through [it] and understanding that this is the reality and how can I work best within that reality.

Getting staff together and building consensus was a common theme. This was especially true when working with unions. Negotiating working conditions, budgets, and policies gave each of the VPs challenges to overcome. One VP spoke about the nuances of unions from working at a public institution with 15,000 people. Because of this, she had to learn what it meant to be in her position at an institution that size. Others spoke in detail about the extended efforts needed to work with contracts and negotiations. Above all, one stressed the importance of building relationships in the process. Strong interpersonal skills developed in other areas of the job can assist even if you have no previous experience with unions. Think of these as a set of portable skills to navigate unfamiliar experiences in a familiar way.

Enrollment Management

Understanding the student experience prior to enrollment is especially important at a USI. Learning how to work with enrollment management, recruitment, and retention was important to nearly all the VPs. Only a few VPs had enrollment management as part of their portfolio prior to being tapped to lead a broader division:

> When I first came here, part of our division had enrollment management and now that's in a separate division. But I learned a tremendous amount about issues around enrollment management recruitment, retention, and graduation. I think just because the initiatives and projects [were many and complex], and some of [the learning gaps were] because of the positional place I found myself in.

Although he did not have experience with enrollment management, he found himself in a position in which he needed to learn about the functionalities of the department, and in doing so, he was able to learn more about how enrollment management initiates at the start of the student's academic experience before they enter college. Similarly, another VP started working with enrollment management without having any experience in that functional area and wondered, "What did I get myself into?" The difference for this VP was that the enrollment management and the student affairs department were not initially merged with one another. In this case, there was already a VP in charge of enrollment

The Vice President Experience   **167**

management, who was doing a great job in leading their division. However, his president recommended that he get more involved with enrollment management to give him more experience with recruitment, retention, and graduation. The specific areas that were mentioned as opportunities for learning had to do with matriculation agreements, dual enrollment, right-sizing enrollment, scheduling of courses, and thinking of institutional positions in the higher education marketplace. These are areas with which student affairs professionals do not usually have experience.

One VP commented that learning about these systems is important for all student affairs leaders to learn. By doing so, it better shaped his understanding of serving students from orientation to graduation, especially with the population served by the institution.

A number of the VPs, while not having positional responsibility for the division of enrollment management, spoke about the need to understand their students' experiences before they entered college:

> My team may not necessarily be the group that is out there recruiting those students, and bringing those students in. We are the team that supports those students when they get here, and so I want to be sure that we're ready for receiving those students to the campus and welcoming them to our community.

It was interesting for me (Gail) to note that a number of VPs have encountered a similar experience to my own with regard to the student experience. As student affairs professionals, we understand the value of providing an engaging student life program and how that contributes to student retention and graduation. Like at my institution, these VPs noted that retention and graduation rates are low. We have had to work on changing the culture of the institution, since this value has not been widely accepted. As one VP stated, "So it's like, well, they're poor, or they're first-generation, or they're ESL, so um . . . it's kind of like paternalistic." Another VP commented, "Providing a better student experience, that's going to take longer than anything else, I think, but it does feed into the enrollment management, it feeds into the student success piece, but that's also a change in culture." VPs at USIs must provide leadership to change the culture in order for the entire institution to recognize and embrace varying ways of increasing retention, a major component of enrollment management, through enriching engagement experiences.

The VPs in this project continue to learn as they lead. One VP summed up her process by using a metaphor:

> I'm starting my fourth year, which would be a senior year in college, and it feels very much like that. I feel like I have junior status at this point, from what I've achieved. I've mastered the learning curve as a freshman, you know, all the things you do: build relationships, learn how to develop

autonomy. Sophomore [year], you challenge yourself more; take some courses that you may not be as familiar with to challenge your own intellectual growth and learning. I did those things, and then your junior [year] you look around and you say, "Okay, what am I really achieving and where do I want to be postgraduation?" And that's kind of how I saw myself and I used that analogy with my team and I think they loved it. But I'm failing in one area, because, again, I'm reaching this senior status but I need the team to graduate, not just me.

Each of the VPs learned a variety of critical skills through their experience working in higher education administration. Some of these were learned from working with students at USIs, some of these lessons were from working with other staff in their division, and some of these lessons were learned from the everyday experiences and crises they encountered throughout their careers. Coming from a background in common with your students (i.e., first-generation, ethnic minority group, low SES) may not be enough to enable you to fully understand and therefore lead your staff and students at a USI. The multiple intersectionalities of the student population, combined with the complexity of the larger institution or union environment, along with the broad scope of the position to connect with the local community, is common for the VPs in USIs. Using your complete toolbox and sharpening your skills is essential in order to be successful as a leader.

Sharpening the Saw . . . and Other Tools

Vice presidents for student affairs (VPSAs) at urban-serving institutions are intentional in their approach to professional development. Many of the VPs found that being part of national organizations—such as Association of Fraternity Advisors (AFA), National Association of Campus Activities (NACA), or National Association of Student Personnel Administrators (NASPA)—was helpful at one time in their careers, but their needs changed as they became VPs at a USI. Seeking new professional associations, reading, sharing with the profession, specialized training, and connecting with other VPs at similar types of institutions were all part of the VPs' toolkits.

Professional Associations

NASPA was by far the most frequently mentioned association through which the VPs in this project had received professional development. Active involvement, conference presentations, holding leadership positions, and attending workshops were identified as the ways in which they were most likely to participate. As VPs progressed in their careers, some pointed out that while they weren't as involved in national conferences as they used to be, their past experiences provided a

The Vice President Experience   169

"stronger base and understanding" around key issues for the current work in which VPs engage. Trying out new opportunities is important for a VPSA, especially at a USI. As one VP put it:

> I went to the NASPA Civic Learning and Democratic Engagement conference, and that was really useful because there I met the guy from the Campus Vote project. Now we're part of this Civic Engagement [initiative] with voting. . . . At this point in my career, I'm excited about that, about going to these different kind[s] of workshop[s] different conferences than NASPA.

In addition to NASPA, some VPs discussed the Association of Public and Land-Grant Universities (APLU) as a source for professional development. APLU is a president's organization with a number of councils, including the Council of Student Affairs, Commission on Access, Diversity, and Equity (CADE) and the Coalition of Urban Serving Universities (CUSU). As a president's organization, it is not always an obvious source of professional development for VPSAs and it is often after having been in the role for a year or two when they discover how to engage with this group. As one VP noted:

> I was not involved, until about a year ago, with APLU. I'm now on the executive committee for student affairs [with] some [institutions with] similar profiles, some big urban [institutions] in that category. So that's interesting to now be part of that conversation. I went to my first conference last fall, [a] very different conference and structure and a lot more conversation around this topic, like the types of students, the challenges of this type of student. I went to a wonderful program on food deficiency, so that's been good because I think that is now a different professional resource for me. I didn't realize how helpful that could have been or I would have been involved a few years earlier.

I (Gail) found that in moving from a predominantly white institution (PWI) to an urban-serving institution that APLU is an even greater resource for student success now that I am working with more ethnically diverse and first-generation students.

The array of professional associations available to those of us who are working with diverse populations is vast. One VP said it best when she discussed numerous professional association with whom she is involved:

> I'm involved a lot with APAHE, Asian Pacific Americans in Higher Education. I carve out where I do professional development. I've been doing a lot of presenting recently at different conferences. We talk about how it's possible to execute a high impact practice on a large urban-serving institution; I'm going to [present] it at the provosts meeting in Baltimore. I did it at AAC&U. I'm going to the CUMU, the urban and metropolitan university

[conference]. We've gotten our proposal accepted at all these different, different places. Which has been really fun because these are conferences I've never gone to before. That's been really fun because then I get to go to all these other workshops I never would have gone to otherwise.

Professional associations offer a vast array of opportunities. While many vice presidents of student affairs have had and/or continue to have connections with NASPA, the urban-serving VPs find themselves engaging broadly in different associations in order to learn, grow, and be supported.

Reading

Reading was a significant form of professional development valued by the VPs in this project. The sources and choices of the VPs varied. Personally, since I (Gail) have come to a USI, I have taken advantage of every opportunity that comes across my desktop to learn more about USIs, minority-serving institutions, and first-generation and DACA students. If I get something across my computer, I stop and look at it. I've read more articles than anything else, worthy articles that somebody brings to my attention. Some of it is skimming, some of it is in-depth reading. I read *The Chronicle*, which might lead me to something else, but I try to read whenever something comes across my eyes.

Other VPs were more specific in their choices of reading materials, including books that were not necessarily related directly to higher education. There appeared to be a strong interest in reading books beyond the student affairs and higher education literature because, as one VP mentioned, "I think that we can learn a lot from other sectors rather than just higher education." These VPs tend to apply what they learn from the books as they share with others through discussion groups or simply by encouraging others to read. One VP mentioned reading *Essentialism* by Greg McKeown and then handing out copies to staff and then having a conversation about the book. She went on to say:

> I'm currently reading, by the two faculty members from Stanford's design school, *Designing Your Life*, so it's based on a course they do—Design Thinking—to help graduate students determine their career path. I'm reading to get a better sense of how to apply Design Thinking in the work we do at the college, as well as thinking through how I can apply these principles in my life.

I (Gail) find that there is a wealth of literature out there, so picking and choosing the books that I read often is a reflection of the moment of time I am in. For instance, when I started building a new team at the University of Massachusetts Boston, I asked the senior leaders and directors to read the book *Start With Why* by Simon Sinek (2009). More recently, we asked them to read *Breakaway Learners* by Karen Gross (2017) as we considered new paradigms for how we do our work.

Turning to Peers

As noted previously, traditional opportunities in student affairs for professional development, such as attending educational sessions at national student affairs–related conferences, had limitations for SSAOs, but connecting with peers at these conferences gained importance. This is especially important for VPs at a USI. As one VP put it:

> One of my former mentors said that for him, at this point [in his career, a conference] is literally more about talking to his peers, like "How are you handling this? What are you doing?" So, I've been trying to work to make sure I can connect to VPs who are at institutions similar to this one because if I were at the flagship, I'd be [fine] because I know that world more than I do this one. So, I've had to be kind of intentional in what my development looks like.

Other VPs mentioned more formalized groups of senior leaders who come together based on the geographical area and/or similarity of institutions. All discussed the value of these type of VP groups in similar ways:

> We have a [state] vice president group, for all the vice presidents of public institutions in the state, and we meet three times a year: two half-day meetings and then one retreat in the summer. So that's been a really good group because a lot of these topics are very similar across the state. In terms of the population, now some of these are not as urban, but the type of students, the characteristics of many of our students, are the same no matter where you are in the state.

The frequency of the formal meetings of these groups varied from once per year to much more often, such as the previous one.

In addition to tapping other VPSAs as sources of knowledge, campus colleagues were also valuable. One VP looked to her colleagues who had been at her campus for 40 years. She was able to benefit from their wealth of knowledge, which enabled her to understand the limitations of working in a big state system. Colleagues both on and off campus serve as a vital part of a VP toolkit for professional development. As mentioned earlier, the VP position at a USI can be lonely, and connecting with colleagues can be one of the ways to deal with the feeling of isolation. Keeping connected to these individuals and sharing insights and providing support was a common theme for the participants of this project.

Niche Education

Specialized education includes workshops and training around particular topics and becoming involved with special interest organizations. This type of professional development was highly personalized and intentional, based on the needs of the individual VP and needs of their sector. A VP at a community college described "one-off" trainings specific to functional areas, such as educational opportunity or disability services programs. Other VPs discussed how they were able to weave learning into serving and how this met their particular educational needs. On- and off-campus opportunities to be on advisory boards and/or task forces enable us to learn from others and connect with new partners. One VP discussed their involvement on a state level:

> I just spent a year on a state-wide task force for sexual assault, and that allowed me to meet and talk on a regular basis with other vice presidents, with lawmakers, with community advocates, and have the conversations around sexual assault and sexual violence in a way that I had not previously. Any time I can get into something that's fresh [so] I can look at what I'm doing a little differently, change the perspective, or maybe take a different lens, I like doing that.

These VPs did not necessarily carve out a specific learning opportunity but rather used ad hoc committee appointments to allow them to develop new insights, connections, and skills. USIs are often replete with opportunities to serve that exist within the community and across the state, and VPs often step up to not only serve but also to sharpen their skill sets and open doors for collaborations. In addition to training and service learning, other forms of niche education mentioned by project participants included using an executive coach or participation in webinars.

Sharing With Others

Teaching and presenting at conferences was a theme often mentioned by VPs as a tool for enhancing themselves professionally. Through the process of sharing with others, VPs gained valuable insights. As one VP put it:

> I learn through sharing sometimes. When I engage in certain things and I share with colleagues, or I go and sit on a panel or do something like that, while I'm sharing many times, the information I have, knowledge I have [connects in different ways].

Unfortunately, becoming a VP can detract from professional development opportunities that have great meaning. The loss of teaching opportunities had a profound impact on this VP:

> In terms of professional development, I . . . teach. And I have not been in the classroom since I came to this role. So, 2 years since I've had my own class, and I miss it terribly. It was one of the best ways that I was able to reflect on and improve my practice.

The practice of sharing with others was mentioned by a number of the project participants. In addition to presenting and teaching, at least one VP mentioned attempting to publish at least once a year. So, it appears that being engaged through offering one's own expertise is an often-used tool that enables VPs to develop their professional practice.

Advice for Current and Future VPs

Throughout this chapter we have seen how different the pathways to the VP position were and the learning that came with some of those experiences. While the VPs were not asked specifically to provide advice for aspiring and/or current VPs at USIs, there were some valuable nuggets that are worth pointing out.

First, get in touch with your personal passion. Ask yourself WHY? Why are you in this field? If the answer is to make a difference in the lives of individuals who are striving to make a contribution to our world, then you may be called to a USI. As these VPs have demonstrated, the true joy of working at a USI comes from the connection that these VPs have had between their work and the combination of their life experiences and values. If, after reflecting on your own journey—family, education, career path—you recognize that you are called to serve at a USI, you will be rewarded greatly because you will be able to be your most authentic self. Being in touch with your personal passion will get you through the most challenging times . . . and there will be many.

Next, be open to learning opportunities. Embrace what you don't know and then go after gaining the knowledge and skills to address these deficiencies. Some of our VPs took on areas of responsibility where they may have had competent staff managing on the front lines in areas like enrollment management and Title IX, yet they recognized the importance of being familiar with the new area in order to provide effective leadership.

In addition, we heard from a number of VPs that learning about the dynamics of the institution and the division is critical. It is important to take the time to understand the people, the relationships, and the informal operating procedures. The student stories will be rich, so listen to them. A USI community will likely have high expectations of involvement, service, cooperation.

And while you may be entering a diversity-rich environment, don't presume institutional racism does not exist or that cultural clashes won't happen. Take the time to get to know your team and learn from the individuals who have been at the institution for a long time. You may not want to fall into the old patterns or necessarily continue the programs and services that have been offered in the past, yet understanding why things are done the way they are, respecting the traditions that have been established, and knowing how to get things done at the institution will be great assets when you are ready to make change.

And you will want to make change. Students at our institutions deserve programs and services equal to or better than the best. When working at a USI, you need to recognize that you are in an environment where the traditional models and best practices in student affairs may not be relevant. More students may have less access to programs and services due to students' greater need to work, care for extended family, and/or deal with a host of personal issues (such as immigration status and trauma). Consider how you can contribute to creating new models that can be useful in USIs and may very well be the way of the future for traditional campuses. USIs can lead the way in creating access and inclusion. Additionally, keep in mind that we don't just affect the individual student; we are likely impacting their families and communities. Therefore, the effect of these new models can be exponential.

Finally, we did want to make note that one VP learned something from their own research of 162 VPSAs. It is not clear that this counsel is unique to VPs at USIs, however it is certainly worth sharing: "One of the recommendations that a lot of [VPs] made that still sticks in my mind, and when I give presentations to grad students or teach classes, I tell them that the number one recommendation was 'when not moving up, move out.'" This suggestion is likely very appropriate, given that in this study, most of the VPs had moved into their roles from other institutions, and all of the VPs were currently working in institutions different from where they started their careers. This does not mean that you build a career of job hopping. It does mean, however, that you might need to consider the option of moving to a new institution if you want to progress to higher levels of responsibility because, for any number of reasons, there may not be opportunity to do so at your current institution.

And when you finally make the leap to the VP position, be prepared to take the heat, test all your skills, and develop new perspectives. It is lonely at the top. Connecting with other VPs at other USIs will not only help with addressing the isolation of the role but those connections also will be essential to providing a new direction for student affairs practice at a USI. Collectively, VPs at USIs can make a dramatic difference to the field. No matter where you go in your career, your true passion will direct your path. It is important to stay true to yourself, because your authenticity will help your students in the most challenging times. Remember to be open to learning skills, traits, and opportunities. Finally, reach out and connect with other practitioners because your support circle is wider than you think.

Discussion Questions

1. The position of vice president for student affairs (VPSA) on today's campus is as challenging as it has ever been. What would you consider to be the unique challenges of the VPSA in an urban-serving institution?
2. Being a successful VPSA requires a combination of certain personal characteristics and professional skills. How would your specific personal qualities affect students at a USI? What skills would you need to develop?

3. Being a VP at a USI requires flexibility and willingness to learn new roles. What are some of the functional areas that you believe a VP should be knowledgeable in?
4. Each VP has a unique path to leading an urban institution. What is your current path? What are some similarities or differences you see between yourself and the VPs in this chapter?

References

Gross, K. (2017). *Breakaway learners: Strategies for post-secondary success with at-risk students.* New York: Teachers College Press.

Knaggs, C. M., Sondergeld, T. A., & Schardt, B. (2015). Overcoming barriers to college enrollment, persistence, and perceptions for urban high school students in a college preparatory program. *Journal of Mixed Methods Research*, 9(1), 7–30. doi:10.1177/1558689813497260

Price, D. V., & Tovar, E. (2014). Student engagement and institutional graduation rates: Identifying high-impact educational practices for community colleges. *Community College Journal of Research and Practice*, 38(9), 766–782.

Sinek, S. (2009). *Start with why: How great leaders inspire everyone to take action.* New York: Penguin Books.

9

STUDENT AFFAIRS IN URBAN-SERVING INSTITUTIONS

Reflections and Looking Forward

Anna M. Ortiz

The senior leaders in this project have given us much to think about when it comes to being successful in urban-serving institutions. They have shown us that the nature of these institutions is fundamentally different from traditional and private universities or liberal arts colleges. They were established and developed with different purposes and serve specific students. Throughout time, they have become institutions that are multipurposed and serve many masters—becoming the proverbial all things to all people. Whether they were 2- or 4-year institutions they were built to serve their immediate communities and their citizens who did not find higher education alternatives that met their needs. Thus, these institutions are adept at specializing resources and services for a diverse array of students: the career changer, the returning student, the student with a family, the student who can't quit his job to go to school, the student who can't afford to go away to school, or the one whose high school preparation was insufficient to go straight into a university. These are the populations that USIs historically serve, but today they are often tasked with becoming more like traditional universities by becoming more selective and changing their campuses to better reflect the collegiate ideal. These expectations are many, and many are conflicting. It's doubtful that their private, traditional, or liberal arts peers could do the same with the limited resources afforded to USIs.

Therefore, rather than lament the sorry lot that the USI has drawn, these leaders, their staffs, and institutions have become champions for the opportunities they offer and the communities they serve. They are the place of second chances and first tries, where families send their college-student children daily to enact their version of the American Dream, where the 30-year-old Gulf War veteran cashes in her GI Bill for a college education. Our vice presidents, vice chancellors, and presidents have devoted their careers to transforming these institutions into places in which communities and their citizens thrive. They have shared important lessons with us about what has worked for them in helping students succeed and how to be effective leaders. Hopefully, they have inspired you to think about a career at an urban-serving institution. With the wisdom offered here, you'll have a good start. In this chapter, I bring my own experiences at a USI and draw conclusions from our leaders about the future of these institutions. I share what I believe we need to do differently and what we look forward to.

Embracing Multidisciplinary Approaches to Student Services

Chapter 4 talked about wrap-around services as a way to meet the needs of students in USIs. These are often needed because we need to optimize the time students spend on campus and do what we can to make their interactions with us as productive as possible, with every efficiency we can muster. Often their needs are many: financial aid, academic advising, mental health services, career planning, to name a few. Our leaders spoke of the need for cross-training staff so that students can get what they need no matter whose office they visit. This is an admirable goal and one that would go a long way to making students' lives less complicated. Our authors of Chapters 2 and 4 referenced taking a case management approach to student services. Borrowing from social work, where this is a common methodology, a case management approach provides students with a single point person, who assesses needs, creates a plan of action, and then helps students access resources to get the assistance they need. While it would be unrealistic to think that every student at an institution would have an individual case manager, through cross-training, it can me more likely that the first person a student sees, is able to garner needed information and resources so that student isn't having to visit multiple offices, or if they do, at least it is purposefully planned. Several VPs mentioned that students needed to feel like the institution had a way of keeping a "memory" of them so that every time they met with a staff member they weren't starting over. A case management approach with good documentation supported by technology may be a good way to accomplish this.

A second multidisciplinary approach we can take in student affairs at urban-serving institutions is to borrow from the tenants of Uri Bronfenbrenner's theory of human ecology to embrace an approach to working with students, their families, and communities (see Renn, 2004 for an integrated description of his works and application to the college setting). Fundamental to this is understanding that the interplay of structures of the *microsystem* of an individual has important implications for a number of psychological outcomes, and when applied in the higher education setting, academic outcomes. When higher education ignores basic structures such as family and community involvements, this not only may cause undue stress for students but also fails to draw upon the many positive outcomes that may result from (a) being cognizant of family and community responsibilities and then making accommodations for them; (b) providing

178 Ortiz

training and advising to assist students in managing competing demands in their immediate environment; (c) instituting child care or other social services on campus that helps to streamline life for students; and (d) integrating students' family and important others into the life of the institution. Many of the senior leaders talked about a myriad of ways in which their campuses are involving family in orientation and campus-wide programming, through child-care centers, and through instituting policies and practices that students may need to put family first.

A third multidisciplinary approach considers student services from a wider view. Many leaders talked about how important the physical space was to increasing student engagement and feelings of belonging on their campuses. Moving student services from the top floor of a building down to the bottom or moving like offices to the same space or building student unions with classrooms were all ways in which they saw that if they could move services, students would be more likely to use them. This kind of thinking borrows broadly from urban planning where development, such as land use and building design, are intended to enhance public welfare. On an urban campus there are multiple considerations here. First, using the physical plant design to promote engagement should be at the forefront of any new building or renovation projects. One-stop-shops or moving critical student services to the same part of campus are examples of these, but so is actually moving our programs and services to where students already congregate. On my campus the library is constantly filled with students—but all the advising and student services are on the opposite side of campus. How effective might it be periodically to move some programming or advising to this space? Second, there is the need to attend to the ways in which the campus impacts the surrounding community. From a student affairs perspective, this is usually from the vantage point of making students less annoying to the surrounding community, be it excessive noise or illegal parking. But, as these leaders talked about, finding ways to serve the community was a way for students to connect to each other and develop a sense of belonging at the institution, while simultaneously meeting important community needs. Finally, the institution itself must also be conscious of its impact. Ideally these are positive, such as examples at the University of Houston, Florida International University, and Coppin State University where medical and other social services were important resources for the city. But they can also be a detriment when aggressive building campaigns gobble up community space or when universities intentionally or unintentionally inspire gentrification.

Ray and Radimer, in Chapter 7, described many theories within education, but not often used in the training of student affairs professionals. Stanton-Salazar's (2010) concept of institutional agents calls on student affairs professionals to become agents of change for students by developing opportunities to provide bridging capital to students. When institutions hire staff and faculty who reflect the demographic and cultural characteristics of its students, then possibilities for bonding capital can be actualized. Yosso's (2005) community cultural wealth model gives student affairs professionals a way to see that, what have been commonly considered deficits for many students, such as family, bilingualism, and growing up in difficult communities can actually be considered assets that students can draw upon to be successful in college. Fighting deficit frameworks is hard, as often our well-intentioned help, is deficit thinking in disguise. In the work of student affairs, critical race theory (CRT; Delgado & Stefancic, 2017) offers important lessons. Of the tenants most applicable to our work, *interest convergence*, requires that we question how dominant structures and policies benefit from the continued effects of racism. We need to ask ourselves if our policies and practices sustain oppressive structures or break them down. The *social construction of race* is another that is useful when we are working with students. This will help us from essentializing what we anticipate to be student experiences and backgrounds. There is no one way to be Latina or African American. And in fact, because we have intersecting identities, ones that may not be apparent, engaging students as their own *story tellers* gives us an opportunity to learn the most from them and then better design our services with that knowledge in mind.

Changing the Way We Think and the Way We Do: Culturally Responsive Student Services

In Chapter 1 we introduced *culturally responsive student services* (CRSS) as a translation of Ladson-Billings' concept of culturally relevant pedagogy (CRP; Ladson-Billings, 1995) to the higher education context. Our leaders gave several examples of why this is important and what this looks like in the USI setting. The first step in this process is work on changing the way we think about students. This entails learning as much as we can about our students, their backgrounds, their living situations, what is important to them in their family and community lives, and what role race, ethnicity, culture and other relevant social identities play in their sense of personhood. It would be inappropriate for us to delve into an in-depth interview about all these factors when we meet with students, especially for the first time, but we can use questions like this as a template in the back of our minds when we do work with students; seeking to understand what students consider important and what may impact their lives in school (and the impact of school in their lives). It might even be helpful for institutions to collect these kind of data on a regular basis so that there is a current profile of student characteristics, as suggested by one leader.

CRSS also calls us to change our attitudes toward students. This can be as seemingly simple as proclaiming, "We are not doing students a favor by serving them; they are doing us a favor by giving us the opportunity to do so," as they do at Florida International University. Or it can be as profound as the example one leader gave when he sought the student's perspective when a faculty member sent a student to judicial affairs for being disruptive in class. He gave the student the opportunity to show that resistance is not the same as disruption. Because students at USIs have a variety of student characteristics that research has commonly deemed as "at risk" (i.e., first-generation, low-income, commuter students, etc.), they are, actually, at risk of being the recipient of our well-ingrained (yet usually well-intended) deficit thinking. An example of this thinking came from a meeting I attended recently where a college president said to a room full of Latinx students, faculty, and staff that students' families are often barriers to their success in college. I'm sure she was trying to be empathetic; at times everyone's family can be a barrier to success. But in this setting, we see a deeply held stereotype about Latinx families not supporting the education of their children. Something that research has proven false, we insist as seeing as a deficit if we aren't careful. CRSS mandates that we examine our fundamental beliefs about the students we serve, and much like working to undo the racist tapes in our heads, we need to undo the deficit thinking that impairs our ability to truly serve our students. They know when we think less of them, when we pity them, and when we want to save them—the deficit thinking isn't so well disguised.

When we practice culturally relevant student services, we strive to meet students where they are and help them develop the tools to succeed. We don't do the work for them, but we also don't make their work more difficult. Throughout this book there are numerous ideas about providing students with opportunities for growth and development while considering that their lives are already full and complex. The VP who requires that in every student activity, the staff members help students to reflect on how they can translate what they learned and accomplished into bullets on their résumé, is practicing CRSS. The president who increases the number of student positions on campus so that students work there instead of commuting to school to work to home is practicing CRSS. The campus that gives free tickets to students and their families for campus soccer and basketball games is doing the same. In the context of the urban serving institution any time student affairs partners with academic affairs to strengthen the sense of belonging in the classroom, major or academic department, they are practicing CRSS. I say this because culture is more than race or ethnicity—it is also the culture of the city, the culture of the family, and the community. There is a culture of being a student at a USI. Adapting our work to meet their unique needs is culturally responsive student services.

Considering the previous sections' discussion on multidisciplinary approaches to student affairs and this sections' call for culturally relevant student services, it's obvious that we need to educate and train master's and doctoral students differently. Ray and Radimer offer many suggestions for doing this in Chapter 7. Speaking as a full-time faculty member, I concur with their critique, but I also understand the challenges in enacting this paradigm shift. There is only so much room in a curriculum that can entail as little as 30 credit hours for master's students. Doctoral students may not even get 30 credit hours of higher education content in their degrees. Canons are hard to give up. Residence life has all the assistantships. There isn't time in a huge teaching load to completely revamp my classes. All these are understandable reasons to not fully commit to a curriculum ready to deliver culturally relevant student service providers and leaders. If most of our higher education institutions are going to become even more diverse than they are now, as predicted by every demographic forecast, as a whole higher education will become more like USIs. Our preparation programs will have to change.

Partnering With Academic Affairs

Throughout the book, it has been stressed that for students at urban-serving institutions, their primary place of connection is the academic unit—whether that be individual courses, majors, or departments. Thus, the work of student affairs at USIs must traverse organizational silos to deliver services, to enhance engagement, and develop a sense of belonging among students. When asked who their closest colleagues were on campus, most senior leaders mentioned the provost or vice president of academic affairs. They all knew that student affairs needed to partner with the academic enterprise in order to fully meet students' needs. Rather than compete with academics for students' limited time, they became more integrated into the academic lives of the students.

They did this through early alert systems, training faculty on different topics related to student success, and supporting department programming. They seemed to work most closely with faculty and departments through supporting internships or other career-related programming. They also were connected through the many student organizations that were major or department based. These different places of collaboration gave their academic colleagues a set of resources and staff support that they could not access on their own and they gave student affairs greater access to students without requiring more effort or time on the behalf of students. One highlight of the many that they described, was when the outdoor recreation unit at one campus partnered with a faculty member offering an interdisciplinary course on history and the environment by organizing aligned activities such as white-water rafting.

At the USI, senior leaders knew that they had to be deeply involved in efforts to increase student success. They were keenly aware of the sacrifices that students and families were making to attend college and that one student's success or failure would have an impact on future college-going for all those connected to that student. They took seriously, their role in supporting the academic mission of the institution. Throughout the interviews, I never heard any of the usual rhetoric about student affairs feeling less than at these institutions. They may have felt less than, compared to their flagships or more prestigious universities in their states, but on their own campuses they knew they were integral to students' academic success and were able to operationalize that in ways that were outlined in Chapters 4 and 5. The pressure that performance-based funding was placing on institutions was felt by the student affairs leaders. In states where this was already taking place, they were concerned about how formulas would unfairly punish their campus and saw their partnership with academic affairs to increase student success metrics as more urgent. Others knew this was on the horizon and were already working with their staffs to ingrain that their primary position was to support student academic success.

Leadership Beyond the Institution

When I spoke with each of the leaders, one of the things that most impressed me was how holistically they approached their positions. They were strong leaders in their own units, but they also saw that their impact and reach had to go far beyond the division of student affairs. The leaders worked with the surrounding community in almost a symbiotic relationship. The needed to become part-time development officers, connecting to corporations and foundations. They also became a part of groups or professional associations to support their own development as SSAOs and to find support among colleagues familiar with the USI context.

Almost every leader discussed their relationship with the local community as an exchange of resources and good will. They were excited to share the many ways in which their students and programs supported the local community. Whether it was a series of mentor programs that targeted specific areas of need or monthly days of service, they were regularly out in the community. There were also specific services and clinics run through their medical or allied health graduate degree programs that involved undergraduates. They also welcomed the community to events on campus. The community college leaders in the project described a relationship built with students that lasted beyond their last course. Community members who had been students, saw the college as a life-long resource center, coming back to campus to use different services. Rather than talking about this like a burden, these leaders welcomed the chance to continue to serve. Conversely, the leaders looked to the community to meet students' needs that the institution could not fulfill. They partnered with community organizations to support student programs. They looked to community agencies to fill in gaps for students' basic needs. They sought out specialized community services such as legal clinics to provide services to students that the institution could not afford.

Relatedly, each senior leader was involved in philanthropy and development in one way or another. Some were just beginning this effort, realizing that local and national businesses might want to invest in their talented students. One leader was animated when he talked about the success of a small career-related program and how strongly it impacted students. He knew that the only way to scale-up the program was to look outside the university for support. He was determined to find that corporation to make that happen. One campus restructured a dean-level position to include development officer duties as a way to strengthen the campaign to fund their DREAM center for undocumented and DACA students, and their basic needs services for housing and food insecure students. All realized that part of their job was to raise funds to support programs and students.

Involvement in professional associations was a constant in the careers of the senior leaders. Early in their career they found that the large conventions that ACPA and NASPA offered the professional development they needed. As they ascended to their senior leadership positions their professional development needs changed. They used these conventions as ways to connect with other vice presidents, to reconnect with friends and colleagues, share ideas and consult around issues and problems they were experiencing. A few had been a part of the NASPA board of directors at one time or another in their careers. While they acknowledged that in their vice president roles, NASPA was their association of choice, most found that it just was not enough to meet their professional development needs. There were two reasons for this. First, some found that the large convention offerings were too generic for their needs and they valued the smaller conferences that are focused on one topic or issue. Second, although NASPA has many avenues to support SSAOs, they found those supports to be lacking because they led at an urban serving institution. They mentioned the special programming for SSAOs at small colleges and wondered if that same kind of programming would be valuable for SSAOs at USIs. They would have a place where they could focus on their distinct context and share resources and ideas to support their work. Thus, they looked to other places for professional development. The two most commonly mentioned organizations were the Coalition of Urban Serving Universities (one of the seven commissions in the Association of Public and Land-Grant Universities) and the Coalition of Urban and Metropolitan Universities. In these they connected with colleagues who serve at other USIs and participate in programming specific to their needs. Most of the leaders also participated in informal networks of vice presidents in their states or regions. Many found these to be most helpful, especially those who were at institutions that were a part of a system. Here they met formally once or twice a year, but what they found most valuable was that they could pick up the phone any time to consult with one of their colleagues.

Involvement in Promise and Career Pathway Initiatives

Two vice presidents were intimately involved in college promise and career pathway initiatives within their cities, and others saw these on the horizon. It seems appropriate to highlight these kinds of initiatives here as they reflect a future impact on the work of student affairs in urban settings. I have been involved in the Long Beach College Promise in a number of ways, as a professor in education and as a principal investigator on a James Irvine Foundation grant called *Bridging the Gap*. The Long Beach College promise seeks to solidify the pipeline between the school district, the community college, the state university and the city. Through this, students are promised admission if they meet basic eligibility requirements for the higher education institution they wish to enter or transfer to. At the community college, the promise even gives them one year free of tuition. The city is involved by facilitating internships for high school, community college and university students to help students explore careers earlier as a way to facilitate their commitment to higher education and increase student outcomes, including time to degree.

Through the *Bridging the Gap* grant, we developed a pipeline of student services to support students in high school as they took dual enrollment courses and prepared to enter the college or university. We designed training for faculty who would be teaching dual enrollment courses so that they knew how to better work with high school students. We worked with college counselors in high schools so that they could advise their soon-to-be high school graduates on involvement opportunities to seek when they went to either institution of higher education (IHE). We also offered a career-exploration-based summer-bridge program to any Long Beach Unified high school graduate matriculating into either IHE. This residential program also gave local students who would not normally live in the residence halls that experience and a head start on making new friends, knowing about resources and developing a sense of belonging. An academic course and peer mentoring followed these students into the first semester of college. Perhaps the most challenging project was to connect the student data between all three institutions so that students did not start anew when they progressed to the next level.

I describe this program here because these college promise programs and an emphasis on career pathways provide new opportunities for student affairs in USIs to become an integral part of increasing college access and new ways to promote student success. For 3 years, the mayor's office and counseling personnel from the school district and community college, joined career development, advising staff, and faculty from the university to create these programs. The size and complexity of these urban institutions, at first, seemed to threaten our progress, but as relationships formed and as we realized the potential of the partnership, we were able to just make things work. I doubt that any of the student affairs staff ever thought they would be sitting down with leaders from the school district to design programs, but being involved in this project changed the way they thought about their work. They realized that to help students be successful, they needed to reach out before they even got to campus. Several also taught the first-year career course that they helped developed.

Preserving the Urban-Serving Institution

USIs in this project are mission driven, as that was a criterion for inclusion. As is evident throughout the book, but especially in Chapter 8, these leaders take that mission to heart. They have chosen to work at USIs, many seeking them after experiences at some of the most prestigious universities in the country. They believe in the access mission and that institutions of higher education should be positive contributors to the communities where they reside. Many fear external pressures that threaten their mission; primarily through funding and accountability mechanisms, that fail to take into account their unique mission and the challenges that they face enacting it.

Public USIs have traditionally served the public good by receiving most of their funding from their states. Few have histories of development leaving them with large endowments. Revenue from grants and contracts is often limited as these are teaching-oriented institutions where faculty are often left little time for traditional research funded by large government or foundation grants. Additionally, many of them see other institutions in their states, especially the flagships, funded at higher levels. There is a convergence of factors at play here. Some are governed by boards of trustees that represent all public universities in the state, thus their advocacy is split among many competing demands. Flagship institutions often are able to have influence on legislatures through their government relations lobbying staffs and offices. Sometimes the legislators themselves are advocates for their alma mater's, which likely also favors those flagships. One institution in the project had recently converted from a state-wide governing board to a local one, giving the institution greater advocacy that has resulted in increased resources. Many leaders spoke of the need to "tell their story," but admitted that their institutions aren't very good at singing their own praises. However, they knew that they needed to become more skilled at conveying their impact. They realized that it was critical to the health of the institution to advocate for themselves in order to get their share of available public resources.

The national call for accountability in higher education also has these senior leaders concerned. Funding formulas that use metrics such as graduation rates and time to degree fail to recognized that for some institutions, making progress in these areas will be slow and incremental. As many of the leaders said, measures of engagement and success for their students may not simply be represented by graduation and retention. When the state funding formula involves ranks or comparisons, like one in the project, there is virtually no way the USI can compete with the more selective public institutions in the state. Thus, they are left with difficult choices. They can raise admission standards, becoming more selective, but less accessible- as some USIs across the country have done. As Astin's (1991) input-environment-output (IEO) theory explains, the easiest way to increase academic outcomes is to admit students with higher academic inputs (GPAs, standardized test scores); the institution itself needs to do very little to ensure that academic success continues. They cannot continue to do more with even less, if state funding dwindles as they are punished for not keeping up. Or they can use resources that could be used elsewhere to increase fundraising efforts and seek corporate sponsorships. In worst case scenarios, declining support means pulling back on services, eliminating academic programs and laying off personnel. The financial picture is even more complex when we consider that these campus are also working with union contracts and policies that may limit the kinds of income they can generate independently, such as raising tuition or adding revenue-generating programs. Using the CRT's tenant of *interest convergence*, we to go back to Astin's (1985) concept of counterproductive views of excellence and see the need to protect USIs from policies and funding that serve the best interest of flagships and more prestigious institutions, at their expense.

Thus, preserving the USI and its unique mission of access and service is not just a starry-eyed notion. The success of these cities and their citizens rely on the survival of these institutions. When these institutions not only survive, but thrive, there is the opportunity for them to become vibrant community institutions. Perry and Wiewel (2005) described institutions that develop real estate by thoughtful urban planning and development. USIs provide important community needs such as health care. They also partner with schools and agencies to enhance the experience of the USI student, but also those who will be future students. They become economic engines for their urban areas through employment, construction contracts, and workforce training. Although, our leaders did not speak at length about becoming cultural centers for their cities, they can certainly play that role through performing arts and other cultural programming.

Choosing to Lead a USI

Urban-serving institutions need talented student affairs professionals with a personal passion for service. Working at or leading a USI needs to be an intentional, well-informed choice. As many leaders said in this project, not everyone can be successful at a USI. The work is different, because the student needs are different and the urban setting is complex. Throughout the advice of our leaders, I heard an undertone of patience and perseverance as mandatory dispositions for their staffs and themselves. Creativity was also a theme that was apparent. Creative use of resources; creativity to revamp programs. It also seemed that to be successful at a USI you need a strong internal compass or locus of control and a great deal of humility. Associated with this is being good at self-reflection and evaluation. These leaders had courage and initiative, necessary characteristics indeed.

When programs don't work or when services aren't used, these leaders searched for the reason why and then re-tooled; often very quickly. There was a sense that they were in constant motion. Whether it was a crisis, a new program, realigning services, or forming new partnerships; they needed to persist so that they did not get easily discouraged when something failed or turned sideways. This required strong relationships, skilled negotiation, and high creativity. They could look to their colleagues and peers for ideas and support, but often, they had to make moves immediately relying on their own personal resources, and those of their staffs. Which is why careful selection of their staffs was so important. Many told stories of staff members who just couldn't make it because they weren't "cut out" to work at a USI. They also found that they inherited staff members who may not have been trained in student affairs or who may have lost the passion for working with urban students through a long career. Thus, they needed to be creative and firm in how they worked with staff dispositions that needed to change. Having the resolve to address poor staff performance and then the talent to make it better was something that was important to making sure the students got the best service possible. Serving students well was not just a slogan or a given- it was a passion and they knew that failing to do this would do students harm.

Working at a USI requires self-direction, self-authorship, a strong locus of control- which ever word you may choose to use. No leader reported that they were getting externally rewarded for their work on a regular basis. When I spoke with each of them, there was very much an ethos of working as hard as they could for the benefit of students. They placed that above all else. Since many of them share backgrounds similar to their students, they understood student, family and community issues from an insider perspective. When they did not share that background, they made efforts to make sure their own privilege and experiences did not get in the way of their work. Every one of them took lessons from their long careers. They were able to self-evaluate and reflect on when they made mistakes and could quickly transform that to new directions. They were also incredibly humble people. They had accomplished a great deal, but knew they still had learning to do. Working in a USI requires that you are able to self-direct and reward yourself for a job well done, knowing that it is never really over.

It also appeared that one needs a great deal of courage to assume the senior student affairs position at a USI. They knew they would be unpopular at times, as any SSAO would, but in their complex environments, with the challenges they met, it was a much more common occurrence. The group of leaders in this project was highly diverse. Only one would be considered "majority"- a cisgender, straight, white male. Of the six women in the project, five were women of color. The rest of the men were men of color or non-heterosexual. They progressed in their careers by the usual channels of progressive leadership roles, but for most of them this also meant that they faced stereotypes and discrimination as they become the generation of SSAOs that moved beyond the predominantly white male demographic. Choosing to work at USIs also meant that they bypassed the privilege that being at more prestigious, better resourced institutions would afford them. Most had been at those institutions in the past and now were making intentional choices to be in their mission-driven institutions where they feel they were called to serve.

Throughout the duration of the project, two of the leaders became presidents, showing that in these institutions, student affairs vice presidents or vice chancellors are poised to take leadership positions. If we are going to successfully serve the students of the future, we need the voices, experience and wisdom of those who work at urban-serving institutions. We need that to better prepare our student affairs professionals to do excellent work at USIs and to assist those who transition to USIs. Furthermore, at all institutions we need those models, practices and strategies because, as some note in the book, urban students are being heartily recruited at traditional institutions, thus, those student affairs professionals need to know how to meet the needs of urban students and promote their success. The future of higher education squarely sits on the shoulders of new populations of college students. Those who have been left behind in the past are now the source future college enrollments. Learning how to meet their needs by creating vibrant environments where they can succeed academically and be ready for fulfilling careers, will be the task of all institutions in the future. To do so, we need to look at these accomplished senior leaders as our experts.

References

Astin, A. E. (1985). *Achieving academic excellence: A critical assessment of priorities and practices in higher education*. San Francisco, CA: Jossey-Bass.

Astin, A. W. (1991). *Assessment for excellence: The philosophy and practice of assessment and evaluation in higher education*. New York: American Council on Education and Macmillan.

Delgado, R., & Stefancic, J. (2017). *Critical race theory: An introduction* (3rd ed.). New York: New York University Press.

Ladson-Billings, G. (1995). Toward a theory of culturally relevant pedagogy. *American Educational Research Journal*, 32(3), 465–491. Retrieved from www.jstor.org/stable/1163320

Perry, D. C., & Wiewel, W. (2005). *The university as urban developer: Case studies and analysis*. New York: Routledge.

Renn, K. A. (2004). *Mixed race students in college: The ecology of race, identity, and community on campus*. Albany: State University of New York Press.

Stanton-Salazar, R. D. (2010). A social capital framework for the study of institutional agents and their role in the empowerment of low-status students and youth. *Youth & Society*, 43(3), 1066–1109.

Yosso, T. J. (2005). Whose culture has capital? A critical race theory discussion of community cultural wealth. *Race Ethnicity and Education*, 8(1), 69–91.

CONTRIBUTOR BIOS

Mariette Bien-Aime Ayala, M.A is a researcher at the University of Massachusetts, Boston and has also worked in the Student Affairs Division, the Urban Education Department, and the Institution for International and Comparative Education. A native of Boston, Ayala has close ties to family in Haiti and enjoys working as an advocate for underrepresented youth in her community and church congregation. Ayala holds a B.A. in Economics and Chinese from the University of Massachusetts in Amherst, a certificate in Advanced Chinese and Business from Shanghai University, an M.A. in Student Affairs and Higher Education from Indiana University of Pennsylvania, and is currently pursuing a Ph.D. in Urban Education, Leadership, and Policy at University of Massachusetts, Boston.

Dr. Anthony Cruz, Ed.D is the Vice Chancellor for Student Affairs of the St. Louis Community College District. Dr. Cruz has served in student affairs and student services roles at institutions across the United States from Florida to Ohio, including Sinclair Community College, Cincinnati State Technical and Community College, Broward College, Kaplan University, and Florida International University. A native of Chicago, Dr. Cruz grew up in Miami and has a doctorate in Education from Florida International University, a master's degree in Public Administration from Florida State University, and a bachelor of arts in Political Science from Florida International University.

Dr. Tiffany J. Davis, Ph.D is clinical assistant professor of Higher Education at the University of Houston, where she also serves as Program Director of the Higher Education master's programs. Dr. Davis' classroom teaching, scholarly work, and professional service broadly focus on issues related to diversity, equity, and inclusion within postsecondary contexts and professional pathways and socialization for the higher education profession. Dr. Davis has published in several journals and contributed chapters to the following books: *The Handbook of Student Affairs Administration (4th ed.); Diversity, Equity, and Inclusivity in Contemporary Higher Education;* and *Contested Issues in Troubled Times: Dialogues about Equity, Civility, and Safety.* Dr. Davis holds a Ph.D. in College Student Affairs Administration, University of Georgia, 2013, an M.A. in College Student Personnel, Bowling Green State University, 2006, and a B.S. in Human Ecology, University of Tennessee, 2004.

Dr. Gail DiSabatino, Ed.D is the Vice Chancellor for Student Affairs at the University of Massachusetts Boston. Dr. DiSabatino believes public universities serve an important role in society based on her experience in student affairs positions at mostly public institutions, including Clemson University, Georgia Institute of Technology, Cal Poly Pomona, and University of Nebraska–Lincoln. A Delaware native, Dr. DiSabatino has more than 30 years of experience in higher education with a doctorate in Higher Education Management from the University of Pennsylvania, a master's of education from Colorado State University, and a bachelor of science from University of Delaware.

Dr. Michael A. Freeman, Ph.D is the first Vice President for Enrollment Management and Student Affairs at Coppin State University. Dr. Freeman has over 30 years of experience in higher education as an administrator and teacher, which includes previous posts at the University of South Florida, Tennessee State University, and St. Mary's College of Maryland. He is a Chicago native, and earned his bachelor's and master's degrees from the University of Iowa and his Ph.D. in Counseling and Personnel Services from the University of Maryland, College Park.

Dr. Jenny Jacobs, Ed.D is an adjunct professor of Theatre and a Theatre Artist. She has served as a theatre professor, dramaturg, designer, and director for undergraduate and graduate theatre departments at institutions including Temple University, Rider University, and Cypress College. Jenny has also served in artistic, administrative, and education capacities for theatre companies and performing arts centers on the East and West Coasts. A native of southern California, Jenny wrote her dissertation about the link between the performing arts and leadership at Long Beach State University, where she completed her doctorate in Educational Leadership. She earned her M.A. in Dramaturgy from Villanova University and a B.A. in Theatre and English from Santa Clara University.

Dr. Larry W. Lunsford, Ph.D is the VicePresident for Student Affairs at Florida International University. Dr. Lunsford has served FIU for nearly four decades in roles ranging from Associate Dean for Student Life and Associate Vice President for Student Affairs to University Ombudsman and Assistant Professor in the

Department of Leadership and Professional Studies in the College of Education. He received a bachelor's in Communications from the University of Tennessee, a master's in College Student Personnel Administration from Indiana University, and a Ph.D. in Higher Education Administration from the University of Pittsburgh.

Dr. André McKenzie, Ed.D is Vice Provost for Academic Support Services and Faculty Development at St. John's University in New York City. His career spans over 30 years and includes positions as Associate Dean of Student Development to roles in the Office of Opportunity Programs, as well as Student Advising and Retention. Dr. McKenzie has also worked for Northeastern Illinois University in Chicago and as a Training Specialist for the Anti-Defamation League's *A Campus of Difference* diversity training program. In addition to his administrative role at St. John's, Dr. McKenzie is also an Adjunct Associate Professor in the University's School of Education. Dr. McKenzie holds a Doctor of Education and Master of Education in Student Personnel Administration in Higher Education from Teachers College, Columbia University, a Master of Science in Guidance and Counseling and a Bachelor of Science in Education from Illinois State University.

Dr. Anna M. Ortiz, Ph.D has been in the profession of student affairs for over 30 years, serving in multiple roles from graduate assistant to director of residence life to professor. She has served on the faculty of Michigan State University and has been at Long Beach for 15 years where she is Professor of Educational Leadership. Her publications cover a range of topics from student ethnic identity development to professional issues in student affairs and new faculty development. She has been active in leadership roles in ACPA, ASHE, and AERA, and recently served as the founding director of the NASPA Faculty Division. She holds a Ph.D. in Higher Education and Organizational Change from UCLA, an M.A. in Higher Education and Student Affairs from the Ohio State University and a B.S. in Human Development from the University of California, Davis.

Dr. Scott Radimer, Ph.D is the Director of Research, Assessment, and Planning at the University of Memphis, as well as an Adjunct Faculty Member in the Leadership department in the College of Education. Dr. Radimer's interests in gender norms and ethnic identity, supervising new professionals, first-generation college students, social media use, and undergraduate men's alcohol use have complemented his years of service in student affairs for institutions such as Boston College, Bentley University, and Vassar College. Dr. Radimer holds a Ph.D. in Higher Education from Boston College, an M.S. in Higher Education from Florida State University, and a B.A. in Political Science from the University of Vermont.

Dr. Darrell C. Ray, Ph.D is the Vice President for Student Affairs for the University of Memphis. He also is a Clinical Assistant Professor of Higher Education Administration within the College of Education. Dr. Ray served as

Assistant Vice President for Student Affairs at Louisiana State University and A&M College, as well as Associate Dean of Students and an adjunct professor. Dr. Ray has served previous institutions as a dean of students, director of student development, and coordinator for housing and Greek life units. He holds a bachelor's in Criminal Justice, a master's in Higher Education Administration from the University of Alabama, and a doctorate in Counseling and Student Affairs Administration at the University of Georgia.

Dr. Franklyn Taylor, Ed.D is the Campus Vice President of Student Affairs for St. Louis Community College Forest Park. Along with an extensive career leading, teaching, presenting, and publishing in student affairs, Dr. Taylor has served at institutions that include the University of Wisconsin-Marathon County, Northern Arizona University, and University of Wisconsin-Whitewater. Dr. Taylor holds an Ed.D. in Educational Leadership from Northern Arizona University, master's degrees in Curriculum and Instruction from University of Wisconsin-Whitewater and Public Administration from University of North Florida, a Graduate Diploma in Education and a B.A. in History and Political Science from the University of Sierra Leone.

Dr. Corlisse Thomas, Ed.D is the Vice Chancellor for Student Affairs for Rutgers University–Newark. Previously, Dr. Thomas served as Assistant Vice President for Student Affairs at both CUNY Baruch College and at Stevens Institute of Technology, Associate Dean of Students and Founding Dean of the Office of Multicultural Affairs at Columbia University, and held positions in Student Activities, Multicultural Affairs, Greek Life, and Admissions at other colleges and universities. She is an Adjunct Assistant Professor in the Higher and Postsecondary Education Program at Teachers College, Columbia University. Dr. Thomas received her Ed.D. in Higher Education and her M.A. in Student Personnel Administration from Teachers College, Columbia University, and her B.A. in Child Study from Tufts University.

Dr. Richard Walker, Ed.D is the Vice President for Student Affairs and Enrollment Services for the University of Houston and Vice Chancellor for Student Affairs and Enrollment Services for the University of Houston System. Dr. Walker was with the University of Miami for 24 years, where he served as Assistant/Associate Dean of Students, Director of Student Life, and Assistant/Associate Vice President for Student Affairs. He also worked at Central Missouri State University and Middle Tennessee State University. Dr. Walker received his Ed.D. in Higher Education Leadership from the University of Miami, a Specialist in Education Administration and Supervision from Middle Tennessee State University, a Master of Education in Education Administration and Supervision from Memphis State University, and a Bachelor of Science in History from Middle

Tennessee State University. He is also a graduate of the Harvard Institutes for Higher Education Management Development Program.

Dr. Edward Whipple, Ph.D is the Vice President for Student Affairs at Williamette University. In over two decades as a Vice President of Student Affairs, Dr. Whipple has focused on student success, academic quality, and institutional effectiveness at institutions such as Bowling Green State University, Montana State University-Billings, University of Alabama, Texas Tech University, and Iowa State University. Dr. Whipple holds a Ph.D. in College Student Services Administration from Oregon State University, an M.A. in Teaching from Northwestern University, and a B.A. in English from Willamette University.

INDEX

Page numbers in bold refer to tables.

academic advising 54, 60, 66, 77, 92; *see also* wrap-around support, and advising services

academic affairs: engagement through 91–93; senior officers 125; and student affairs 51, 59, 60, 125, 180, 181–182

access-oriented mission 21–22, 27, 28, 31, 34, 35, 186

administrative bureaucracy 61

admissions 183; cycle, automated process in 21–22; and performance-based funding 31; selectivity 31, 32, 185; *see also* enrollment(s)

advocacy, for students 52–54

African American students 40, 51; academic services for 77; community cultural wealth 134; commuters, family responsibilities of 48; cultural conflicts 145; different kinds of capital possessed by 134; and family 97; food insecurity of 43; retention rate of 78; *see also* Latinx students

Alfano, H. J. 8, 48

alternate night schedules 53

alumni associations 90

American College Personnel Association (ACPA) 138, 183

American Community Survey (2009–2011) 1

American Council on Education 52

anchor institutions 20–21, 35

Anderson, C. 63, 64

Asian American and Native American Pacific Islander–Serving institutions (AANAPISIs) 19, 21

Asian critical theory (AsianCrit) 135

Asian Pacific Americans in Higher Education (APAHE) 169

aspirational capital 134

assessment 119; plan 120; program 120; types of 120

Association of American Colleges and Universities (AAC&U) 169

Association of Fraternity Advisors (AFA) 168

Association of Public and Land-Grant Universities (APLU) 33, 169; Council of Student Affairs 169; Innovation and Economic Prosperity Universities award program 73

Association of Public Land-Grant Universities 65

Astin, Alexander 2, 3, 4–5, 85, 90, 185

Ayala, Mariette Bien-Aime 151

Barbatis, P. 53, 69

belonging, sense of 8–9, 14, 54, 84–87, 91; and academic success 8–9; and campus climate 98–100; and community involvement programs 93–95; and commuter students 8–9; and culture 96; and degree completion 86; development, strategies for 101–102; and

intentionality 87–89; and poverty-alleviation supports 44; and validation 49; and wrap-around approaches 66; *see also* engagement
Black History Month 92
Black identity development, theory of (Cross) 130
Blixt, A. B. 126
board of trustees/regents: and funding 185; governance of 29, 30
bonding capital 133, 178
Bourdieu, P. 133
boutique programs 61
Bresciani, M. J. 120
bridging capital 133
Bridging the Gap grant (Irvine Foundation) 183, 184
Bronfenbrenner, Uri 177
Broton, K. 44
budget *see* fiscal management
bureaucracy, administrative 61
Burlison, M. B. 47, 48

California State University (CSU) 42, 87
campus *see* urban campuses
campus climate: and belonging 98–100, 102; and student affairs professionals 146
campus communities 53, 95, 96, 98, 107, 121, 124
campus culture 64, 97, 113
campus security 121
campus violence 120–121; shootings 120
career advising 60
career development 70–73
career pathway initiatives 183–184
career purposes, of vice presidents 154–155
career readiness 71, 72, 73, 80
career-related activities, and engagement 93
CARE Teams 76
Carnegie Community Engagement Classification 11
case management approach 25, 65, 66, 177
Center for Counseling and Consultation 74
challenge and support, concept of (Sanford) 130
Chavez, A. F. 50, 51
Chickering, A. W. 129, 132
chief fiscal officer 116
child care services 53
Chronicle of Higher Education, The 122
City University of New York (CUNY) 30, 43; Black Male Initiative (CUNY BMI) 77–78

Clark, M. R. 9, 60, 67, 68–69, 113
classroom(s) 51, 140; disruptive behavior in 121; engagement of professionals with students in 92, 93; instruction format 141; materials/activities, culturally relevant 75; validation 49
Coalition of Urban and Metropolitan Universities (CUMU) 11, 33, 34, 39, 169–170, 183
Coalition of Urban Serving Universities (USU) 11, 25, 26, 27, 33–34, 65, 169, 183; 21st Century Workforce Development initiative 72
co-curricular programming 92
cognitive-developmental model, of moral development (Kohlberg) 130
College Goal Sunday 52
Commission on Access, Diversity, and Equity (CADE) 169
communication 93, 101–102, 118, 122, 145; between campus and family 97; linguistic capital 134; skills 147, 165
communities 34–35, 177; among students 66, 67; hometown setting, lived experiences in 153–154; impact of campus on 178; and localized board structures 30; members, as validation agents 49; partnership 26, 44; relationship of leaders with 26; services 26, 178, 182; *see also* community involvement programs; USI as resource to 25–28
community colleges 21, 152, 153, 155, 158, 159–160; advising models 77; and child care services 53; district approach 30; first-generation students in 42; food and home insecurity of students 42–43, 44; and foster youth 44; leadership 138, 182; as point of contact for support 24; promise initiatives 183; and resources 25
community cultural wealth model 134, 137, 178–179
community development 7, 29
community engagement 26, 27, 31, 54
community involvement programs 93–95
community organizations, partnerships with 63, 68, 182
community-oriented policing 24
commuter students 40, 54, 60; academic and social integration of 86; academic/nonacademic issues faced by 75; advising initiatives for 76; complexity of 47–49; engagement of 86, 90, 91; experiences

196 Index

of 8; financial aid for 62; homelessness of 43; lack of time 90; loneliness of 67; multiple identities 47; provision of virtual connections to 53; and staff training 111; work and family responsibilities 48–49, 68
completion coaching 77
continuing-generation college students 131
contract negotiations 115, 116
Coppin State University 89, 96, 100, 102, 178
costs, of higher education 28–29
Council for Adult and Experiential Learning 118
Council for Advancement of Standards in Higher Education (CAS) 138
counseling services 69, 74, 123
counterproductive hierarchy, engagement with 3–5
counterproductive views, of excellence 3, 186
crisis management 120–123
critical race theory (CRT) 78, 134–135, 179, 185–186
Cross, W. E. 130
cross-training, staff 60, 112, 177
Crutchfield, R. M. 42, 43
Cruz, Anthony 38
culinary programs, college 44
cultural capital 63, 134
cultural competence 2, 75, 108
cultural diversity strategic plans 95
culturally relevant pedagogy (CRP) 2, 5, 49, 179
culturally relevant/responsive student services (CRSS) 2–3, 5, 73–78, 139, 179–181
culturally responsive teaching 49, 50–51
culturally specific programming 73, 75
curricula: curricular creativity 142; doctoral programs 142; and faculty 139–140; preparation programs 137, 138, 139–140, 147
Cuyjet, M. J. 117, 118–119

Darling, R. A. 54, 77
data driven decision-making 119–120
Davis, J. 143
Davis, Tiffany J. 19–20
Davis, C. H. F., III 78
Deferred Action for Childhood Arrival (DACA) students 44–45, 182
degree completion 64, 65, 76, 77, 78, 79, 86, 96, 156

demographic profiles *see* diversity, of students
DeSantos-Jones, J. 120
Digest of Education Statistics report 43
director-level positions 110
DiSabatino, Gail 151
disabilities, students with 111
disadvantaged backgrounds, students from 60; access to social capital 133–134; different kinds of capital possessed by 134
disruptive behavior, in classrooms 121
distance learning 141
district approaches, USIs with 30–31
diversity, of students 22–23, 39–47, 49, 74, 137, 139, 143, 164; cultural conflicts 144–145; first-generation status 41–42; food and home insecurity 42–44; immigrants 40; LGBTQIA students 45; low-income students 45–47; understanding 144; undocumented and DACA status 44–45
doctoral preparation 141–143, 146, 147
Doctor of Education (EdD) programs 141, 142
domestic violence, victims of 69
Donaldson, P. 77
Dougherty, K. J. 31
Dream Centers 41
dropout rates, of commuter students 48

early alert programs 60
East Baltimore Revitalization Initiative 29
economic development 20, 21, 25, 27, 31
education programs 11
Educators for Fair Consideration 44
Eduljee, N. B. 8, 48
Eisenberg, D. 44
Elliott, Peggy Gordon 6, 7
emergency funds 52, 64, 123
emergency response teams 122, 123
emotional agility, of professionals 144, 146
employment 39, 148; and gaps in preparation programs 138; student 27, 70, 90
engagement 14, 84–87, 101; and community involvement programs 93–95; and commuter students 8; concept, transforming 89–91; and degree completion 86; expectations for 91; family 95–98; and first-generation students 42; and intentionality 87–89; interaction of time and effort 86; measurement of 91; and places of

Index **197**

importance for students 91; and residential spaces 23; spaces for events 88; and specialized programs 89; through academic affairs 91–93; *see also* belonging, sense of

enrollment(s) 51; dual enrollment courses 184; and involvement in community 94; management 33, 166–168; minority 99; rate, of urban-serving institutions 5–6; shifts in 137

entrepreneurship 93

environmentally focused theories 133–135

equity 4, 5, 21–22, 35, 40, 75

excellence: counterproductive views of 3, 186; institutional 5

executive leadership 116–117

expenditures, institutional 28

faculty: and classroom instruction format 141; connecting students with 102; crisis management by 121; culturally responsive teaching 49, 50–51; cultural responsiveness 49, 50; development, involvement of student affairs in 124; and doctoral programs 142; engagement with students 93, 147, 148; identification of internal biases 143; impact on career path 158; involvement in student affairs 124; and preparation programs 139–140; professional development for 75; and programming 92; relationship of SSAOs with 106; role in professional development of staff 112; as role models 50; sensitivity 75; validation of students by 49; *see also* staff; student affairs professionals

familial capital 134

families 177; and belonging 102; and career decision-making 73; and career path of vice presidents 160; communication 97; decision-making 97; educational background 152–153; engagement 95–98; environment 153–154; integration, into USIs 53, 69–70; Latinx 180; members, as validation agents 49; parenting 97; programs for 69–70; responsibilities, of commuter students 48–49, 68; support, for commuter students 67; volunteering 97

family advisory councils 53

Fassinger, R. E. 130

Feldblum, M. 118

field trips 158–159

financial aid 40, 46–47, 51; documents 46; offices 46; programs 62–65; *see also* funding

financial literacy 51, 64–65

financial management education sessions 51

first-generation students 41–42, 109, 113; career readiness of 71; career services programs for 70; and family 96; family members, knowledge of 132; financial aid for 46, 47; job-search-success rates of 70; low-income 46; vulnerability to academic process 114

fiscal management 116–117

Fischer, M. A. 45

Fish, M. C. 69

flagship institutions 30, 31, 101, 185

Florida International University (FIU) 122, 178, 179; access to education 22; Biscayne Bay Campus (BBC) 122–123; Hurricane Irma 122–123; pedestrian bridge collapse 123; Student Affairs 106

food banks 44

food insecurity 42–44, 69

food pantries 42–43, 53, 69

foster youth 43–44

Free Application for Federal Student Aid (FAFSA) 52

Freeman, Michael A. 84, 85

Friedman, D. 26, 27

funding 51, 65, 116, 182; emergency funds 52, 64, 123; formulas 185; metrics system 31, 32, 181–182; performance-based 31, 32, 181; and student success 76, 80; *see also* financial aid

fundraising 116–117

gap grants *see* retention grants

Garland, J. L. 47

Gefen, D. R. 69

Georgia Board of Regents 30

Goldrick-Rab, S. 44

governance: board of trustees/regents 29, 30; institutional 29–31, 35; shared, within institutions 29; system/district approach 30–31

graduation rates 6, 31, 32, 76, 78, 87, 123, 167, 185

grievance procedures 115

group-focused theories 130

Grutzik, C. 54, 77

Hagedorn, L. S. 9, 61

Harper, S. R. 78, 113–114

198 Index

Harris, M. 21
health, of institutions *see* institutional health
health problems, students with 43
health services 25, 26; *see also* mental health
hierarchy of needs (Maslow) 42, 43
high-impact educational practices 85, 90, 94, 95
Hispanic Federation 94
Hispanic-serving institutions (HSIs) 19, 21, 25, 96
historically Black colleges and universities (HBCUs) 21, 99
Holley, K. 21
homecoming 100
home insecurity 42–44, 69
homelessness *see* home insecurity
hometown settings, lived experiences in 153–154
Hoxby, C. M. 46
human capital, and community engagement 27
human ecology, theory of 177–178
human motivation 42, 43
human resource management, in doctoral programs 142
Hurricane Irma 122–123

immigrants 40, 54, 155; child care services for 53; and educational mobility 152; undocumented 41, 44
inclusive excellence 72, 98
Inclusivity Resource Center (IRC) 74
individually focused theories 129–133
innovation 27, 33, 73, 143
innovative programs 90
input-environment-output (IEO) theory 185
institutional agents 133–134, 178
institutional diversity 20
institutional excellence 5
institutional governance 29–31, 35
institutional health 31–33
institutional leadership 28–31
institutional sensitivity 75
institutional silos 59–60, 77, 79
institutional striving 32, 35
institutional sustainability 31–33
Integrated Postsecondary Education Data System (IPEDS) 5
intentionality: and engagement/belonging 87–89, 98, 101; and operational aspects of administration 142
interest convergence 179, 185–186
internships 93, 116, 140, 158, 183–184

intersectionality 38, 130
intrusive advising programs 61, 77
Irvine Foundation 183
Ishitani, T. T. 48

Jackson, M. 107
Jacobs, Jenny, Dr. 1
Jacoby, B. 43, 47, 53
job honing 110
job-search-success rates, of first-generation students 70
Johns Hopkins University 27, 28
Joiner, T. 48

K-12, partnerships of USIs with 27
Keeling, R. P. 120
Kilgo, C. A. 8
Kodama, C. M. 48
Kohlberg, L. 130
Krause, K. D. 8
Kretovics, M. 8, 53
Kuh, George D. 65–66, 85

Ladson-Billings, G. 2, 179
Larimore, J. 109
"last-dollar" scholarships 64
Latina/o/x critical race (LatCrit) theory 134, 135
Latinx students 41, 180; career services for 73; food insecurity of 43; retention rate of 78; *see also* African American students
leadership 52, 54, 108, 115, 125–126, 182–183, 186–188; commitment to community 26; and conventions 183; and creativity 186; dual-leadership roles 30; executive 116–117; holistic approach of leaders 182; influence of parents on 162; institutional 28–31; servant 162; system/district approach 30–31; and trust 145; of vice presidents 161–163; *see also* senior student affairs officers (SSAOs); vice presidents, experiences of
learning communities 102
Lee, M. 77
legal services 69
Lesbian, Gay, Bisexual, Transgender, Queer, Intersex, Asexual (LGBTQIA) students 45
Leveson, L. 48
life-long learning, by students 147–148
life skills 70–73
linguistic capital 134
lived experiences, early 153–154

loans 46; and economic background of students 131; micro 51; *see also* financial aid
local organizations/agencies *see* community organizations, partnerships with
Long Beach College Promise 183–184
Long Beach Unified high school graduates, summer-bridge program for 184
Longerbeam, S. D. 50, 51
low-income students 45–47, 109; college outcomes of 46; financial aid for 52, 63, 64; retention grants for 63–64
Lumina Foundation for Education report (2010) 156
Lunsford, Larry W. 105

McClellan, G. S. 109
McCullough, B. C. 136
Mckenzie, A. B. 49
McKenzie, André 58
Mackie, W. 8
McKinney, K. 121
McKinney, L. 77
McNeil, N. 48
Maguire, J. 42, 43
marginality (Schlossberg) 135–137
Martin, G. L. 8
Maryland Higher Education Commission 95
Maslow, A. H. 42, 43
mattering (Schlossberg) 88, 130–131, 135–137; appreciation 136; attention 136; dependence 136; ego-extension 136; importance 136
Maxwell, W. 9
mental health: issues, of students 121; needs, students with 23; programs and initiatives 67–70; services 121
mentoring 71, 184; culture, campus-wide 72–73; programs 90, 94, 182; and staff diversity 109
metrics system, for funding 31, 32, 181–182
metropolitan universities *see* urban-serving institutions (USIs)
Miami Dade College District 30
micro loans 51
microsystem, and psychological outcomes 177–178
minority student populations 39–40, 99; access to social capital 133–134; and institutional agents 133–134
Misra, K. 8
mission, of USIs 33, 34, 113, 115, 181; access-oriented mission 21–22, 27, 28,

31, 35; equity 4, 5, 21–22, 35; and leadership 29; statement 11
Moneta, L. 107
morale, staff 112–113, 118; supervision of motivated staff 113–114; working with unions 114–116
Mueller, J. 49
multicultural competency, of staff 49–50, 109
multicultural services 158, 164
multidisciplinary approaches, to student services 177–179
multiple identities, of commuter students 47
Muslim students 41

National Association of Campus Activities (NACA) 168
National Association of Colleges and Employers (NACE) 70, 71, 72
National Association of Student Personnel Administrators (NASPA) 52, 64, 138, 168–169, 183
National Center for Education Statistics (NCES) 27; Condition of Education report 43
Native American critical theory (TribalCrit) 135
natural disasters 122–123
navigational capital 134
Nelson, D. 8
Nelson, K. A. 107
networking, between USIs 33–34
Newbold, J. J. 8, 60
Nicpon, M. F. 8
nonprofits 25, 26, 51, 63

O'Donnell, K. 85
off-campus housing 88
O'Meara, K. 32
on-campus career centers 70
on-campus work experiences 70–71
online-advising case management 61
online counseling 69
online learning 141
online students 111
opioids, training for 95
orientation: faculty 121; parent/family 70, 96, 114; staff 110; student 66, 70, 114
Ortiz, Anna M. 1, 84, 176

parents: and career path of vice presidents 160; educational background of 152; financial management education sessions for 51; of first-generation students 96;

200 Index

influence on leadership 162; integration, into USIs 53, 69–70; parents' weekend 98; programs for 69–70; students living with 48; *see also* families
Pascarella, E. T. 41
peers: and belonging 102; peer to peer learning, of first-generation students 42; and professional development 171–173; support systems, of commuter students 67
Pell Grants 6, 40, 52, 63
Pellicciotti, B. 45
Penn Graduate School of Education Center 11
performance-based funding 31, 32, 181
Perrakis, A. I. 9
Perry, D. C. 7, 186
physical spaces: and community 178; and engagement 87–88, 89, 178
Pierson, C. T. 41
Pino, D. 77
placement testing 61
planning, by SSAOs 117–119, 122
Player-Sanders, J. 45
policies 52, 54; financial aid 62–65; institutional 75, 122, 179
Pope, R. 49
Portland Community College, Achieving the Dream initiatives 51
Potter, M. 64
practicum experiences 140
preparation programs 137–141; achievement, and institutional setting 143; becoming a life-long learner 147–148; community college leadership 138; competencies/dispositions critical for professionals 143–147; and curriculum 138, 140; doctoral preparation 141–143; and institutional dynamics 140, 143; institutional type 146; lack of curricular focus 137; misalignments 140; practitioners 138–139, 140, 143; self-care 147; soft skills 145; student experience, contextualization of 140
prestige, institutional 32
problem-solving events 69
professional associations 168–170, 183
professional conferences 148
professional development 50, 75, 111, 112, 168–173, 183
promise initiatives 183–184
psychological resources, of students 131
public health partnerships 25

public spaces, policing of 24
Puente 78

racism 134, 173
Radimer, Scott 128
Ramos, S. 54, 77
Ray, Darrell C. 128
reading 170
real estate development 7, 186
regents *see* board of trustees/regents
Reid, A. M. 48
Reisser, L. 129, 130, 132
relationship building 24, 77, 88, 97, 124, 125, 144, 145, 165–166
Rendón, L. 40, 48, 49, 136
residential development 29
residential spaces 23
residential students 8, 48; *see also* commuter students
resistant capital 134
restroom accommodations, for transgender students 45
retention grants 63–64
retention rates 167; of Black and Latino students 78; and funding 31; of vulnerable populations 156
Reynolds, M. 49
RISE (Reach, Inspire, Succeed, Empower) Network 78
risk management 121–122
Robin Hood Foundation 63
Rodin, J. 7
role models: faculty/staff as 50; for first-generation students 71
Rosenberg, M. 136
Run to the Top initiative 64

safety, on urban campuses 24
St. Louis Community College 30, 42, 45; Retention Grant 52
San Diego State University 32
Sanford, N. 129, 130
scalability, of interventions 61
Schlossberg, Nancy 129, 130, 131, 135–137
scholarships 90; for commuter students 90; "last-dollar" 64; student athletes 89
schools, local 27–28
school teams 66
Schuh, J. 117
Scott, J. 112
selectivity, admission 31, 32, 185
senior student affairs officers (SSAOs) 14, 105–106, 187; as change agent 117–119;

Index 201

characteristics necessary for 106; connecting with and learning from students 164–165; crisis management 120–123; critical skills for 163–168; data driven decision-making 119–120; developing partnerships 123–125; dynamic team, establishing and maintaining 107–109; enrollment management 166–168; executive leadership 116–117; fiscal management 116–117; hiring of staff 107, 108, 109; interpersonal relationships across the institution 165–166; orientation and training of staff 110–112; planning 117–119; recruitment plan 126; risk management 121–122; special programming for 183; staff morale 112–116; theoretical conversations 118; training and education of 107; *see also* vice presidents, experiences of
servant leadership 162
service-learning programs 26
sexual harassment training 95
sexual identity development model (Fassinger) 130
shared governance model 29
Shevalier, R. 49
silos, institutional 59–60, 77, 79
Single Stop USA 25, 63
Smith, E. 78
Smith, L. N. 126
social capital 133, 134
social construction, of race 179
social justice 74
socioeconomic status (SES) 45–47
soft skills 145
sporting events, inclusion of family in 96
staff 107; attitude 113, 179; boredom of 114; contract negotiations 115, 116; cross-training 60, 112, 177; with culturally similar backgrounds 74–75; diversity 108, 109; engagement with students 8; hiring of 107, 108, 109; indoctrination period 113; investment in 126; learning about students' characteristics 111, 114; morale 112–116, 118; multicultural competency of 49–50, 109; orientation and training 110–112; professional development of 111, 112; professional experiences and preparation 108–109; relationship of SSAOs with 106; as role models 50; sensitivity 75; and student success 74;

training in student development theories 50; unions 114–116, 166; validation of students by 49; *see also* faculty; student affairs professionals
Stanton-Salazar, R. 129, 133–134, 178
Steele, P. 63, 64
Steinacker, A. 54
stress, of students 67; commuter students 48, 68; reduction, and family programs 70; and wide range of responsibilities 68
student activities programs, and student affairs 92
student affairs professionals 3, 8, 14, 35, 50–54, 128–129, 187; competencies 50; developmental needs of students 50; financial education strategy 51; and funding 51; partnership with academic affairs 51, 125, 180, 181–182; preparation programs, needs/gaps in 137–148; professional development for 50, 75; and programming 92; student development theories 129–137; *see also* faculty; staff; senior student affairs officers (SSAOs)
student development theories 43, 50, 129–137; critique of 129; environmentally focused theories 133–135; individually focused theories 129–133; mattering and marginality (Schlossberg) 135–137
student housing, on campus 33
student involvement 47, 48, 85, 93; *see also* engagement
student learning 75, 86, 106, 110; and culturally relevant pedagogy 5; and engagement 92
student profile *see* diversity, of students
students of color *see* African American students
student success 6, 8, 9, 28, 32, 48, 51, 58–59, 79–80, 85, 181; career development and life skills 70–73; commitment of vice presidents to 156–157; culturally relevant/responsive student services 73–78; definition of 59; effect of personal heritage on passion for 152–157; financial aid programs, policies, and initiatives 62–65; measurement of 91; structural challenges in promoting 59–62; wellness and mental health programs and initiatives 67–70; wrap-around support and advising services 65–67

202 Index

student support specialists 77
student workers 70–71, 93
suicidal behavior 121
supervision, of staff 113–114, 142
sustainability *see* institutional sustainability
Sype, G. E. 8
system approach, USIs with 30–31

talent development approach 5
tax filing services 69
Taylor, Franklyn 38
technology 80, 101–102, 177; connection
    between departments 60–61;
    development and transfer 27;
    information technology 73
Terenzini, P. T. 41
Thomas, Corlisse 58
time management 117
Tinto, Vincent 85
Torres, V. 45
training: cross-training, staff 60, 112, 177;
    faculty 51, 181, 184; for opioids 95;
    related to campus violence 121; sexual
    harassment 95; social justice 74; SSAOs
    107; staff 3, 110–112
transitions (Schlossberg) 130–132; self
    131–132; situation 131; strategies 132;
    support 132
TRIO students 60
Trowler, V. 86
Trump, Donald 41, 44
tuition rates 28–29
Turner, S. 46

UHin4 program 29
underprepared/underserved students 3, 4,
    21, 27, 28, 31, 139
undocumented students 41, 44, 69, 182
unions, staff 114–116, 166
University of California, Los Angeles 27, 30
University of Central Florida (UCF) 27
University of Houston (UH) 19, 73, 178;
    College of Medicine 25, 26; employment
    by 27; institutions of 30; Third Ward
    Initiative 22; UHin4 program 29
University of Houston System Board of
    Regents 25, 30
University of Illinois (Chicago), South
    Campus/University Village project 29
University of Maryland College Park 95
University of Massachusetts (Boston) 73, 170
University of Tampa (UT), Spartan Ready
    Career Readiness Program 72

University of Texas–San Antonio,
    Graduation Rate Improvement Plan 32
University of Texas system 30
urban campuses: and city, boundaries
    between 24, 25; climate 98–100;
    coordination on 60; design of 23;
    environment 23–24; food banks 44;
    multicultural offices in 74; public spaces,
    policing of 24; safety concerns 24;
    services, accessing 62; space, for mental
    health services 68–69
urban college students 38–39; advocacy for
    52–54; average racial/ethnic identity
    across sample institutions **39**; commuter
    students 47–48; first-generation students
    41–42; food and home insecurity 42–44;
    intersectionality of 38; LGBTQIA
    students 45; low-income students
    45–47; minority populations 39–40;
    partnership with staff 38; professional
    development for student affairs
    professionals 50; serving 49–50;
    undocumented and DACA status
    44–45
Urban Experience Program 78
urban planning 29, 186
urban-serving institutions (USIs) 1, 5, **12–13**,
    20–21; broad-based access and equity
    mission 21–22; definition of 10; duties
    associated with leading student affairs 14;
    establishment of 20; institutional dynamics
    140, 143; institutional governance 29–31;
    institutional leadership 28–31; institutional
    sustainability and health 31–33; leading
    186–188; literature about 7–10;
    networking between 33–34; paradigm
    shift and cultural change in 53–54;
    performance pressure 6; as point of
    contact for support 24; preservation of
    184–186; professional experiences and
    preparation necessary to work at 108–109;
    project description 10–14, **12–13**;
    qualitative research 9; quantitative research
    9; as resource to cities 25–28; student
    pipeline to 27–28, 183, 184; student
    profile, diversity in 22–23; urban context,
    influence of 23–25
urban-serving research universities 31–32

validation 49, 88, 136–137
vectors of development 132–133
vice presidents, experiences of 151–152;
    bargaining units, working with 163, 165;

campus colleagues 171; career influences 157–160; career purposes of 154–155; commitment to student success 156–157; conferences 171, 172; connecting with and learning from students 164–165; consensus, building 165–166; critical skills for SSAOs 163–168; early lived experiences 153–154; effect of personal heritage on passion for student success 152–157; effect of presidents on leadership 162; enrollment management 166–168; family educational background 152–153; field trips 158–159; formalized groups 171; guiding principles 162; institutional dynamics 173; institutional fit 155–156, 159, 161; institutions, changing 164–165; interpersonal relationships across the institution 165–166; isolation 162–163, 174; leading, experience of 161–163; learning opportunities 173; learning process 167–168; moving to new institution 174; niche education 171–172; off-campus, time spent 163; pathways to vice presidency 160–161; personal passion 173; portable skills 163, 166; professional associations 168–170; professional journey 157–161; programs and services 173–174; reading 170; sharing with others 172–173; state-level involvement 172; turning to peers 171–173; variations in institutional type

157; *see also* senior student affairs officers (SSAOs)
Virginia Commonwealth University (VCU) 11
Virginia Tech, shootings at 120
Vygotsky, L. 129, 133, 135

Wake Forest University, Mentoring Resource Center 72–73
Walker, Richard 19–20
weekend colleges 54
Weitz, S. 117, 118–119
wellness programs and initiatives 67–70
Whipple, Edward G. 105
Wiewel, W. 7, 186
Wolniak, G. C. 41
workforce development 25
workforce readiness 72
Working Students Success Network (WSSN) 63
work responsibilities, of commuter students 48–49, 68
workshops 51, 96, 171
wrap-around support, and advising services 65–67, 69, 177

Yosso, Tara 48, 133, 134, 135, 137, 178–179
Young Americans for Freedom 98

Zerquera, D. 21
Ziskin, M. 45
zone of proximal development 135